# THE
# BEST KEPT
# SECRET:
## SEXUAL ABUSE
## OF CHILDREN

## Florence Rush

**Human Services Institute**
Bradenton, Florida

**TAB BOOKS**
Blue Ridge Summit, PA

*Human Services Institute* publishes books on human problems, especially those affecting families and relationships: addiction, stress, alienation, violence, parenting, gender, and health. Experts in psychology, medicine, and the social sciences have gained invaluable new knowledge about prevention and treatment, but there is a need to make this information available to the public. Human Services Institute books help bridge the information gap between experts and people with problems.

FIRST EDITION
EIGHTH PRINTING

© 1980 by **Florence Rush**.
First McGraw-Hill paperback edition, 1981
Reprinted by arrangement with Prentice-Hall, Inc.
Published by HSI and TAB Books.
TAB Books is a division of McGraw-Hill, Inc.

**Library of Congress Cataloging-in-Publication Data**

Rush Florence.
    The best kept secret.

    Includes bibliographical references and index.
    1. Child molesting.  I. Title.
HQ71.R87   1981        362.7'044        81-8422
ISBN 0-8306-3907-1                       AACR2

Questions regarding the content of this book should be addressed to:

**Human Services Institute, Inc.**
**P.O. Box 14610**
**Bradenton, FL 34280**

Cover photograph by Susan Riley, Harrisonburg, VA          HSI

Unless otherwise specified, all testimonies contained in this book were obtained either by the author or by her research assistant, Helene Silverstien.

Permission to use the testimonies was given by all participants. These testimonies are heavily disguised to protect the privacy of those who so generously contributed their emotions and experience.

The author wishes to express thanks to the following for permission to quote from the works listed below:

"annie died the other day," by E. E. Cummings. © 1961 by Marion Morehouse Cummings. Reprinted by permission of Harcourt Brace Jovanovich, Inc., from *Complete Poems 1913–1962* by E. E. Cummings.

*Sexual Assault of Children and Adolescents*, a paper presented to the Subcommittee on Science and Technology of the U.S. House of Representatives, January 11, 1978, by Carolyn Swift, director of Prevention Projects.

*History of Sacerdotal Celibacy in the Christian Church*, by Henry Charles Lea. © 1966 University Books, Inc. Published by arrangement with Lyle Stuart.

*On Love, The Family and The Good Life*, selected essays of Plutarch, translated by Moses Hadas, The New American Library.

*Greek Lyric Poetry*, translated by Willis Barnstone. Copyright © 1962, 1967 by Willis Barnstone. Reprinted by permission of Schocken Books, Inc.

*THE ORIGINS OF PSYCHO-ANALYSIS: Letters to Wilhelm Fliess, Drafts and Notes, 1887–1902*, by Sigmund Freud, translated by Eric Mosbacher and James Strachey. © 1954 by Basic Books, Inc., Publishers, New York.

*Transformations*, by Anne Sexton. Copyright © 1971 Anne Sexton. Reprinted by permission of Houghton Mifflin Company.

*Women and Madness*, by Phyllis Chesler, Copyright © 1972 by Phyllis Chesler. Reprinted by Permission of Doubleday & Company, Inc.

*Fundamentals of Human Sexuality*, Second Edition, by Herant A. Katchadourian and Donald T. Lunde. Copyright © 1972 by Holt, Rinehart and Winston, Inc.; copyright © 1975 by Holt, Rinehart and Winston. Reprinted by permission of Holt, Rinehart and Winston.

*A House Is Not a Home*, by Polly Adler. Copyright © 1953 by Polly Adler. Reprinted by permission of Holt, Rinehart and Winston, Publishers.

"Hippie Morality—More Old Than New," by Bennett Berger in *The Sexual Scene*, edited by John H. Gagnon and William Simon. Copyright © 1970 by Transaction, Inc. Published by permission of Transaction, Inc.

*Invitation to Sociology*, by Peter L. Berger. Copyright © 1963 by Peter L. Berger. Reprinted by permission of Doubleday & Company, Inc.

86524

For Eleanor, Matthew and Thomas
and all the women who listened while I talked
and talked while I listened.

# Contents

# Acknowledgments

When I switched late in life from working mother to activist/feminist writer, my good friends Sylvia Friedman, her daughters Alix and Diane, Edith Ballin, Anita Roberts and Arthur and Marilyn Baily accepted my transformation with equanimity and, I suspect, pride. During the inevitable periods of doubt and flagging self-confidence incurred by such radical change, my daughter, Eleanor, and my son, Matthew, never lost faith in this project. My brothers David and Emil, my sisters-in-law Minda and Lucy and my mother, Bessie Kortchmar—despite her doubts about "modern women"—consistently propelled me along.

During the seventies I was fortunate enough to be welcomed by groups forming within the escalating women's movement. I am grateful to the National Organization of Women, New York Radical Feminists, Older Women's Liberation, Women Against Pornography, women's centers and women's studies groups within colleges and universities, and the numerous organizations throughout the country which combat sexual assault and violence against women and children, for providing me with a platform from which to voice my ideas and exchange them with others. My thanks, as well, to such understaffed, underfunded, courageous publications as *Women's World, Prime Time, Majority Report, Off Our Backs, The Radical Therapist, Women: a Journal of Liberation,* the London-based *Women Speaking, Plexus, Notes From the Third Year, Time Change Press* and *Chrysalis* for giving me the same opportunity.

It is impossible for me to name all those who sustained me but I wish to express my sincere gratitude to those who read and commented upon my manuscript, supplied me with pertinent information and otherwise contributed to my work: Paul Adams, Jane Albert, Louise Armstrong, Kathy Barry, Minda Bickman, Sol and Ray Chernoff, Phyllis Chesler, Marjory Collins, Lucy Cores, Helen Duberstein, Andrea Dworkin, Holly Forsman, Leah Fritz, Jan Goodman, Susan Griffin, Kirsten Grimstad, Lu Hamet, Lolly Hirsh, Mimi Joulicour, Iris Kanter, Pam Kearan, Barbara Kolber, Joyce Levine, Joyce Lippman, Barbara Mehrhof, Evan Morely, Robin Morgan, Allison Owings, Helen Payne, Rosetta Reitz, Susan Rennie, Adrienne Rich, Gloria Roddy, Ruby Rorlich, Lainnie Ross, Lynne Tschirhart Sanford, Marian Schiffer, John Schlien, Lynne

Shapiro, Judy Sullivan, Dorothy Tennov, Myra Terry, Louise Thomas, Toni Vietorisz and Frances Whyatt.

And to those who, in addition to friendship, contributed their professionalism—my agent, Jim Seligmann, and my editors Gladys Topkis, Diane Cleaver and especially Mariana Fitzpatrick, who finally helped me to pull it all together, along with production editor Shirley Stein—my deepest appreciation.

I owe the troubling personal testimony found here to my longtime friend and colleague, Helene Wierse. Her skill and sensitivity enabled hundreds of courageous people to reveal a particularly painful part of their lives in order to possibly free others who are trapped in silence.

And to my mentors: Joan Mathews, who encouraged me to write, and Susan Brownmiller, who inspired me to undertake this book, my everlasting gratitude.

# Introduction:
# Susan Brownmiller

Florence Rush made her spectacular debut in the women's movement on April 17, 1971, a day I remember well. We in New York Radical Feminists were holding a two-day conference on rape in rented spaces at Washington Irving High School in New York City, a follow-up to our January speakout at Saint Clement's Church at which for the first time in history women had testified to their own rape experience in an open forum. Our speakout had been an emotional event, a classic in consciousness raising, but now it was time to go beyond personal testimony and attempt to make theory, to build from experience, and to piece together from scholarships an analysis of sexual assault.

Several hundred women participated in this weekend conference, which was a model for many feminist conferences to come, borrowing techniques from academia, conventional politics, social work and psychology. Papers were presented in the musty auditorium in the morning sessions, registrants convened in small classrooms for thought-provoking workshops in the afternoon. There was, of course, a karate demonstration at lunchtime. Looking back, I suppose it was all very cheeky; the outside world was certainly nonplused. Rape in those days was a word that brought on giggles in otherwise intelligent people. Few outside its victims thought it might be an important subject to explore. No one considered that it might have a history, and only a handful believed it was going to become an issue of international feminist concern.

Florence Rush was a member of our Westchester chapter (actually we used the word brigade, but it was hard to think of a brigade in suburbia) and a member as well of OWL, Older Women's Liberation. She was an activist in the Congress of Racial Equality and a professional social worker in a residence for dependent and neglected girls. I should also report that she was a mother of three—one whose outward appearance belied a lifetime of political activism, and one of the few of mature age who was able to make the transition from the left to feminism with ease, giving our movement a special savvy and depth. She had gone to the rape speakout in January, and like the rest of us, her eyes had been opened. At the urging of her good friend Joan Mathews, one of our conference planners, she agreed to present a paper at the meeting in April. Drawing on her work with young girls, her files of case studies, the few available articles (written by Freudian psychologists), her own knowledge of the field and her own true instincts, she developed her thesis on the sexual abuse of children.

Now she says she was nervous; then she was merely magnificent. Her presentation was fresh and startling, her documentation was sound and impressive. I have been to many feminist meetings, but never before and not since have I seen an entire audience rise to its feet in acclaim. We clapped, we cheered. I doubt that many of us had given much thought before that day to the implications of the sexual abuse of children. After listening to this calm woman from Westchester, we would never forget.

Much of the material that was in that early paper is presented in this book in greatly expanded form. It quickly took on a life of its own as its author was besieged for reprints. Cited, quoted and anthologized a score of times, it became a landmark contribution to feminist thought. But while others were eagerly quoting her material, with or without permission, she came to believe that she had barely scratched the surface, that there was much more she wanted to say.

An entire movement has been warmly awaiting this book. Unquestionably her ideas have already had the strongest impact. It is fair to say that the new nationwide interest in the sexually abused child has largely come about because of Florence Rush's efforts, whether or not the mental health establishment cares to acknowledge the source. She is categorically, the first theorist on the subject who does not blame the child in any way, shape or form. She is also the first thinker to see child sexual abuse not as an isolated incident but as a pervasive pattern with antecedents of social acceptance that reach far back into history.

This could not have been an easy book to write, and for many it will not be an easy book to read. There are those who would prefer to safely sentimentalize past traditions rather than look them squarely in the face. As Rush tells us, even Freud himself preferred to alter the historic record rather than come to terms with certain unpleasant truths. This is a book that faces unpleasant truths head on. She tangles with history because she seeks to untangle history; she confronts the present offender because she wishes to end the offense, for all time. This book is a testament to one woman's concern for civilization.

# Preface:
# Growing Up Molested

During my many years as a social worker I observed that the pattern of the sexual abuse of children consisted of a male adult and a female child. The victims who came to my attention were primarily socially and economically deprived, but as others from advantaged backgrounds came to my attention I realized that the problem cut across all areas of society. Indeed, I painfully remembered that I, despite the amenities of a middle-class upbringing, had also been sexually abused as a child.

I was born into an extremely stable family. My parents left a small town in Czarist Russia to escape my father's imminent conscription into the Russian army and the suffering imposed on their lives by anti-Semitism and poverty. They were quite poor but optimistic and confident that they would do well in America. They labored in the sweatshops of New York's Lower East Side until finally, with the help of relatives and my mother's determined wish for his education, my father attended and graduated from the Brooklyn College of Pharmacy. He opened a drugstore, then another, and finally accumulated enough money to buy into a machine shop. Eventually he became a relatively wealthy man.

My two older brothers and I enjoyed summer camp, an uncommon luxury for children from immigrant families, and later we all went to college. At the time of my father's death some years ago, my parents had known each other for sixty years.

Friday night was a festive time in my parents' home. The candles burned for the Sabbath and the dining room table was spread with a lace cloth and covered with a variety of cakes, fruits, nuts, wine and tea for guests who customarily dropped in. Among our regular visitors was our family dentist, whom I shall call Dr. Greenberg, and his wife. This couple, along with many others, would share in the warmth and laughter, discussing politics, singing old Russian and Yiddish songs and telling stories.

My mother always accompanied me to the dentist, but one day, when I was about seven, she sent me off to my appointment alone. The office was not far from our home and in those days the

streets of New York were safe. That particular morning, Dr. Greenberg greeted me pleasantly as usual (I never remember seeing a
nurse or receptionist in his crowded office). Although I was old
enough and big enough to get into the chair myself, he lifted and
seated me with a flourish. He put the usual bib around my neck,
filled the cup for rinsing but placed the instruments in my lap rather
than on the swinging tray used for that purpose. Each time he picked
up an instrument to examine my mouth, he fondled some part of
my body. Soon he began dropping instruments on the floor. After
retrieving them, he managed to slip his hand under my dress and
force his way between my legs. His fingers produced sensations
which made me shamefully uncomfortable, and sensing that something was terribly wrong, I began to cry. Dr. Greenberg laughed at
my tears and accused me of being a "silly child" to be afraid of the
dentist. But his hands continued to move over my genitals. Truly
alarmed, I began to sob louder and louder. I finally made so much
noise that Dr. Greenberg drew back, washed his hands, scolded me
for being such a baby and promised me a nice present if I could
manage to be a brave little girl next time.

   I ran home as fast as I could and told my mother everything.
Momentarily shaken, she regained composure by reassuring herself
that I was lying and had invented the story to avoid the necessary
dental work. She must have been very eager to believe this, since
heretofore my visits to the dentist had never created a problem.
When I refused to keep my next appointment, she apologized to
Dr. Greenberg, who benevolently commented on how difficult it was
for children to overcome fear of the dentist. He continued his Friday
night visits, but whereas formerly I had been outgoing and friendly,
reluctant to go to bed, I now retreated to my room without pressure.

In retrospect I now wonder about this dismissal of my upsetting
accusation, particularly in light of another incident which occurred at
about the same time. I loved the drugstore, and when he wasn't busy
with customers, Danny, the young clerk and my friend, concocted
for me the most extravagant and imaginative sundaes, with nuts,
fruit, whipped cream and various fruit syrups. He also fed me
Hershey bars while consuming a few himself and tucking a few more
into his pocket. One evening I overheard my father complaining
of loss of inventory, and wanting to gain his approval, I told him
about Danny and the Hershey bars. To my dismay, Danny was fired

immediately. Why, I now wonder, was this story so readily believed and acted upon while my molestation by the dentist was first questioned and then dismissed?

The years passed and with early adolescence came the sharing of confidences with close friends. Jane and I were inseparable, and along with making plans for our futures, we exchanged library books, five-and-ten-cent-store lipsticks and secrets. I told Jane about Dr. Greenberg. She told me about her experience with a local merchant. More cautious than I, she had never repeated what happened to her in the back room of the fruit store to anyone.

We reported regularly to each other on the number of exposed men we saw, compared techniques on how to ward off being touched, grabbed at or even mauled in buses and subways, and created strategies for extricating ourselves from uncomfortable and even dangerous situations. For example, Jane and I were addicted to the movies but discovered that we could scarcely get through a double feature without finding the hand of some strange man up our skirts. So we worked out a system. Whoever was being annoyed would stand up and say in a very loud voice: "I must go home now because my mother is expecting me." We would then change seats, hoping to be left alone long enough to see the end of the film. This was our problem and it never occurred to us to tell our parents or the police.*

Subsequently I have heard countless stories similar to and far worse than mine, and have come to know that child molestation by a trusted family friend or relative, as well as a stranger, is in no way unique. It is time we face the fact that the sexual abuse of children is not an occasional deviant act, but a devastating commonplace fact of everyday life.

---

*During the 1930s, movie houses were so often invaded by men searching for children that some theaters (in New York, at any rate) roped off a "children's section" for youngsters who were not accompanied by an adult. This section was sometimes supervised by a matron.

annie died the other day
never was there such a lay—
whom, among her dollies, dad
first ("don't tell your mother") had;
making annie slightly mad
but very wonderful in bed
—saints and satyrs, go your way
youths and maidens: let us pray

e. e. cummings

*Pedophilia:* The sexual desire in an adult for a child

*Pedophile:* An adult who sexually desires children

*Pederasty:* Unnatural sexual relations between two men especially when one is a young boy

*Pederast:* A lover of young boys

Definitions from the *Random House Dictionary*

# 1. A LOOK AT
# THE PROBLEM

Children are the least articulate and most exploited
population suffering from society's failure to confront
realistically the phenomenon of human sexuality.
Carolyn Swift, *Sexual Assault of Children and Adolescents*[1]

It is difficult to be patient with contemporary attitudes toward the
sexual abuse of children. A current inclination to view child-adult
sex as harmless and a reluctance to hold molesters responsible for
their behavior has encouraged sexual liberationists to insist that in
matters of sex "children aren't always children anymore,"[2] that
pedophilia is a victimless crime[3] and, comes the sexual revolution,
"the taboo of pedophilia will fall away."[4] This new morality has also
spurred organized pedophiles to come forward and claim sex with
children as a civil right, and encouraged some professionals to
"scientifically" defend the practice.

  At a national conference on the sexual abuse of children,
held in Washington, D.C., last year, one speaker, a professional who
has worked on problems of incest, told an audience of 300 people
that, according to as yet unpublished evidence, some incest may be a
positive, healthy experience or at worst dull and neutral. (This
statement is, to say the least, controversial. Dr. Suzanne M. Sgroi,
former chairman of the Sexual Trauma Treatment pilot program in
Hartford, Connecticut, countered by stating, "I have never know-
ingly talked to a happy, well-adjusted, unconcerned incest victim."[5])
Unfortunately, professionals and lay people alike tend to focus upon
the debatable but exotic emotional aspects of the problem rather
than indisputable concrete physical hazards. Inequality between a
child and adult should alone forewarn of emotional problems, and
the physical dangers inherent in difference in size and strength
present clear-cut medical hazards. A tiny mouth, anus or vagina

1

cannot accommodate an erect penis. One surgeon reported the following to the National Commission on Pornography and Obscenity:

*Lately, I've been in gynecology and obstetrics. It's absolutely frightening to see what's going on. The wards and private rooms are filled with young girls. . . . Their insides are torn to pieces. It is impossible to describe the repair jobs we do. These girls suffer from every kind of sexual abuse. It used to be that doctors treated prostitutes in such condition but now we have to treat young girls from the best of families. . . . Every day we see girls in their teens with disease and infection.* [6]

## A FAMILY AFFAIR

Incest and other forms of sexual abuse of children are subjects clouded by myths, contradictions and confusions. There is disagreement among doctors, therapists, sexologists and researchers as to whether as many boys as girls are molested, whether they are equally traumatized, whether child molesters are normal, neurotic, psychopathic or psychotic, whether the child victim in some way offers herself for a sexual encounter or whether the molester derives his behavior from a disturbed mother or a fractured family. Speculation as to the number of incidents varies from five to five hundred thousand to one million per year and from five to thirty-five million persons who will experience a sexual encounter with an adult during childhood.

There seems to be a consensus, however, that the offender is overwhelmingly male (from about 80 to 90 percent), that about 80 percent of the time he is a family relative or friend of the victim and her family, that actual incidents are grossly underreported and that offender behavior crosses all social, economic and racial lines. Beyond this, most opinions do not match with one another, or my own. To my thinking, the molester is not the product of a disturbed or dysfunctional family and may be as normal or abnormal as the rest of the so-called normal male population. The reason he seeks out a child as a sexual partner is because a child, more than a woman, has less experience, less physical strength, is more trusting of and dependent upon adults and therefore can be more easily coerced, seduced, lured or forced. And because the molester is also a friend of or relative of the family, even concerned adults cannot cope with him.

More than one devoted parent has vowed, "If anyone so much as lays a finger on my little girl, I'll kill him." But when a mother or father, let us say, discovers that it was their good friend Jack (who just lent them money and took Mary to the hospital when the baby arrived two weeks ahead of schedule), who, their child reports, "touched me all over" rather than some "degenerate" stranger, they will have difficulty acting upon their anticipated rage. They will calm down. They will be more reasonable. Exposure might cost Jack his job. Sally might leave him. How will she manage? How will the families act if they meet in church or the supermarket? Could the children still play together? Problem is heaped upon problem and it is soon agreed that the whole thing is best ignored. Some may even sympathize with Jack. "We never knew he had this thing for kids. The poor guy needs help." At most, in the future they will not leave their daughter alone with Jack.

One mother, in a story told to *Woman's Day,* stormed to the home of the neighborhood child molester after he had approached her child. There she was met by the man's wife, who pleaded that, but for this one peculiarity, her husband was an exemplary spouse and father. In exchange for a promise that the molester would enter psychotherapy, the mother agreed not to press charges.[7] Child molesters are notably resistant to treatment, but for those reluctant to inflict hardship upon innocent relatives, therapy is a welcome if ineffective solution. There are in fact so few solutions that often the child victim must protect the man who has endangered her. One young woman, in an attempt to rescue her niece, told this typical story:

*Jill, my sister's daughter, is fourteen. Her stepfather has been feeling her up and going into her bedroom at night for the past six months. I know she's telling the truth because he did the same to me when I lived with them. Jill couldn't stand it and finally told her teacher. The teacher told the school psychologist, who said that either the child was lying and very sick or the family was in great trouble. The father could go to jail.*

*When confronted, the stepfather said Jill lied. Jill's mother believed her husband. Wringing her hands, she pleaded with her daughter to "confess." Otherwise who would support them and her younger brothers? Jill tried to stick to her story, but with persistent pressure and increased guilt at depriving the family of support, she finally "confessed" that she lied. She was denied a request to live with me and placed under psychiatric care.*

Russell George, convicted child molester, in testimony to English criminologist Tony Parker clearly illustrated how adult inability to cope with his behavior guaranteed him free sailing. One Christmas, at a family gathering, he took his six-year-old niece into a bedroom, pulled down her underpants and fondled her. The child's father "caught me right in the act," he said. Without a word the father took the child and his wife and left. Everyone seemed "embarrassed" but no one said anything. George assured his wife that the father "simply got the wrong idea." Because he was not confronted, he continued to molest little girls whenever there was a family gathering. George well understood that "it's not easy for people to start making accusations"[8] because no matter how much people may wish to protect a child, few will risk placing a woman and her child in financial and social jeopardy. The sexual abuse of children is consequently the most muted crime.

## DIMENSIONS

Vincent De Francis of the American Humane Society, whose study of 263 child victims of sexual abuse has become a standard reference, proposed that though incidents are of unknown national dimensions, "findings strongly point to the probability of an enormous national incidence many times larger than reported incidents of physical abuse of children."[9] Carolyn Swift, Director of Prevention Projects, Wyandot Mental Health Center, Kansas City, in a presentation to a Congressional committee estimated that "fifty to eighty percent of all incidents go unreported."[10] In a random study of 4,000 American women done by the Kinsey team, 25 percent were found to have experienced a sexual encounter with an adult before age thirteen.[11] David Finkelhor, research scientist at the University of New Hampshire, in his study of 796 college students found that of the 530 female subjects, 19.2 percent had been victimized in childhood, and of the 266 male subjects, 8.6 percent had been victimized.[12] The Kinsey percentage is often projected as representative of 25 percent of the female population; hence, approximately twenty-five million women in the United States will experience sex with a male adult before age thirteen. If we take the same liberties with the Finkelhor study, then twenty-eight million of our combined male and female population will experience a sexual encounter with an adult in childhood.*

National statistics, though helpful, are unnecessary for us to grasp the vast extent of the problem. There is scarcely a study, report or investigation into aspects of human sexuality which does not indicate that child-adult sex is an active, prevalent pastime. Of 5,058 reported sex crimes in New York City in 1975, 27.2 percent of the victims were under fourteen (20 percent female, and 6.4 percent male).[13] In a study of over 1,500 imprisoned male sex offenders, who had committed over 1,700 offenses, 998 were against children under fifteen.[14] More than one-half of all victims of reported rape are under eighteen, and 25 percent of this number are under twelve. Seventy percent of all young prostitutes and 80 percent of all female drug users were found to have been sexually assaulted in childhood by a family member.[15] The director of Shalom, a temporary shelter for girls in California, said that from 25 to 50 percent of all the children in the shelter have experienced sexual abuse. (The majority were removed from their homes for other reasons, but their sexual victimization is usually disclosed during counseling.)[16] Dr. Pascoe, Professor of Pediatrics at the University of California, estimated that "upwards of 80 percent of the kids at Juvenile Hall had been sexually molested regardless of the reason that placed them there."[17] The Brooklyn Society for the Prevention of Cruelty to Children reports that from 75 to 85 percent of all reported crimes against children are of a sexual nature, and of the 850 cases brought before the court in one year by the agency, 405 were sex crimes against children.[18] The number of children referred to the Sexual Assault Center in Seattle, Washington, has been increasing steadily since 1973. During 1978 over 25 percent of the cases referred were children under age fourteen, and 13 percent of these were under nine.[19] Dr. Frederick Green of George Washington University, Washington, D.C., found that sexually abused children "are more common among the Children's Hospital patients than broken bones and tonsillectomies";[20] psychiatrists, doctors, nurses, social workers, teachers and child-care workers are discovering so many cases as to suggest a national epidemic.

---

*These figures are based upon an American population of two hundred million.

## MEDICAL CONSEQUENCES OF THE SEXUAL ABUSE OF CHILDREN

Adult sex with children presents an increasing serious health problem.* Cases of rectal fissures, lesions, poor sphincter control, lacerated vaginas, foreign bodies in the anus and vagina, perforated anal and vaginal walls,[21] death by asphyxiation, chronic choking from gonorrheal tonsillitis, are almost always related to adult sexual contacts with children.[22] Of twenty cases of genital gonorrheal infection in children aged one to four, nineteen had a history of adult-child sex. A history of adult-child sex was obtained in all twenty-five cases of infected children between five and nine, and the same was true of all 116 cases of children between fourteen and fifteen. In another study, 160 of 161 cases of this illness in children resulted from sexual contacts with adults.[23]

And with the high risk of teenage pregnancy, young females are victims of premature sex no matter what the age of their partners. The Alan Guttmacher Institute, Research and Development Division of Planned Parenthood, published the following disturbing information:

*The death rate from complications of pregnancy, birth and delivery is 60 percent higher for women who become pregnant before they are fifteen, while the rate for fifteen- to nineteen-year-olds is 13 percent greater than for mothers in their early twenties. . . . Mothers fifteen to nineteen are twice as likely to die from hemorrhage and miscarriage and 1.5 times more likely to die from toxemia, while mothers under fifteen are 3.5 times more likely to die from toxemia. Toxemia has been cited as a "special hazard" of pregnancy among the very young because of lack of development of the endocrine system, emotional stress of such early pregnancy, poor diet and inadequate prenatal care.[24]*

The number of children having children is hardly insignificant. According to Department of Health, Education and Welfare statistics, four million teenage women from fifteen to eighteen are heterosexually active. Of this number, four out of ten, or one million, become pregnant each year. This does not include the under-fifteen set who, less fertile and less able to conceive, but no less active, get

---

*Studies on rape have attested to the fact that infants, six months and less, have been penetrated.*

pregnant at the rate of 30,000 each year. Between 1971 and 1976, when the general birth rate declined, teenage pregnancies escalated by 33 percent, resulting in 600,000 live births. Percentage-wise, the greatest increase occurred in the under-fifteen group, especially among those between the ages of eleven and thirteen.[25] We must remember that many children involved are often so young that they cannot understand the birth process or even assimilate, when taught, the proper use of birth control. And in a social climate which boasts of vanishing virginity and "the flowering of teenage sex," where the media blast daily that sex is love, sex is fun, and that if you reach for a mate instead of a plate, sex will even keep you thin, but ignores the dangers of venereal disease, pregnancy and death on the delivery table, most youngsters ready or not, are pressured into premature sex. In our sex-obsessed society, even the most sophisticated adolescent can be convinced that sex at an early age is more revolutionary (certainly easier) than overthrowing capitalists and landlords.

## THE EMOTIONAL CONSEQUENCES OF ADULT-CHILD SEX

Dr. Joseph Peters, Director of the Philadelphia Sex Offender and Rape Victim Center at Philadelphia General Hospital, has pointed to potential danger signals such as loss of appetite, nightmares, bed-wetting, clinging to mother, resistance to going to school or playing with friends, as symptoms possibly arising from sexual encounters with adults. In the child who has had repeated and continued premature sexual experiences, severe depression, inability to function, psychosis and suicide can result.

Peters was particularly concerned that therapists "distinguish between fantasy and the fact of child molestation. Ascribing these events to psychological fantasy," he continued, "may be easier and more interesting for the therapist, but may also be counterproductive for the most efficient resolution of symptoms."[26] Furthermore, incidents which are overlooked usually surface in adulthood when a person is overwhelmed by the demands of adult sexuality. Peters cautions that, "In their aversion to what are often repulsive details, psychotherapists allowed and continue to allow their patients to repress emotionally significant, pathogenic facts."[27]

Therapists who relegate childhood sexual encounters with adults to fantasy unfortunately reflect a general reluctance to deal with the problem. Professionals and lay persons alike prevent the problem from surfacing by claiming it is imagined, that the child lied or by denying that the experience is harmful. Dr. James Ramey, a member of the Department of Psychiatry at the Bowman School of Medicine in North Carolina, in an article "The Last Taboo," mitigated the danger of father-daughter incest by classifying it with victimless crimes such as homosexuality and masturbation. Researchers David Finkelhor and Judith Herman question Ramey's conclusions. They explain:

*Many women who have experienced incest report Ramey's arguments are nothing new; they have heard them all their lives from fathers, stepfathers, uncles or older brothers. Incest offenders often rationalize their behavior by saying that they see nothing wrong with incest, that its dangers have been overblown, and that it would cause no harm if it were not for the interference of busybodies, that it is not a universal taboo. This by no means unpopular position has been furthered by an enormous infusion of pornographic and popular men's magazine literature in recent years, advertising the benefits of incest.*[28]

Others who have worked with victims and their families have also illustrated how the general tendency to conceal or minimize incest operates. In an article entitled "Divided Loyalty in Incest Cases," Courtney, who was seduced by her father at age ten, admonished him in a letter when she reached adulthood. "Can you understand how ironic it is being in my position where I kept my mouth shut about your sexual abuse of me to protect you from the destruction of one family?"[29] she said. She further detailed the constraints which fed her anguish:

*Since I was a little ten-year-old child, I had to deceive and hide from all the world and my mother that my father took a sexual interest in me and initiated sexual activities with me. Remember how you taught me that art of deceit? First you put me in a situation that had to be kept secret (for your protection) and then you pledged me to secrecy. . . . As a ten-year-old child, what was I supposed to do? You are an intelligent man—you figure out the options available to a ten-year-old in that position.*[30]

Of course a ten-year-old child who is exploited by her father has no options. If the man who is supposedly her prime protector is also her seducer and exploiter, where can she go? Courtney bitterly understood that "As your daughter, you were in charge of protecting me, overseeing my development toward adulthood." But instead, at thirty-one, she found herself "still trying to come to grips with the devastating effect that [the incest] has had on my life."[31]

Katherine Brady, in her book *Father's Days: A True Story of Incest,* threw light upon the painfully false stance she adopted to cover the serious emotional disturbance caused by her incestuous experience:

*Each increase in my guilt, shame and disgust caused an equal increase in my need to create a glossy pleasing surface. The darker the inside the brighter the outside must be to hide it. . . . By the time I reached high school, I had two absolutely separate personalities. The public one, exhibited to family and friends alike was friendly, stable, honest, thoughtful, courteous, trustworthy, reliable and cooperative. The private one was fearful, isolated, anxious and depressed.*[32]

The inclination to mollify injury to the child as the result of child-adult sex, injury which is carried into adult life, is additionally reinforced by our ubiquitous double standard. For example, both the clinical and popular concept of a healthy male differs significantly from the picture of a healthy woman. A healthy woman will meet the behavior norms accepted for her sex even though these traits are less desirable than those attributed to the healthy male. A healthy male is seen as positive and assertive and is taught to strive for self-actualization and mastery. The female, however, is judged literally at "face value," i.e., for her physical charms. She is seen as normal when she is passive, yielding, accepting of her second-class status, charmingly unsure, ambivalent and slightly confused.[33]

The experience of Virginia, a twenty-three-year-old woman who came to me for help, illustrates the double standard in evaluating mental health. Her stepfather started having sex with her when she was twelve and stopped, at her insistence, when she was seventeen. Virginia, too, managed to attain a "glossy pleasing surface" but as soon as she reached eighteen, she consulted a psychiatrist. Impressed by her attractive appearance, her social grace and charm, the psychiatrist refused to acknowledge or deal with the conflicts she was convinced stemmed from her relationship with her father; he maintained that Virginia was upset by "what was going on inside my head rather than what actually happened between me and my stepfather." When she visited her family in their spacious suburban home, she found the same disregard for her distress. "Everyone acts as though nothing happened," she declared. "But for me anger is always threatening. My family and friends, including my stepfather, admire my self-confidence. The truth is that I am not, nor do I feel, self-confident. This inability to talk about the most appalling and traumatic occurrence in my life leaves me feeling split in two and paranoid. He's my father. He did this thing to me and yet he acts as though everything is just fine."

Because our culture does not openly deal with the hazard of incest, it offers no help to a child who is entitled to a protective father and not a destructive adult lover; particularly when that adult is her father or a member or friend of the family. Denial or mitigation of the problem leaves the victim alone to bear, perhaps for a lifetime, the burden of this shameful secret and its consequences.

## WOMEN TALKING

The women's movement, by turning the spotlight on sexual assault, has encouraged open discussion of childhood sexual abuse. Louise Armstrong interviewed 183 women who, like herself, had been involved in an incestuous relationship with their fathers. "What is our commonality?" asked Armstrong. "First and foremost, it is that sharp sense of betrayal of trust, a kind of trust we can now never have. Certainly some of us learn to trust again." But, she insists, "We have to grow up. We will never have a loving, caring father."[34] Painful as it is, women can better order their lives within this reality than within the futile psychiatric fantasy that their sense of betrayal is a figment of a disordered female imagination. But even before the Louise Armstrongs searched for and found female "commonality," experiences were aired, in rare but significant women's literature.

As far back as A.D. 900, Lady Murasaki, in her classic description of royal Japanese court manners in *Tales of Gengi*, told of her adoption by Prince Gengi when she was ten. Had she been Gengi's real daughter, "convention would not have allowed him to go on living with her on terms of such complete intimacy,"[35] she wrote. A sixteenth-century anonymous poet voiced a young girl's dread of her forced child marriage as she lamented, "How should I Love and I so Young."[36] The nineteenth-century poet Charlotte Mews portrayed a farmer's child-bride whose eyes beseeched whenever men folk appeared, "not near, not near."[37] An American slave wrote in her diary that, even before the age of twelve, when the slave child hears her master's footfall she knows that she is no longer a child, and the writer herself was forced to submit to her master when she was barely fifteen.[38]

The Maimie Papers are a collection of letters written by a New York prostitute early in the twentieth century. Maimie was placed in reform school by an uncle, "the same who did me wrong when I was a tiny girl and any number of times since then."[39] Agnes Smedley, in her autobiographical novel, *Daughter of Earth,* tells how she was approached by an elegant barber at fourteen. When he assaulted her, she bit, scratched and fought him off, and finally in "loneliness mingled with my misery and tears"[40] found her way home. Thereafter she never ventured from home alone without carrying a knife.

Susan Brownmiller pointed to the biographical works of Billie Holiday, Maya Angelou and underground actress Viva, all as accounts of girls raped before age ten,[41] and Virginia Woolf in later life still shivered with shame as she recalled her half-brother, George Duckworth, "standing me on a ledge at about six or so exploring my private parts."[42]

During the second wave of the women's liberation movement in the 1970s, women more freely and frequently aired such experiences. Claudia Dreifus in *Woman's Fate* described a meeting of a consciousness-raising group at which Victoria told of how at six she was undressed and fondled by a male baby sitter and then at ten was approached by his father who asked if she would pull down her pants for him as she had for his son; Claudia remembered a janitor who gave her money and candy in exchange for touching his penis; and Liza recalled that when she was four or five her grandfather put his hand in her underpants whenever she sat on his lap.[43] In *Combat in the Erogenous Zone* Ingrid Bengis describes how at age twelve she panicked and froze when a man in the subway, looking straight at her, managed to lift her skirt with a hidden hand and touched her.[44] In *Flying* Kate Millett describes taking a ride with a man she thought was her father's friend until he grabbed her breasts and exposed his penis. She escaped, but because she thought *she* had sinned, she told no one.[45] Joyce Ladner in *Tomorrow's Tomorrow* learned early in life about the "rape man," a middle-aged child molester who wandered the streets,[46] while Susan Griffin's initiation to sexuality was "typical." Every woman, says Griffin, "has similar stories to tell: the first man who attacked her may have been a neighbor, a family friend, an

uncle, her doctor or perhaps her own father."[47] Robin Morgan, in
her poem *The Father,* remembered being "felt between my legs at age
twelve."[48] And Linda Marie, in *I Shall Not Rock,* tells of being sold by
her stepfather, Lester, to an old man as payment on a house:

*Helda, my little sister, and I were included in the deal and he managed to get*
*each of us when he could. . . . On the street he was a kindly old man; in the*
*house he was a beast. When I was in a body cast (had fallen and broken a hip),*
*he'd come into my room and squeeze my breasts and kiss me with his shriveled*
*toothless mouth. I was embarrassed and there was no one I could trust enough to*
*talk about it. When Lester was at work the old man would take Helda to his*
*room, tell her dirty stories, sexually abuse her, and then give her candy. After the*
*old man went out, Lester would come in for his daily ration. . . . I'd lie quietly*
*and hope for Mary to come down from Heaven and save me. . . . I hated them*
*but couldn't stop them. I was the child bride of my mother's husband who had*
*chosen to share me with his brother. I was ten years old.*[49]

Women, however, are now doing more than giving testimony. They
are questioning, challenging and interpreting. Nancy Gager and
Cathleen Schurr, in their book *Sexual Assault: Confronting Rape in*
*America,* explain:

*Little girls like their mothers learn at an early age to endure being sexually used.*
*A few experiences with the disbelief, shock, shame and embarrassment of those*
*closest to them provide good training in silence.*[50]

Susan Brownmiller in *Against Our Will* presented a historic analysis:

*The unholy silence that shrouds the inter-family sexual abuse of children and*
*prevents its realistic appraisal is rooted in the same patriarchal philosophy of*
*sexual private property that shaped and determined the historic male attitude*
*towards rape. For if a woman was man's corporal property, then children were*
*and are a wholly owned subsidiary.*[51]

Sandra Butler in *Conspiracy of Silence, the Trauma of Incest,*[52] calls into
question some of society's most basic attitudes toward sex, the
sanctity of the nuclear family unit, male-female role expectations
and, above all, the rights of children to their own bodies. And Louise
Armstrong explored the motivations behind the incestuous father:

*The abusive father must have a sense of paternalistic prerogative in order to rationalize what he is doing; playing doctor with his own kid. Weak or authoritarian nature, he must have a perception of his children as possessions, as objects. He must see his children as there to meet his needs rather than the other way around.*[53]

Lucy Berliner, a social worker who has been working with sexually abused children, does not accept that "dysfunctional" families produce incestuous fathers. Since Masters and Johnson have indicated that 50 percent of all marriages are dysfunctional, "does that mean that 50 percent of all families are incestuous?"[54] she asks. And Linda Tschirhart Sanford, in her forthcoming book, *The Silent Children,* advises: ". . . The offender is not out of the ordinary. He did not land from an alien planet. He came from amongst us . . . and is a mirror of our culture."[55]

## MEN TALKING

Men generally do not take sex with children seriously. They are amused by it, wink at it and allow adult-child sex to continue through a complex of mores which applauds male sexual aggression and denies a child's pain and humiliation, confusion and outrage. How else is it possible that a book such as *The Discreet Gentlemen's Guide to the Pleasures of Europe* can recommend places where one can find "Lolita-aged nymphettes who make pocket money with every orifice but the natural one"?[56] Or that *Mankoff's Lusty Europe* can suggest locations outside of Paris where one can find little girls as young as ten for sex, a spot where children dance nude and fondle men as they watch a film, and bordellos supplied with teenaged prostitutes?[57] Back in the 1920s Edwards West Browning, dubbed "Daddy Browning" because of his sensational interest in little girls, at fifty-two married "Peaches," or the fifteen-year-old Frances Belle. The childless couple drew spectacular headlines when Peaches sued for a divorce because Daddy displayed "too much affection" for their ten-year-old adopted daughter. In a circuslike atmosphere, Daddy was awarded custody of the child.[58] A swashbuckling movie star was never convicted of the several charges of statutory rape brought against him; at age fifty-two he died in the company of his seventeen-year-old girl friend. A fair-haired boy of American football pleaded guilty to the charge of indecent exposure in front of a little girl.

During his trial, he received popular support and was placed on probation. A forty-three-year-old film director who pleaded guilty to having unlawful sexual intercourse with a thirteen-year-old girl fled to France before sentencing.

A. Nicholas Groth, Ph.D., Director of the Sex Offender program at the Connecticut Correctional Institution in Somers, remarked that in his twelve years' experience he never encountered self-referral for help by a child molester,[59] and among those who have been apprehended "genuine remorse or shame is uncharacteristic."[60] Dr. Joseph Peters found that men attracted to children are remarkably insensitive to the needs of others and it is likely that this insensitivity "permits them to be oblivious to the problems created by their destructive behavior."[61]

The fact is that child molesters rarely understand that they have done anything wrong. An incestuous father is surprised to learn that his behavior is punishable by law because he believes that sexual access to his children is his right. And this right is reinforced by the media in films, advertising and pornography, which constantly eroticize children, and by professionals who endorse father-daughter incest and adult-child sex. Offenders find further support in history, where our Hebrew, Christian, Greek and Roman forefathers sexually used male and female children. Indeed, men can point to a past in which little girls became brides at age ten, and argue that marriage and cohabitation between men and children is still common in certain parts of the world. In Lepcha, for example, old men of eighty copulate with girls of eight and nobody minds. The fictional prototype pedophile, Humbert Humbert, justified his interest in Lolita by pointing to Dante, who fell in love with his Beatrice when she was nine, and Petrarch, who fell in love with his Laura when she was twelve.

My impatience with current treatment programs which purport to rehabilitate the child molester or incestuous father, stems from the fact that they ignore a social milieu where male sexual power over women and children is institutionally integrated. These programs tend to consist only of apprehended offenders who are more distressed by discovery than by what they have done, and enter treatment as an alternative to prison or as a condition of their probation. And with the shared tendency of the molester to blame the victim or his wife, the popular "family therapy" method, while insisting that the offender admit responsibility for his own behavior, reinforces the customary strategy of blaming the victim, wife or mother. In family therapy it is expected that the wife will ultimately admit that "she was party to the incestuous situation" and the victim will discover that "she was not entirely a helpless victim."[62]

Behavior modification attempts to alter molesting behavior by mechanical reconditioning devices. Treatment is based upon the theory that the molester is "overresponsive to sexual cues involving prepubertal physical development."[63] The offender undergoes aversion and reward reprogramming; that is, he is exposed to images of children in combination with unpleasant stimuli such as electric shock or an ongoing commentary on the sexual unattractiveness of children. He is also exposed to images of seductive, attractive adult females with an ongoing commentary on the delights, pleasures and gratifications which can be obtained from a sexual relationship with them.

One imprisoned child molester claimed that upon completion of a behavior modification program he was cured. When asked why he was in jail, he answered, "Oh, last time I was picked up for going after little boys. Now I'm better. I was picked up for going after girls." The prisoner got the message—not the one intended by those who supervised the program, perhaps, but one where sexual use of female children is written in history. For example, Christian decrees prohibiting marriage between persons of disparate age were so riddled with loopholes as to render them useless. During the nineteenth and early twentieth centuries protective legislation was enforced with so little enthusiasm that respectable men, however cloaked with pretensions of prudery, sexually used children in a lively Dr. Jekyll and Mr. Hyde double life. And the belief that the United States has suffered from a repressive Puritan history is unsupported by ineffective penal codes, few prosecutions and extremely light sentences meted out to sex offenders.

One way or another, child molesters get permission for what they do. Adult-child sex is not a phenomenon that emerges from nowhere but is a legacy from the past which continues on in our everyday life.

# 2. THE BIBLE AND THE TALMUD: AN INFAMOUS TRADITION BEGINS

We have a little sister, and she hath no breasts;
What shall we do for our sister
In the days when she shall be spoken for?
If she be a wall,
We will build upon her a turret of silver;
If she be a door,
We will enclose her with boards of cedar.
*Song of Songs 8:8, 9*

A millennium before the Hebrews wrote their first Bible and the Greeks their *Iliad* and *Odyssey*, there existed a rich literature in the cuneiform system of writing, which was inscribed upon clay tablets. These tablets gave us the myths, lamentations, epic tales, proverbs and laws of the ancient civilization of Sumer, ancestor to our own modern culture. One tablet related the story of the god Enlil who, when he encountered the goddess Ninlil bathing in a pure stream, desired her. The goddess, however, was unwilling:

> *The lord speaks to her of intercourse.*
> *She is unwilling.*
> *Enlil speaks to her of intercourse.*
> *She is unwilling.*[1]

Ninlil felt she was too young for sex and politely explained:

> *My vagina is too little.*
> *It knows not how to copulate.*
> *My lips are too small.*
> *They know not how to kiss.*[2]

On still another tablet a Sumerian who vehemently disapproved of child marriage declared, "I will not marry a wife who is only three years old as a donkey does!"[3]

From these meager fragments we have some small indication that approximately five thousand years ago there was a young girl who felt she was too "little" for intercourse and said so, and at least one man who objected to sex with children. The Bible and the Talmud, however, encouraged sex between men and very little girls in marriage, concubinage and slavery. The Talmud held that a female child of "three years and one day" could be betrothed by sexual intercourse with her father's permission. Intercourse with one younger was not a crime but invalid. If a prospective groom would penetrate the child just once more after her third birthday, he could legitimately claim his promised bride.

## THREE YEARS AND A DAY

One might ask whether ancient age calculations matched modern standards, particularly since Abraham at the dubious age of one hundred and Sarah at age ninety became the proud parents of Isaac. In fact, as Biblical narratives moved from Genesis or from myth to history, chronological computations came to resemble our own. The Talmudic decree of "three years and a day" was derived from the Book of Numbers, and this book followed Genesis by a comfortable distance.

Numbers contains the story of the Midian women who successfully seduced Hebrew men from their faith. In vengeance, the Israelite army attacked this pagan community, but when it returned victorious with spoils and captives, Moses greeted the conquerors with surprising fury. His reaction was provoked by the presence of the Midian women, the very same who had lured the men into sexual abominations, and Moses wanted no further heathen contamination. He commanded the death of all the women but ordered that "all the woman children that have not known man by lying with him, keep for yourselves."[4] During the first three centuries of the common era, rabbis who compiled Talmudic law had the following discourse:

*Rabbi Joseph said: Come and hear! A maiden aged three years and one day may be acquired in marriage by coition.*

*Mishna [the law]: A girl of the age three years and one day may be betrothed subject to her father's permission by sexual intercourse.*[5]

*Gemara [discussion]: Our Rabbis taught, "A girl of the age of three years may be betrothed by sexual intercourse. But the sages say only one who is three years old and one day."*

*It is written: But all the female children that have not known man by lying with him, keep alive for yourselves, but do not spare them if they have known man by lying with him. Consequently it must be said that the Scripture speaks of one who is fit (one of three years and a day) for copulation, not one who has actually experienced it. [Num 31:18]*

The age of three years and one day for betrothal or marriage* grew out of an old Semitic tradition and cannot be dismissed as myth, nor is it simply a Talmudic academic exercise.

According to Jewish folklore, a woman came before the renowned, revered second-century Rabbi Akiba ben Joseph. She complained that sexual intercourse had been forced upon her before she reached the age of three. After pondering the problem, the Rabbi compared the situation to a baby who submerges his finger in honey: "The first time he cries about it, the second time he cries about it, but the third time he sucks it. He ultimately enjoys the experience."[6] The Rabbi drew upon what was then common, everyday wisdom. And Moses Maimonides, the sophisticated twelfth-century physician, philosopher and Talmudist, did not take issue with his ancient predecessors. In his monumental work *The Mishnah Torah*, an organization and clarification of Talmudic law, he reaffirmed that a female child who was "three years and one day could be betrothed by sexual intercourse" with paternal permission.[7] By the twelfth century, age was certainly reckoned as it is today.

Perhaps this striking lack of concern for the female child could be better understood if we remember that the Biblical female, no matter what her age, was a property, and as such stripped of all human attributes. When God commanded, "Thou shalt not covet thy neighbor's house; thou shalt not covet thy neighbor's wife nor his ox, nor his maidservant nor anything that is thy neighbor's,"[8] he categorized a man's wife with his house and ox. And because the female was a sexual property, all heterosexual relationships were

---

*During the Biblical and early Talmudic period, distinction between betrothal and marriage was not clear.*

defined as financial transactions. Marriage was the purchase of a daughter from her father, prostitution was a selling and reselling of a female by her master for sexual service, and rape was the theft of a girl's virginity which could be compensated for by payment to her father. Where the Bible was vague regarding the age of the females involved in these transactions, the Talmud was explicit.

## CHILD MARRIAGE

Although the Talmud recommended that a daughter be given in marriage when *na'rah*, between the age of twelve and twelve and a half, a father could marry her off well before that time. A boy reached his majority at thirteen and was then eligible to negotiate his own affairs. He was not, however, obliged to marry until eighteen, and even then could postpone matrimony until his mid-twenties. When ready, he could acquire a bride in three ways: He could enter into a contract agreement with the girl's father, which, much like today's credit system, was a "buy now and pay later" arrangement; he could make a direct full payment; or an act of sexual intercourse with the father's permission could involve either immediate or delayed payment, but authorized possession of the female.[9] Once married, the daughter was released from her father's authority, became her husband's property and was under his total control. But while under her father's jurisdiction her market value fluctuated with geography, history and current events. She did not enjoy the intrinsic, incalculable moral value we ideally place upon human life.

In pre-exilic days a Biblical tribal chief counted his wealth in actual property and his status was enhanced by a large collection of wives, concubines and slaves. Females were in demand and daughters were an asset. But when the Jews were forced to wander the world over, an entourage of women was a burden. The Hebrews were also governed by the laws of their host country or "the law of the land," and polygyny, concubinage and slavery had been outlawed in Europe in the eleventh and twelfth centuries. A man was then limited to one wife. As the demand to own many women decreased, daughters became a liability and one who was not spoken for by the time she was *na'rah* was an undesirable, over-the-hill spinster.

Even if parents were reluctant to subject their immature daughters to early wifehood, they were hard put to risk being saddled with such a perishable commodity. In thirteenth-century France, for example, parents gave their daughters when money and opportunity presented itself:

*As is our custom now of betrothing our daughters even while they are minors [under 12]. This is due to the fact that [persecution and] Exile overcomes us every day and if one can afford to give his daughter a dowry, he fears that tomorrow he may not be able to do this and his daughter will remain forever unmarried.*[10]

And in the sixteenth century the situation did not improve:

*We are few in number and do not always find the proper match; our practice is to marry our minor daughters early when the proper match presents itself.*[11]

Talmudists had some ambivalence regarding the marriage of under-aged girls* but generally leaned in favor of the practice. Even Maimonides, who opposed the custom, conceded that a father has the authority to betroth his daughter while she is a minor, or a maiden, to whomsoever he wishes.[12] And the lawmakers who pondered the problem of natural sterility in the very young also found a rationale. It was men, not women, who the Bible commanded "to be fruitful and multiply," they argued. And it was men only who were subject to punishment for the crime of Onan.† Coitus interruptus, male masturbation or birth control were criminal acts. The female, who was not considered responsible for procreation, could legitimately masturbate or practice birth control. Her sterility was of no consequence. So, as long as a man placed his penis in a vaginal canal, pointed his sperm in the right direction and did not indulge in any spermal extravagances, "intercourse with a *child* or barren woman" was permitted.[13]

## CHILD RAPE

Because all heterosexual relationships were based upon the sale of a property or the female to a man, Biblical rape was often indis-

---

*The terms underaged or minors refer in this chapter to females under twelve.*

†According to Hebrew law, a man was obligated to marry his dead brother's wife in order to continue his brother's line. Onan avoided impregnation of his dead brother's wife by practicing coitus interruptus, or "spilling his seed upon the ground."

tinguishable from marriage. If a man took an unbetrothed girl's virginity without her father's permission, the culprit had infringed upon another man's property, committed a civil crime which could be erased by payment to the father. And if the father insisted, the rapist had to marry his dishonored daughter. Rape was a crime of theft, legitimatized by payment and marriage:

*When a man comes upon a virgin who is not pledged in marriage and forces her to lie with him and they are discovered, then the man who lies with her shall give the girl's father fifty pieces of silver and she shall be his wife because he has dishonored her.* [14]

The word *dishonor* did not refer to personal insult but to the female's lost virginity. Once penetrated, it was her secondhand status and reduced value which dishonored her. If the rapist paid the bride price, acknowledged possession (if you break it, it's yours) and added her to his household, rape was transformed into marriage and the female was no longer dishonored.

An earlier law differed from this Deuteronomic rendition. In Exodus, the word *seduce*, which implies consent rather than force, stipulated that even if the girl consented, the man was a rapist and payment was required. But unless the father so ordered, marriage was not obligatory.

*When a man seduces a virgin who is not yet betrothed he shall pay the bride price for her to be his wife. If the father refuses to give her to him the seducer shall pay in silver the sum equal to the price for virgins.* [15]

Louis Epstein, student of both Biblical and Talmudic sex laws and customs, has raised the question of whether the child's consent would affect the father's compensation rights. Epstein did not think it would:

*Can a girl's consent matter very much since she does not own herself and when she gives herself gives what she does not own? Furthermore the girl is said to be a minor virgin not yet betrothed, which in Biblical times means she was of very tender age. How can her state of mind make any legal difference?* [16]

And he continued:

*A fair conjecture on the basis of the foregoing is that the Bible treats rape and seduction as one phenomenon legally blaming both on the man.* [17]

Also, since the daughter was the incontrovertible property of her father, Epstein concluded that, unless so ordered, marriage followed by rape was not inevitable:

*It is utterly impossible to believe that the Deuteronomic legislators mean to deny the father the right to object to the girl's marriage to the ravisher for that is contrary to older Biblical tradition.*[18]

Therefore:

*Marriage is compulsory on the offender but subject to the consent of the girl's father . . . this general treatment of rape and seduction remained in force to the end of the second commonwealth (the first and second century of the common era).*[19]

It is Epstein's contention that, whether his daughter was taken by force or not, the Biblical father could demand compensation and give or keep his daughter as he wished.


CHILD PROSTITUTION

But why should a Biblical father whose daughter was raped and dishonored simply take the money and not insist upon marriage? There could be several reasons. He might care deeply for his child and wish to protect her from the slave status of a wife.* He might find her an efficient laborer and wish to keep her services for himself, or he could sell her again at a reduced price as someone's concubine or slave. And finally, if the crime of rape could be obliterated by payment and marriage was not obligatory, there was no crime if a man, with a father's permission, paid a price for repeated sex with an unbetrothed daughter. Biblical prostitution was rape which was paid for and permitted without any obligation to marry. Just as rape and marriage were barely discernible, so were rape and prostitution. Since a father was not compelled to give his daughter in marriage, he could keep both money and daughter and hire her out again and again.

---

*Since it was the male and not the female who was obligated to be "fruitful and multiply," a father was not legally compelled to marry off his daughter; her unmarried, celibate state was not sinful. A male on the other hand was not permitted to remain unmarried or celibate.*

Today we are taught that the sin of the prostitute is the sale of her body and the virtue of the good woman is the discriminating gift of her body. But the female of the Old Testament, who did not own herself, could not dispose of herself, and if she gave her body of her own free will, she was taking illegitimate liberties with her father's property. The Old Testament definition of prostitution is surprising. It was not the woman who sold herself but the daughter who deprived her father of his fee (or the defiance of paternal authority) who was shamed and disgraced. Just as the man who stole a child's virginity was a thief, so was the daughter who gave herself without her father's permission a harlot.[20] When a father disposed of his daughter's sexual favors in a legal monetary transaction, sex between a man and an unmarried, unbetrothed daughter was both legitimate and respectable, and the girl was not a harlot nor the man a rapist.[21] In fact, a daughter who was legitimately prostituted could marry a Jew, and later some rabbis even agreed she could marry a priest.[22] True, a father was advised not to prostitute his daughter, but if he did so he broke no laws and was not subject to punishment.*

If the father who prostituted his daughter was not disgraced, then the female who engaged in the sale of her body under paternal auspices was not an outcast; social approval depended upon whether or not she accepted her property status and properly submitted to being bought and sold. But if she was willful and gave herself to a man of her own volition, she committed a capital crime. The daughter of a priest who gave herself without permission suffered death by fire,[23] and the daughter of an ordinary citizen who "played the prostitute in her father's house" was stoned to death.†[24] There was no Biblical prohibition against prostitution, only against the child who defied paternal authority.

There are even indications that a husband could also exchange his wife for profit and privilege. When Abraham, the first patriarch, was traveling with his beautiful wife, Sarah, he feared that strangers would kill him in order to possess her. They pretended, therefore, to be brother and sister. As foreseen, Abimelech, King of Gerar, took a fancy to Sarah, and thinking she was Abraham's sister,

---

*There is some question as to whether or not the Biblical admonition against prostitution is limited to temple or sacred prostitution—an idolatrous, pagan Canaanite custom.

†If the female who played the prostitute in her father's house was under twelve, the stoning was postponed until she reached her twelfth birthday.

took her for himself. But because he had slept with another man's wife and sinned, God threatened him with death. Abimelech set about to rectify his unwitting crime. He returned Sarah to her husband, heaped land, cattle and other wealth upon Abraham, and because he had sinned unknowingly, repented and made retribution, he was forgiven. But Abimelech was almost duped again by Abraham's son, Isaac, who, when passing through Gerar, also claimed his wife, Rebecca, to be his sister. This time Abimelech discovered the truth before it was too late but was horrified to think what might have happened if Rebecca had been taken to bed. Such pranks were expensive and though Abimelech was penalized, Abraham and Isaac went unpunished; in fact, Abraham was rewarded.[25] Later in Biblical history, the prophet Ezekiel was more disturbed by the woman who gave herself without compensation than by the married prostitute who demanded a fee; because "an adulterous wife who owes obedience to her husband takes fees from strangers." Society favored the prostitute who plied her trade for her husband's benefit over the woman who squandered her talents. To the woman who gave herself without compensation Ezekiel preached: "You are opposite of other women in your fornications; you don't receive a fee, you give it."[26]

Although prostitution in ancient Israel suffered no moral disapproval, in the cities of Europe its practice proved embarrassing. However, when the Talmudists debated the question of father as pimp, they were at a loss as to how to control the problem. They counseled fathers against surrendering their children to "all comers" to have sexual intercourse with them at any price the father might choose,[27] but since the father's right to exploit his minor daughter was inviolate, he could not be fined or punished. General disapproval demanded some control and some punishment. Since the rapist or seducer could be legally penalized and daughters were inconsequential, the daughter and violator, rather than the father, were held accountable:

*Such a man [the father] is not liable to the fine because the Torah has imposed this fine upon the violator and the seducer, while this woman [under 12] who had prepared herself for such misconduct, whether of her own volition or at her father's behest, is a prostitute.*[28]

The sages concluded, therefore, that both the daughter and man are "subject to lashes."[29]

## THE FREE FEMALE

The Bible did not contemplate the free female. In pre-Exile days she was always someone's wife, concubine or slave. In the Diaspora, however, many females had no masters, but men of wisdom were not about to alter a woman's slave status, and in the growing world of art, science and commerce, made no effort to offer her financial security or independence. In fact, free status of the female represented no more than her decreased value to men. When many fathers found themselves saddled with overaged, unmarried daughters, a Talmudic decree relieved fathers from this unwanted responsibility by releasing all overaged daughters from paternal authority. All those "of age" were given their freedom.

If such "freedom" had assured the child, young as she was, of an education, skill and employment, liberty might have been welcomed, but such options were neither offered nor intended. Poor, uneducated and unprotected, like all such women in history, the free female child turned to prostitution as her only means of survival. Even if she managed to obtain menial work, stigma and sexual exploitation were inevitable and therefore a "free" woman was a loose woman, and freedom meant whoredom.*

But in Exilic days, age twelve was not the bottom line for freedom or whoredom. A man previously able to take a widow or divorcee as a third wife, a concubine or a slave could no longer make such accommodations, and therefore a minor widow or divorced female under twelve was also on her own:

*If a father has given her [his daughter] in marriage and she was widowed or divorced while her father was yet living, she is subject to no authority but her own even though still a minor; for once she is married her father has lost authority over her.*[31]

And with the elimination of certain forms of capital punishment, other minors also achieved freedom. The minor rebellious daughter who played the "prostitute in her father's house" and the adulterous

---

*As an interesting aside, the Hebrews of remote antiquity participated in a metronymic family system wherein the wife remained with her own kin and her husband visited for short or long periods; if he displeased her, she dismissed him. Her children belonged to her and bore her name. Originally, the metronymic wife, or zonah, was respectable, but in the wake of the patriarchal family her reputation suffered. Later the free woman was also labeled zonah, but by then the word was transformed from its positive to a negative connotation, and the zonah or metronymic wife came to mean prostitute or whore.*[30]

minor wife who "of her own free will played the harlot" and were previously stoned or burned to death, were now released from either a father's or a husband's authority. And a captive bride might also be released from her husband.

During the European pogroms, the rabbis decided that if a captive Jewish woman could produce two witnesses swearing she had not been raped, her husband could take her back; but even with a witness, if mere suspicion discomforted him, he could divorce her. Some argued that minor child brides should be excluded from this regulation, but they were overruled. So captive child brides who could not produce the necessary witnesses, or those who did have witnesses but were nevertheless suspected of being defiled, were divorced. And the last to join these ranks was a minor whose father had died before he could arrange her marriage and who was given by her brothers or mother. Such a child could dissolve her marriage by declaring her "right of refusal."

If she was six or younger and wished to leave her husband, the marriage was automatically dissolved. If she was ten or over, a formal declaration in front of two witnesses of her wish to leave her husband was necessary. If she was between the ages of six and ten she had to be examined by the authorities to determine whether or not a formal declaration was required. The minor female who was given a "right of refusal" was on her own.[32]

Even if these discarded children were mercifully sheltered by kind relatives and neighbors, neither they nor their relatives could escape the stigma of shame. These children were after all the rebellious deflowered daughter, the adulterous minor wife, the minor captive, the minor bride who declared her right of refusal and the minor widow and divorcee, all rendered cheap by lost virginity and probable sexual use and abuse. They were sexual rejects, unwanted because of their reduced marketability, and, unprotected, they were "free" to be prostitutes, to be molested and to be raped.

STATUTORY NONVIRGINS

Although some women were freed, rape remained a crime of stolen virginity. But the widow, divorcee, rebellious daughter and adulterous wife were free precisely because they had lost their virginity, and if compensation in case of rape depended upon an intact hymen rather than sexual violation, reparation was an empty promise. Some females managed somehow to reach freedom and still retain their virginity, but since the lawmakers were determined to disqualify those who could possibly collect, the law established a category of "statutory nonvirgins"—women and children whose hymens were intact but whose life circumstances made them susceptible to liberties and abuse. Such a one was counted a nonvirgin. She was the overaged twelve-year-old unmarried daughter who was released from her father's authority. Whether she experienced coitus or not, she was ineligible for compensation if raped.

With the elimination of the "overaged," there were those under twelve whose life circumstances made them vulnerable to sexual liberties, and these too were counted as "nonvirgins."[33] These were the redeemed captive minor, the emancipated minor slave, a minor deaf-mute and imbecile and, finally, any virgin under twelve who had a bad reputation.[34] If a minor virgin claimed to have been raped and two witnesses testified that she had been known to abandon herself in unseemly ways since childhood, she too was disqualified. Nor do we end here.

If the law can contrive a "statutory nonvirgin" there is no reason why it cannot conjure up a "statutory virgin."[*] And it did. It decreed that a female under the age of three was too immature to have sexual validity and therefore had no virginity to lose. Copulation with one so young was not illegal but invalid. Maimonides assured us that the rape of one under three was no cause for alarm for, once past three, "she will recover her virginity and be like other virgins."[35] No matter how often a child under three was penetrated, she legally retained her virginity; therefore, any claim against the penetrator could not be pressed and he went unpunished. This peculiar principle of invalid sex below a certain age applied also to the male child. Though male children received full adult status at thirteen, as minors they were classified with women and slaves and therefore also subject to sexual abuse. Rape, or the crime of stolen virginity, did not apply to males, but the crime of homosexuality did, and participants were either put to death or exiled.[†] However,

---

*The term is my own.

†Lesbianism, sex between women, was not illegal. No matter what her relationship with other women, a female was still someone's daughter or wife and subject to male control. But since all men were free, a male who rejected women also rejected his obligation to marry, multiply and perpetuate the patriarchal family. He had to be stopped.

since the male child under nine, just as the female under three, was
not considered a sexual person, a homosexual relationship with a
male child under nine went unpunished.*³⁶ The rape of male
children under nine was overlooked but sex between two consenting
male adults was a capital crime. Thus, all female children under
three and male children under nine could be raped with impunity.
Consequently, the only person eligible to sue for rape was the virgin
not under three nor over twelve, not counted a statutory nonvirgin,
with a good reputation, who could produce two witnesses to testify
that she had been forced into a sexual relationship in the normal
manner. The motive was clear. When the raped daughter was a
property and owned by her father, he was compensated in any case,
but when the daughter became eligible for reparation, exceptions
proliferated and she *could not* collect in any case.


## YESTERDAY AND TODAY

Child marriage is rare in modern industrial cultures but among
communities which have not been exposed to the changing Western
world, the practice continues. In order to prevent child brides, the
state of Israel in 1950 forbade a father or groom to contract a
marriage for a girl under sixteen. This prohibition, however, did not
nullify a marriage performed in defiance of the law since the cere-
mony was valid under Jewish law. A more stringent amendment in
1960 declared that any person involved in the matrimony of a girl
under 17³⁷ (father, rabbi, cantor, groom), whether or not the marriage was validated by ancient law, was subject to imprisonment or
fine or both.

    Tradition, however, is not so easily overcome by legal stric-
ture. We are presently far removed from the world of our ancestors,
but the concept of the female as a sexual property persists. We still
allow that a man cannot rape his wife because we believe that he
cannot be held liable for sexually abusing that which belongs to
him.† Although current legislations demand penalties, the weight of
centuries proves more effective than statutes, and laws are broken

---

*Later flogging was recommended for the rape of little boys.*

†*This is now being contested in some states.*

every day. Sally, who lives in the United States, told us the following story in the early seventies, when she was sixteen:

*My grandmother died when I was thirteen and I was placed in a foster home. I was all alone and my biggest fear was that I would lose this family. One morning the father came into my bedroom when the mother went to work. He made me do things. I am ashamed to say what I did. He said, "Everybody should learn to do this and you are a big girl anyway." I was scared because I thought if I didn't do what he wanted I would be sent away. But he came to my room a lot and then I would gag and felt very sick. Then he began to have intercourse with me. I told him not to do this again because it made me sick but he wouldn't stop. So I told my teacher in school. They didn't believe me and said I had to have a doctor's examination. The doctor hurt me and when I screamed he said, "That shouldn't hurt; you're big enough for a truck." Then I saw a psychiatrist and he didn't believe me.*

*Everyone asked if I realized how serious this was and that the family had been good to me; they said I was too old to go to another foster home. They asked me if I had sex with anyone else and then said that I enticed him.*

*I had to go to the police and I wrote a statement three pages long. Most of the questions were whether I played around with boys and nobody asked me what he did. We went to court and he got away because the judge said I led him on. I told the judge and the police that he did the same to other foster girls in the house. In fact he said to me I shouldn't make a fuss because the other girls liked it. But no one ever asked the other girls what happened to them.*

*I was scared and ashamed. I felt like I had done something wrong; like it was my fault.*

The image of the sexually insatiable female remains. As of old, Sally is held accountable for a sexual offense that was committed against her.

Hebrew law is far from unique in its injustice. Judaic codes did not miraculously appear in the wilderness of the Sinai desert but were derived from those of earlier, more aggressive and powerful nations. The Bible and the Talmud are remarkably similar to, and often imitations of, the Assyrian and Babylonian codes. And though many other Judaic laws were altered, basic sexual decrees and customs, as we shall see, remained unchanged under Christianity.

# 3. THE CHRISTIANS

One lived in a world of brutal lust, where disregard of moral law is accepted as a matter of course by all parties. Where the aim of the confessor is to inflame passions or overcome resistance by coarse violence; where women regard it as natural that the lawful authority of the priesthood is to be exercised by their undoing and their consciousness is to be soothed with pardon granted in the name of God . . . where the Inquisitor busies himself not with moral or spiritual questions involved but with ascertaining whether certain technical rules have been violated.

Henry Charles Lea, *History of Sacerdotal Celibacy in the Christian Church*[1]

Sexual abuse thrived under Christendom. Christian knights, noblemen, crusaders and princes of the church regularly ravished women and children, and for money and power little Christian girls were regularly traded in marriages.

The most striking contrast between Mosaic and Christian doctrine is the materialism of one and the spiritualism of the other. The Hebrews offered both fleshly rewards and worldly punishments, whereas the Christians belittled the treasures of this life and directed all aspirations and fears to eternity. When earthly sin could be forgiven by lining a priestly pocket, and when vows of celibacy did not restrain the clergy from sexual activity, even license, the laity saw no reason to deprive themselves of similar pleasures.

## CHILD MARRIAGE

Canon law ostensibly forbade child marriage. Twelve was the legal age for the bride and fourteen for the groom. The church ruled against a union between persons of dissimilar age and without mutual consent. Marriage of the underaged, between those of dissimilar age and without mutual consent, was, nevertheless, common. Occasionally, a boy was wed to an older woman, but child marriage was primarily the destiny of female children. In fourteenth-century France, a sixty-year-old *burgher* (householder) who had married a fifteen-year-old girl, said: "Seldom will you see a man who will not marry a young woman."[2] It was not at all uncommon for a girl to be a bride at ten, or for one of tender years to be married to a septuagenarian while "church laws did not rescind the nuptials."[3] And since girls were traditionally a property, a *marriage de convenance* was the normal arrangement in every class. In the thirteenth century, Grace, the daughter of Thomas of Saleby, was a great heiress. The king gave her as ward to Adam Neville after her father died. When she was four years old, Adam proposed to marry her. The Bishop forbade the marriage, but while the Bishop was away, the marriage was performed by a priest. And later:

*King John sold Grace to his chamberlain Norman for two hundred marks; and when Norman died, the King sold the poor girl once more for three hundred marks to the third and worst of all husbands, Brian de Lise.*[4]

When acquiring a wife, men were advised to examine her as one would when purchasing a mare. When Edward II searched for a wife for the future Edward III, he sent the Bishop of Stapleton to inspect Philipa of Hainult. The Bishop dutifully submitted the following report:

*The lady whom we saw has not uncomely hair, betwixt blue, black and brown. Her head is clean shaped; her forehead high and broad and standing somewhat forward. . . .Her nose is fairly smooth and even save that it is somewhat broad at the tip and also flattened yet it is no snub nose. . . .Her lips somewhat full and especially the lower lip. Her teeth which have fallen and grown again are white enough but the rest are not so white. . . .Her ears and chin are comely enough. Her neck, shoulder and lower limbs are reasonably well shapen. . . . Moreover she is brown of skin all over and much like her father. . . .And the damsel will be nine years on St. John's day next to come [emphasis mine], as her mother saith. She is neither too short nor too tall for such her age, she is fair in carriage, etc.*[5]

The church considered extreme youth or "nonage" an "impedi-ment" to matrimony, and recalcitrant parents or guardians who married off the underaged were subject to punishment. But so many exceptions were introduced that impediments to nonage or mar-riage when underaged, became meaningless. If a family wished to form an alliance for economic reasons, to consolidate power or avert hostilities, marriage of the underaged was permitted.[6] Where child marriage was customary among converts such as Hindus, the cus-tom was retained.[7] If a child and an adult were illegally wed, a simple act of church "convalidation" would "remedy" this unfortunate situation,[8] or if an underaged child was judged bright enough to comprehend the meaning of marriage, she was deemed old enough to consent and a church dispensation validated the union.[9] The church fathers further reasoned that since extreme youth was only temporary, a child bride would inevitably outgrow the impediment and passage of time would validate the marriage.[10]

With impediments so easily ignored, the church had diffi-culty in establishing just what it was that constituted a valid marriage. Judaism ordained that a bride could be legally acquired by contract, money or sexual intercourse, but since the church eschewed materi-alism, sexual intercourse emerged as the validating factor. As early as the sixth century, Pope Gregory decreed that "any female taken by a man in copulation belonged to him and his kindred."[11] And since copulation with or without consent established male possession of the female, vaginal penetration superseded all impediments. Gratian, twelfth-century Italian ecclesiastic and founder of canon law, set forth that while consent was desirable, conjugal union was rendered in-dissoluble, regardless of age or mutual consent, by coitus. And twelfth-century Pope Alexander III also advised that consent was desirable, but that copulation established a marriage as forever binding.[12] Even if a union was unproductive, if sexual intercourse had taken place with a *child* or barren woman, the marriage could not be dissolved.

Canon law also had far greater regard for copulation than for age, for if the parties "be ripe for marriage, it is a good marriage whatever the age may be."[13] When during the twelfth century a woman asked to be released from a union because she was given below the age of twelve and not in a position to give consent, papal permission was denied because her husband swore that sexual inter-course had taken place.[14] Children who were illegally given when underaged or without consent could, according to church law, repudiate the marriage when legal age was attained. But if vaginal penetration had taken place, the female was bound to her husband for life.

One cannot help but wonder what the church fathers had in mind when they established that penetration qualified a child as "ripe for marriage." Although males have the capacity for penile erection from birth on, they must still be mature enough to have knowledge of and desire for the process in order to copulate. Precocious youths of seven and eight can and do sometimes engage in coitus. So by church definition they are possibly "ripe for marriage." But for the female, neither knowledge nor desire is necessary. All that is required is that she be penetrated, and, equipped with a vaginal canal from birth, she can, from birth, be penetrated. If one can discount her pain and consequent physical damage, the female is constituted for conjugal union from the day she is born. And the church accounts of "impediments" to incest or "affinity" made it clear that male adults were copulating with their betrothed who were age seven or younger.*

### THE "ONE FLESH" PRINCIPLE

The "one flesh" principle appeared in the New Testament: "A man shall leave his father and mother and be made one with his wife; and the two shall become one flesh.[15] This principle was affirmed by Paul and became a tenet of the later church: "You surely know that anyone who links himself with a harlot becomes physically one with her for the Scriptures say 'the pair shall become one flesh.' "[16]

The act of coitus constituted a man and woman as one person; therefore, those who copulated became "one" and were forbidden to each other's relatives. A man who had sexual relations with a woman was in a state of "affinity" to all her kin, and marriage to her sister, for example, was forbidden.[17] Let us say a man who was betrothed to a child wished to dissolve the betrothal and marry her mother. If the man had had carnal knowledge of the child, he was in a state of affinity with her mother and the "impediment of affinity" (or incest) prevented such a marriage. However, *if copulation with the child took place before the child was seven,* the man was then free to marry the

---

*Seven was recognized as the age for transition from infancy to adulthood. At seven boys were eligible for school or apprenticeship. However, since marriage only was contemplated for females, seven was the legal age for female betrothal.*

mother. Why? Because, as in the Hebrew tradition, where sex with a child under three was invalid, so under Christianity was sex with a child under seven invalid. In fact, sex with a child under seven was inconsequential, for *"from betrothal to a girl less than seven the impediment of affinity does not arise."*[18] [Italics mine.] The man who copulated with his betrothed if she was under seven did not violate the impediment of affinity, and was therefore free to marry her mother.

In the twelfth century, the Prince of Norway, for example, became the subject of legal discussion when the woman he was to marry was known to have had carnal relations with the Prince's uncle. The uncle was betrothed to this woman when she was under age seven and he had, by common knowledge and a deposition of witnesses, slept with her. Since all this took place before the child's seventh birthday, the Pope declared both betrothal and sexual relations null and void and the Prince was permitted to marry the woman in question. But soon after this decision, the Pope received additional information. The uncle, now dead, had traveled during the time of his betrothal, but when he returned he married the child *after* her seventh birthday. Since the uncle had had full marital relations with her after she was seven, the Pope was compelled to revoke his earlier decision. If the Prince married her, he would violate the "impediment of affinity." The marriage did not take place.[19]

Christian law did not focus upon whether a man *did* copulate with a child but rather *when* he copulated with her. Sex between men and children was debated not out of concern for a child but out of regard for the technical violation of the impediment of affinity. And since canonists defined sex with a child under seven as invalid rather than illegal, some subsequent jurists took this distinction to mean that rape of one so young was not possible. When the delineation between childhood and adulthood was raised from age seven to ten, jurists who were presented with a case of rape of a seven-year-old "doubted whether rape could be committed upon a child under ten years old."[20]

## CHILD RAPE

Civil law was separated from church law in England under the statutes of Westminster in the thirteenth century. The crime of statutory rape evolved from this event and it became a misdemeanor for a man to ravish a female under the age of twelve even if she did not resist.

Three centuries later, in 1571, one W. D., a Scotsman, was accused of and indicted for the felonious rape of a seven-year-old child. The act was verified by several reliable witnesses. The arrest, however, took place at a time when England was attempting to assert her authority over Scotland and there was greater interest in establishing a precedent of authority over a Scottish subject than in convicting W. D. as a rapist. The court found W. D. subject to British rule but acquitted him of the charge of rape. He went unpunished. Why?

Under the statutes of Westminster, rape of a nonresisting child was a misdemeanor and not a felony, so it appeared that the court was correct in assessing judgment. Though W. D. escaped the charge of felonious rape, he most certainly could have been charged with a misdemeanor. But legal minds could not even agree that he had committed a misdemeanor. According to canon law, sex with a child under seven, just as Hebrew stipulation of sex with a child under three, was invalid and therefore it was legally ignored. Without a precedent, the jurists absurdly read into the court records that they "doubted a rape in so tender a child," and even more absurdly concluded that "if she had been nine or older it would have been otherwise."*[21] Five years later this absurdity was rectified and the possibility of child rape was no longer doubted. In 1576, jurists ruled age ten to be the legal age at which a female child could consent to sex, and twelve remained the legal age at which she could consent to marriage. As a result, carnal knowledge of a "woman-child" below ten was cited as a felony (whether she consented or not), while carnal knowledge of an unresisting "woman-child" between the ages of ten and twelve was a misdemeanor.[22] But no sooner was one absurdity eliminated than another took its place. Unless proof was offered to establish a child's age (at a period of very informal record keeping), the charge of felonious rape could not hold. As late as 1832, a man was freed of the charge of felonious rape

---

*This case was discussed in a modern law journal under the title "A More Than Ordinary Case of Rape." The author was understandably puzzled, for without knowledge of the legal tradition he speculated that "it may be that the justices doubted rape could take place unless procreation was possible." He could not have been aware that in Judaic and Christian tradition, from which most of our common law descends, coitus with immature children was not considered impossible but simply invalid, and therefore legally ignored.

not because he did not rape a child, but because her baptismal certificate indicated that on the day the rape took place, she was two days beyond her tenth birthday.[23] Although the new law recognized the possibility of child rape, child welfare was sacrificed to a legal technicality.

## THE PRIESTHOOD

If ordinary citizens could rape and ravage with impunity, members of the clergy enjoyed even greater sexual privileges. From the most humble to the most exalted, they wielded the power necessary to exact sexual submission. Women and children, mothers, wives, daughters, penitents on a pilgrimage or in the confessional—all were violated by their spiritual fathers. The confessional was so conducive to lechery that Rome issued edicts calling for the punishment of sexual solicitors. But the church had little enthusiasm for imperiling its own authority. The medievalist, Henry Charles Lea, in his *History of Sacerdotal Celibacy,* reasoned that to admit that the confessional was being abused "is to deter people from seeking it. . . .Respect for the sacraments will be destroyed and Christianity will be overthrown."[24] Devoting its greater concern to avoiding scandal and undermining church power, the clergy made it almost impossible to charge or convict an offender. To press a charge, the solicitation could take place neither before nor after, but precisely during the confessional hour; not one, but two denunciations were required. But if a father confessor chalked up two denunciations, the character and motive of the accusor were under greater examination than those of the accused. Church fathers declared that, "Besides it is usually the women who are temptors and when their advances are repelled they will bring false charges to ruin the innocent."[25] And if by any remote possibility a priest was found guilty, his punishment was so light that it hardly deterred future offenses. Naming a sexual solicitor was so difficult, incurred so much suspicion and embarrassment upon the accusor and finally resulted in such light punishment that the process was hardly worth the trouble.

Though discussions of sexual violation by the priesthood are to be found in church records, the victim's age is rarely stated. Occasionally we find references to "infamous things" inflicted upon female children and adolescents, or hear of a father confessor who fondled and copulated with very young penitents. But considering general clerical behavior and the fact that female children and young girls were placed in constant contact with the priesthood, sexual exploitation of female children was inevitable.

In a Christian family of four or five daughters a father could hardly provide dowries for all, so one child was selected for matrimony while the rest were packed off to convents. By age six a girl's fate, marriage or a nunnery, was decided. The less favored usually entered a convent by nine and took their vows by thirteen. And since entry into monastic life necessitated forfeiting all worldly goods, it was not unusual for a child heiress to be shut away by relatives who coveted her inheritance. Convents controlled by ministers and prelates became the "dumping grounds" for unmarried, unwanted female children, and they were soon so crowded with underage novitiates that by the twelfth century parents and guardians were prohibited from taking vows on a child's behalf.[26] These stipulations, as so many others, were ignored.

In the beginning of the eighteenth century the prioress of the convent of St. Caterian di Pisola openly declared that monks and confessors alike treated nuns and young novitiates as wives, but their victims' mouths were sealed by the "dread of excommunication threatened by their spiritual fathers."[27] And since convents were schools for very young girls, she further stated that "when it is considered that convents converted to dens of prostitution were the favorite schools to which girls of the higher classes were sent for training," the sexual exploitation of schoolgirls "can be readily imagined."[28] As late as the nineteenth century, with records revealing only the barest of information, one half of the accusations of clerical sexual abuse were connected with educational institutions.

## THE WITCH HUNT

The witch hunt took place in Europe from the fifteenth to the eighteenth centuries. In 1484 Pope Innocent VIII issued a papal bull empowering the Inquisition (the judicial arm of the church) to find, imprison, examine, torture and execute witches. To facilitate the process, the Dominican friars Heinrich Kramer and James Sprenger compiled the *Malleus Malificarum*, a document which became the guideline for witch hunting and, dog-eared, appeared upon the bench of every Inquisitorial court. This guideline labeled a woman guilty of witchcraft when she merely practiced her traditional role. As midwife she was said to offer newborn babes to the devil, as abortionist she slayed infants in their mothers' wombs and, because of her knowledge of vegetation and birth control, she was said to blast the produce of the earth and prevent wives from conceiving. Coming from a long line of pagan mothers and grandmothers, the document declared, females did not shrink from the foulest abominations and filthiest excesses, and copulated with the devil.[29] Men, however, were exempted from such treachery because "blessed be the Highest who has so far preserved the male sex from so great a crime."[30] But if men were preserved from the crime of witchcraft, children were not.

Witches are generally envisioned as "old, lame, bleary-eyed, foul and full of wrinkles."[31] But since sex was integral to witchcraft, those charged were young, in their prime, and within the age range of sexual activity. The progeny of witches were considered to be automatically contaminated, for "how else would it happen that . . . tender girls of eight have raised up tempests and hailstorms unless they have been dedicated to the devil under such a pact by their mothers . . . which is the way all witches begin."[32] Jean Bodin, sixteenth-century law professor and Carmelite monk, in order to root out this heresy established that the usual legal measures were not applicable. Little girls at age six (legal age for sexual consent in France) were of an age to copulate with the devil, and therefore old enough to stand trial. Bodin found burning by fire too swift (half an hour from beginning to end) and preferred the extended agony of cautery by a hot iron for both children and adults.[33]

Henri Bouget, a prominent lawyer of the same century and nationality, reasoned that once in Satan's clutches, the reform of children under twelve was impossible. He systematically tortured eight-year-old Loyse Mailley until she named accomplices and thus created the basis for a mass witch hunt.[34] Nicholas Remy, demonologist and Inquisitor, found "no lack of examples to prove that their age does not restrain children from committing deeds of witchcraft."[35] In England, Jennie Device, age eight, after incriminating her mother, burned with her as a witch. In the same country both Mary Hicks, age nine, and her mother, Elizabeth, were burned at the stake.[36] In America, five-year-old Sara Good was found capable of "casting an eye" and was imprisoned in chains with her mother.[37] In Luther's Germany,* in 1628, Anna Rausch, age twelve,

---

*Even after the Protestants replaced Catholic authority, the witch hunt and executions continued with the same intensity.*

Sybille Lutz, eleven, and little Murchin, eight and a half, all confessed to having had sexual relations with the incubus (male demon). Sybille and Anna were put to death, but Murchin and some other children were remanded to their fathers for reformation.[38] In a letter to an unidentified friend in 1624, the chancellor to the Prince-Bishop of Wurtzburg stated that "there have been 300 children of three and four who are said to have intercourse with the devil. I have seen children of seven put to death."[39]

In Mora, Sweden, in 1669, authorities claimed that the devil had hundreds of children in his power; fifteen were burned and thirty-six between nine and fifteen were condemned to be scourged at the church door weekly for a year.[40] In the Hague at the close of the seventeenth century, eight youths under age fifteen and one girl age twelve "confessed" to fornication with the devil and died at the stake.[41]

In a society where sexual abuse went unhampered and people believed in evil spirits, it was not difficult to attribute a sexual offense to a supernatural spirit. Remy was satisfied that a child who "could not suffer a man" could accommodate the devil, and in his treatise on demonology he wrote:

*Although Catherina Latomia of Marche at Haracourt, February 1587, was not yet of an age to suffer a man, he [the devil] twice raped her in prison being moved with hatred for her because he saw that she intended to confess her crime; and she very nearly died of the injuries she received from that coitus.*[42]

Victims of sexual abuse, without a recourse, found it simpler to blame or even believe that spectral demons rather than flesh and blood men had violated them.

During the three hundred years of Europe's witch hunt it was recorded that the daughter of Donald McGrigor said that she had been confronted by the devil in the shape of a man who "offered her a dollar if she should go with him."[43] Margaret Duchall "did freelie confess hir paction with the diwell, how he appeared first to hir in the likeness of a man in braun cloathis and ane blak hat."[44] When Isobell Smyth was alone gathering heather, "the devil appeared to hir alone lik ane braw gentelman."[45] Thirteen-year-old Annabel Stuart declared that the "devil in the shape of a black man came to her mother's house and required that she give herself to him,"[46] and Maria deAllara at age eight became a witch when a man wearing white long trousers fondled her and he was Satan. "She had intercourse with him 20 times."[47] One unfortunate child who claimed to have been abused by an incubus was discovered to be infected with virulent gonorrhea, and, to divert attention from her pregnancy, another girl claimed to be possessed by three devils.[48]

Since evil spirits conveniently substituted for sex offenders, the incubus or male demon was, not surprisingly, far more enterprising than the succubus, the female demon. Scores of girls "furnished evidence of having yielded their virginity to creatures of the male gender," who they said were "none other than the devil."[49] Considering the general eagerness to brand females as sexually culpable, some wondered if these feminine complaints were not simply a disguise for sexual indulgence. After all, a sinful nun might try to palm off her lover as an incubus, and undoubtedly when a nun was disgraced by lost virginity or pregnancy, attempts at deception occurred. Demonologists who believed in devils and witchcraft were not, however, easily deceived, and wondered why they should not suspect that these women used spirits to cover their adulteries and sin.[50] As late as the twentieth century, the Reverend Montague Summers, firm believer in the supernatural and renowned scholar of witch hunts and witchcraft, interpreted the complaints by seventeenth- and eighteenth-century nuns of molestation by spirits as a diversion from their own lascivious behavior. The history of Sister Marie Renata was a case in point. During the eighteenth century, after fifty years of devotion, she was accused of bewitching other nuns. Under torture she confessed that she had given herself to Satan at age eight and at thirteen had entered into a sexual alliance with two demons. Alerted to imposture, and, after meticulous research, Summers revealed that Sister Renata had in fact lent herself "to the foul desires of a man of high estate," and the two whom she claimed were demons were actually "two officers."[51] Until the moment she was beheaded, Sister Renata insisted it was the devil who took possession of her body and copulation with him was all too real.[52]

In seventeenth-century France, nuns, novitiates and schoolgirls came to God's emissaries in alarming numbers begging for relief from sexual torment inflicted by demons. Their complaints were accompanied by dramatic convulsions, writhings and vomiting that made it impossible to ignore the "epidemic." France soon became the showcase for the bizarre behavior of females residing in convents and, in some instances, the prosecution of heretical priests.

## SEX OFFENDERS AND POSSESSED WOMEN AND CHILDREN

Witchcraft was primarily a female sexual crime, but when on rare occasions a man was prosecuted, charges of seduction, rape or lechery were incidental to the greater crimes of wizardry, sorcery or magic.* Fathers Louis Gaufridi, Urbain Grandier and the priests of the convent at Louviers had all violated women and children but each was executed, not for sexual violation, but for sorcery or magic. Each could have escaped torture and death if the charge had only been one of sexual immorality, but each father confessor was unfortunate enough to have been the victim of local rivalries, power politics or to have influential enemies who wanted him eliminated.

Father Louis Gaufridi was a charming, handsome parish priest who was Madeline de la Palud's father confessor and seducer. When gossip of his prolonged visits with thirteen-year-old Madeline reached Mother Superior Catherine, the child confessed that Gaufridi had stolen her "most beautiful rose." Since such indelicacies were not unusual, Madeline was discreetly transferred to the more distant convent at Aix-en-Provence. But when at fifteen Madeline was taken with violent convulsions, she averred that she was first debauched by Gaufridi at age nine and as the result of "his magic," was possessed by three devils. Father Romillion, director of the convent, had no love for the carefree Gaufridi. Dominican Inquisitors were always pleased to bring ignominy upon a secular priest and the French laity, generally resentful of Roman power, was more than eager to expose church corruption. The Inquisitors, wishing to be rid of Gaufridi, preferred to associate Madeline's contortions and vomiting to devilish possession caused by this "Prince of Magicians" rather than to the torment she suffered from priestly sexual abuse. Without any evidence whatsoever that Gaufridi practiced wizardry, he was subjected to extreme torture and asked to name accomplices. He named no one. On April 11, 1611, he was first strangled to death and then burned. Ironically, Gaufridi, guilty of child molestation, was punished for a crime of which he was innocent.

As soon as Gaufridi was executed, Madeline, age nineteen, seen as tainted by sexual use, was rejected by both the church and her family. At forty-nine she was accused of being a witch and

---

*One male for every twenty females was executed for compaction with the devil.

imprisoned. Ten years later she was released into the custody of a distant cousin and died at the age of seventy.

Father Urbain Grandier, confessor at the convent of Loudin, also a charming, audacious scoundrel, had the temerity to impregnate the twelve-year-old daughter of the public prosecutor. As a result of this offense and his open sexual activity, he was charged with lechery but received only mild censure. Grandier had also written a treatise opposing priestly celibacy and had fallen into the bad graces of Richelieu, so when Sister Jeanne des Agnes of the convent of Loudin swore that he was a sorcerer who had bewitched her, she found much support. Some say that Sister Jeanne was involved in a plot to undermine Grandier and others, that she pretended possession when he spurned her advances. In any case, sixty women from among nuns and laity bore witness to his sexual misconduct. Charges of sorcery followed and Grandier was found guilty of heresy. Under torture he confessed to having entered into a pact with the devil. Horrified, some nuns testified that their charges of sorcery had been dictated by his enemies, but the courts refused to acknowledge their retractions. Grandier was found guilty of magic, demonological possession and malefactia. He was tortured until the "marrow oozed from his bones," but he, too, refused to name accomplices. He was burned alive on August 18, 1634. After Grandier's demise, his enemies, including Cardinal Richelieu, withdrew the financial support they had contributed to the sisters who testified against him.

Despite inhuman torture Grandier had the strength to refrain from incriminating fellow human beings, but he could not refrain from sexually seducing a twelve-year-old child. Neither Grandier nor Gaufridi lacked courage or integrity, but impregnating and disgracing women and children never offended their code of ethics or their honor.

The members of the clergy who were involved in the Louviers affair were devoted to a mystical sect known as the "quietists," a group neither approved nor recognized by the Vatican. When the pious Madeline Bevant, orphaned at nine and apprenticed to a linen establishment, was seduced and disgraced at age twelve by a monk, she entered the convent at Louviers. The chaplain, Father David, devotee of the quietists, demanded total surrender to his will, instructed the nuns to worship in the nude and submit to his "lustful embraces." After Father David died, Father

Picard, of the same religious inclination, replaced him. Madeline became pregnant by him; he gave her an abortive which resulted in a "painful evacuation"; he also shared her with his aide, Father Boullé. When, after fourteen years, Picard died, Madeline and other nuns exhibited the symptoms of possession and at public exorcism the inhabiting devils revealed the convent's erotic secrets. Since Madeline's experience was presented in greatest detail (she kept a diary), the Bishop charged her with witchcraft and copulating with devils. She was expelled from the order and thrown in prison, where she was "wantonly" abused and miserably treated. She attempted to take her life by stopping her menstrual flow with rags, swallowing spiders and bribing a boy to bring her arsenic. She finally died in prison at the age of forty. In 1644, quietists Boullé and his aide, Duval, were charged with witchcraft and heresy and were burned alive.[53]

## POSSESSION: FANTASY OR HYSTERIA?

We are too sophisticated today to believe in devils but have substituted scientific "fantasy" for superstition. In his rather superficial study of witchcraft, Freud speculated that to the befuddled witch, her broomstick represented the "great god penis" and her stories of copulating devils were derivations of a chaotic psyche. We are informed today that the case of sixteenth-century Jeanne Fery, who was seduced at fourteen and then later claimed to be tormented by devils, "reads like a classical diagnosis of hysteria,"[54] while the cloistered nuns at the convent at Lille who insisted they cohabited with devils were "attempting to compensate for their sad experience [isolation from the male sex] with daydreams."[55] Whether one believes that irrational behavior stems from original sin or from repressed sexual guilt depends also upon one's superstition. I have no quarrel with students of human fantasy, but their credibility is strained if they prefer dubious psychic experience to concrete facts. How is it possible that Freud and some of his followers could not acknowledge that the confessions of witches, extracted under torture, reflected the projections of theologians, lawyers and Inquisitors? Would not these unfortunate women have confessed to anything, including copulation with the devil and flying on broomsticks, in order to stop the pain?

Even today, powerless, frustrated, sexually abused children

exhibit symptoms similar to those of the nuns and children who claimed to be invaded by an alien force. Take, for example, Virginia, who was systematically abused at family gatherings:

*It was nothing like penetration, just the pawing and feeling and "Come on, you're so pretty. Give your uncle a little kiss." There was one uncle in Reichian therapy and he would press against me with a big penis. First I used to make believe I was sick and go to the bathroom, but after a while I did get sick every time and vomit in the toilet. I begged not to go but I was only ten, so my mother made me.*

Betty also behaved very strangely when she was sexually used by a man she trusted and liked:

*When I was 11 we lived in the country and I would visit the cows on a neighboring farm. The old farmer there was always nice to me, very friendly and kind, but when I was 11 he began to tease me a lot and wrestle with me. He got excited and frightened me, and I knew something sexual was going on. I used to love to go to the farm, but because he kept putting his hands on me and teasing and wrestling, I couldn't go anymore. After a while I knew I didn't want men to get excited when they saw me, so when my breasts began to develop, I bound them very tight with bandages but first I cut the skin with a razor so the bleeding would explain the bandages.*

The tendency to disbelieve a victim's understanding of her own disturbance, the refusal to recognize that a sexual advance by a trusted adult, priest or an uncle can be extremely detrimental, will only compound a child's sense of isolation and confusion. This psychiatric analysis of Judy is one such example:

*Early in puberty Judy was frightened by sex; she told of an incident at her uncle's house when she was baby-sitting for her cousin and the uncle asked her to undress in front of him. Judy added, "Of course I didn't," and continued her account by describing how the uncle touched her "all over." She could not imagine what his intentions were; she only knew that she could not stand his touching her much longer. "I nearly went out of my mind," she added.[56]*
*The seduction scene with the uncle seems to have been a prepubertal trauma following the model described by Greenacre. "These trauma were provoked by the victims and were compulsive repetitions of pre-Oedipal conflicts influencing the intensity of the Oedipal phase and subsequent severity and deformation of the superego. . . . "*

*This incident [the seduction] was followed by an avoidance of any situation which might arouse sexual feelings. When Judy eventually found herself alone with a boy she feared being attacked by him; obviously she feared her own loss of control. To an impasse of this kind she reacted with nausea and vomiting. We recognize in these transient symptoms an ingestive which seems to extend back into the period of oral ambivalence.*[57]

If the psychiatrist had listened to Judy he might have hit upon the problem. It was not loss of control over her sexual feelings or "pre-Oedipal conflict" that overwhelmed Judy, but rather her adult uncle's flaunting of his own lack of control; Judy, within her rights, did not want him to touch her, and in a society that refuses to recognize the violation of this right, she did indeed nearly go out of her mind. And just as the possessed nuns were tormented by real people, so was Judy equally tormented by a flesh-and-blood relative.

Today as in the past, spiritual fathers, like other father figures, continue undisturbed to molest their spiritual daughters. Along with teachers, psychiatrists, uncles, fathers and stepfathers, many revered men of the cloth find some small pleasure in tormenting little girls. Testimonies regarding sexual abuse by men of the church are not difficult to find. In 1975 Barbara spoke as follows of her molestation by the local priest:

*When I was quite young, about six or seven, my sisters, who were older than I, and myself used to go to tea at our local priest's house and he would always sit me on his lap and start touching me. He'd touch me between my legs and touch my bottom and put his hand up my skirt. I didn't have any breasts but he would kind of feel me around there and it felt very uncomfortable for me, I knew it was wrong. I did in fact tell my guardian when I got home that I didn't want to go there anymore. First of all I said that I didn't like the smell of his house, any reason but the truth. But she did not believe me and made me tell her the truth.*

*When I did I was punished for being so evil as to think this about a priest. I was not given desserts and had to do all the washing and wiping up for about a week. It was never mentioned again but I still had to go to his house. Nobody mentioned it to him at all and he still continued to do it. Since I was told that the priests didn't do this sort of thing and I was to blame, I really began to think that perhaps he hadn't done it. I just had a nasty imagination.*

Claire had her experience with a guitar-playing local minister:

*When I was about 14, living with my aunt and uncle, I needed a summer job.*

*They were very friendly with the minister of one of the biggest churches in the community. This minister gave me guitar lessons; that's how I met him originally. Then he gave me a job in his office.*

*I would be running things off on the mimeograph machine or addressing envelopes and all of a sudden he would come over to me and put his hands on my breasts. And he would say, "Hmmm, you're really growing into a fine young lady." I didn't know how to handle it. I didn't know what to say. I knew deep down he shouldn't be doing that . . . He was much older and he was a minister. I never said anything to my aunt and uncle because I knew they wouldn't believe me because they were very involved with the church and really liked the minister. And so it kept on happening. Finally, I told my aunt I was going to quit that job. I left but never forgot it. He was in his forties, married with children my age. I would have told my aunt and uncle but I didn't want to be in a position where I'd have to prove myself when it was this man who was doing something wrong—not me.*

Louise, who became pregnant at thirteen, was not molested but "damned" for life by her father-confessor:

*I became pregnant at thirteen by a high school teacher. My parents took me to a priest. He told me I was a vessel of sin—it was my fault. Nobody, not even a boy my own age, would attempt to seduce a decent girl of 13. I was going to perish in hell.*

*I freaked out. That's the reason I could deal with suicide, because I had already committed mortal sin. I was already damned. For a long time it didn't make any difference what happened to me because I was going to hell anyway. I was already dead.*

Sally's foster father, a deacon, was not deterred either as a father or a deacon from getting his sexual pleasure:

*My foster father was a deacon and he molested me for six years from 11 to 17 years old. He got at me every chance he could; three or four times a week. I was very confused. I knew nothing about sex and could not understand what he wanted of me. He was a quiet, respected man and though he kissed me sexy, he was the only father I had. I never dreamed of telling anyone. I had no choice. Where would I go? I felt it was my fault.*

Historian Jacob Burckhardt recognized that the brutality of the corrupt church destroyed human souls and "drove multitudes of the noblest spirits . . . into the arms of despair."[58] During the period of absolute Roman Catholic power, nuns, novitiates and schoolgirls were in fact the exclusive property of the monks. When without recourse or relief they named incubi as their tormentors, they were indeed possessed, not by spirits, but by actual men who in reality manipulated their bodies as if they were nothing more than pieces of property. Yet such scholars of the human soul as religious leaders and psychiatrists, will not identify those who preach purity while they seduce and rape as contributing to the shattered female psyche. No matter how much history has established the existence of sexual slavery, authorities of every age have found the means to ignore its reality.

# 4. GREEK LOVE

If we examine the truth of the matter, Protogenes, the passion for boys and for women derives from one and the same Love.

Plutarch, "On Love"[1]

The eighteenth-century English statesman Lord Chesterfield advised his son that "women then are children of larger growth."[2] I presume that Lord Chesterfield included little boys among those children he identified with women. Horace, first-century B.C. Latin poet and satirist, also lumped women and children together and recommended sporting with either one. When a man is in a passion, Horace suggested, he should avail himself of a slave girl, but if a slave girl is not about, a boy at hand will do.[3] The ancient Greeks, avowed boy lovers, unlike Horace did not identify boys with females, although they treated them as such.* The mythical Pandora who opened the forbidden vessel and heaped evil upon the world was the Greek prototype of the treacherous nature of all women. Man, who was opposite from woman, approached the ultimate in virtue, and boys in their bloom most approximated perfection. Therefore, the Greeks found youth, or more specifically "youths," and beauty synonymous, and to attain the pinnacle of human perfection Greek men pursued young boys. In addition to philosophy, art, science, mathematics and other incalculable contributions to civilization, the Greeks gave us "pederasty,"† a custom which advocated sexual relationships between mature and immature males. During Greece's Golden Age, pederasty flourished along with divine philosophy. In addition to divine philosophy, pederasty had many practical uses.

---

*Cf. Chapter 14, "The Sexual Abuse of Boys."

†It is interesting to note that the word pederast has the same root as pedagogue, which means teacher or instructor.

## BOY LOVE

To the imperialistic Greeks, war, heroism, art, poetry and youth were not incongruous, and men who courted death and danger were poetically honored:

> *In a young man all is beautiful when he possesses*
> *The shining flower of youth.*
> *Alive he is adored by men and desired by women.*
> *And the finest to look at when he falls dead*
> *In a forward clash!!*[4]

And since war required an ample supply of young men prepared to "fall dead," militarism and pederasty served each other well. Plato proposed that an army of lovers could provide his country with an invincible army:

*Of what am I speaking? Of the sense of honour and dishonour without which neither states nor individuals do any great work. And I say that a lover who is detected doing any dishonourable act, or submitting through cowardice when any dishonour is done to him by another, will be more pained at being detected by his beloved than at being seen by his father or his companions, or by anyone else. The beloved too, when he is found in any disgraceful situation, has the same feeling about his lover. And if there were only some way of contriving that a state or an army be made up of lovers and their loves, they would be the best governors of their own city, abstaining from all dishonour and emulating one another in honour; and when fighting at each other's side though a mere handful, they would overcome the world. For what lover would not choose rather to be seen by all mankind than by his beloved either when abandoning his post or throwing away his arms? He would be ready to die a thousand deaths than endure this....*

*Love would inspire him, that courage . . . which the gods breathe into the soul of some heroes, love of his own nature infuses into the lover. Love will make men dare to die for their beloved!*[5]

Undoubtedly lovers were brave, but Greek militarists were too practical to rely on love alone. Boys, subjected to incessant pressure, were severely punished if they fell short of required standards of courage. The Spartans fined and disgraced an adult lover if his boy cried out "effeminately" in battle, and Pericles, ruler of Athens, cautioned: "Our love of things of the mind does not make us soft,"[6] for "we give obedience to those in authority and obey the laws themselves."[7] And "those in authority" were men, not boys.

The men who ruled Greece kept a tight rein on their beautiful boys. Pederasty was, in fact, a means of raising Greek soldiers in accordance with government specifications, and city-states such as Athens, Sparta, Corinth and Crete issued legal guidelines regulating the practice. Just as each barely pubescent girl was compelled to marry a man from fifteen to twenty years her senior, so each male child of noble family had no choice but to take an adult lover. Greek fathers, distracted by the Olympic games, theater, symposium, courtesans and their own boy lovers, often neglected their sons. Pederasty was thus the prime method of education, with each adult male expected to act as teacher and counsellor to a boy and each boy to be paired off at age twelve. A man desiring a youth was obliged, however, to abide by legal procedures, and any unauthorized abduction was severely penalized. When of age, a twelve-year-old could be courted, and often many admirers would vie for his favor in open competition with gifts, poetry, flattery and even cash. Once a suitor was approved by the father, the lucky man was permitted to possess the boy by rape.

The custom, some say, was derived from divine precedent established in the myth of Zeus and Ganymede. The beautiful boy Ganymede so charmed Zeus that he transformed himself into an eagle and swept the boy to Mount Olympus, where he served as cup bearer and Zeus's favorite. This abduction was a privilege permitted only to a god. When the mortal Laius, father of Oedipus, secretly abducted Chrysippus, the young son of King Pelops, this unauthorized theft by a mortal was condemned as a capital crime. Just as with the Hebrew daughter, lack of paternal permission transformed sex with a boy into a crime. In the tradition of Zeus and Ganymede, the sexual use of boys was allowed, but to avoid the affront committed by Laius, a potential suitor was expected to consult the boy's father for approval and then publicly announce his intentions. Once this was accomplished, in keeping with mythology and custom a mock abduction was staged, with family and friends feigning anger and even pursuit; but when the game was over, the lover received his prize.

The pair then secluded themselves for a month or more from the community, and during this time the boy received rich gifts from his adult lover, among which was full military equipment. Youths thus chosen were honored with special privileges and distinguished from those less fortunate who, unselected, were presumed to suffer from faulty character and held in disgrace. Upon completion of the ritual, the adult was responsible for the conduct of his young comrade. Their time was spent in perfecting dexterity of body and mind, use of weapons, horsemanship, execution of duties and obedience to authority.[8]

No matter how noble this custom was made to appear, adult lovers enjoyed every advantage over their boys. No matter how much pederasty was idealized as the fountainhead of civic and personal virtue,[9] equality was not conducive to a man's sexual pleasure, and despite all aspirations toward masculinity, "oh, sweet boy like a girl"[10] exemplified adult male interest. Boys trained as wrestlers were assessed more for their potential performance in bed than their skill:

> *Yesterday I supped with the boy's trainer, Demetrius,*
> *The most blessed of all men.*
> *One boy lay on his lap*
> *One stooped over his shoulder*
> *One brought him the dishes and another served him with drink—*
> *The admirable quartette.*
> *I said to him in fun,*
> *"Do you, my dear friend, work the boys at night too?"*[11]

Characteristics found attractive in women were sought after.

> *I like them pale*
> *And also I love those the color of honey, and the fair too;*
> *And on the other hand I am taken by the black haired.*
> *Nor do I dismiss brown eyes;*
> *But above all I love sparkling black eyes.*[12]

There's always one who prefers the very young, the forbidden:

> *My neighbor's quite tender young boy*
> *Provokes me not a little,*
> *And laughs in no novice manner to show me that he is willing.*
> *But he is no more than twelve years old.*

*Now the unripe grapes are unguarded;*
*But when he ripens there will be watchmen at the gates.*[13]

Greek poetry abounds with men swooning for the "tender flower of youth" and "the thighs and delicious mouth" of pubescent boys. The man who pitifully pined for a boy's smooth limbs, blushed at the mention of his darling's name, or slept cold nights on his beloved's doorstep, was the man who ruled Greece. But these Greek rulers did not esteem homosexuality per se. Only sex between men and boys was deemed desirable. Congress between equally grown men was unacceptable and scorned. Once a boy matured, custom demanded that the lovers part and the boy, now entering manhood, was expected to, in turn, pursue women and other young boys. Greek men who rejected hairy lovers, however, respected maturity in their colleagues. Solon, lawmaker and pederast, attributed wisdom and authority to men past forty.[14] Adult males did not covet boyish immaturity in themselves, but as one acquires a work of art, so did Greek men possess charming boys. When it came to boy love, they scoffed at equality and brotherhood:

*If you see beauty, strike while the iron is hot.*
*Say what you mean, grab his testicles full-handed.*
*But if you say "I reverence you and will be like a brother"*
*Shame will close your road to accomplishment.*[15]

Oddly enough, we hear nothing from youths admiring the hairy thighs and bristling lips of their bearded lovers. Greek men fantasized that "by the very fact that we breathe our love into beautiful boys we keep them from avarice . . . strengthen modesty and self control."[16] This obsession with superficial beauty and pretensions of virtue was bound to lead to corruption, and beautiful boys were hardly convinced that their advantage lay in modesty and lack of avarice. At an Athenian banquet, one handsome youth immodestly announced: "We beautiful persons, since we produce a certain inspiration in those who are inclined to love, render them more generous with regard to money. . . . "[17] First extolling the glories of masculinity for militaristic purposes, then demeaning boys as females in order to use them sexually, pederasts came to be despised by many youths:

*There is no class of men for whom they [youths] have more persistent suspicion and hatred than their pederasts and when the opportunity offers they exact terrible vengeance. Archelaus was killed by Crateas who had been made a minion and Alexander of Pherae by Pytholaus. Periander, the tyrant of Ambracia, asked his minion whether or not he was with child and the lad was so infuriated that he killed him.* [18]

With homosexual alliances restricted to a man and a youth, this inequality, so like the heterosexual male/female combination, inevitably resulted in men trifling with boys as they did with women. They took them as concubines, bought and sold them in prostitution. Just as women, valued for charm and sexual appeal, employ these assets for favor, privilege and money, so did attractive lads learn to play one admirer against the other to increase their supply of gifts. Yet the very men who encouraged this behavior were horrified to learn that their pets were opportunistic, and that "alluring boys commanded a higher price than a farm." [19] But if men were willing to buy, then boys were willing to sell, and in ancient Greece there were as many boys as females in brothels, with free boys as well as slaves available for hire.

But the Greek interest in young boys went beyond voluntary prostitution. Some boys were violated, raped and forced into sexual slavery. And since soft femininity was so desired, many boys were castrated, for men found in them the height of pleasure. The ruler of Corinth appropriated three hundred boys from the subjugated colony of Cacyra (Corfu) for castration and sale; the eunuch, Hermotimus, had been castrated by Panionius, a man who made his living by kidnapping good-looking boys, castrating them and then selling them at a high price. [20]

Greek men wanted in their boys what they wanted in women: hairless, soft, powerless immaturity; and poets urged lovers to snatch their pleasure in the time allotted by a beardless face:

> *Enjoy the season of thy prime;*
> *All things soon decline*
> *One summer turns a kid into*
> *A shaggy he-goat.* [21]

It has often been said that the tyranny of Greek love could only be severed by a hair.

Eventually, Plato came to despise Greek love. Many boys, first pampered, were later abandoned. His original faith in pederasty soured bitterly:

*Learn the lesson that there is no kindness in the friendship of a lover; its object is the satisfaction of an appetite like the appetite for food. As wolves for lambs, so lovers lust for boys.* [22]

And some boys who were never able to make the required leap and transform themselves into proper wolves, continued in their attempts to please men by maintaining soft girlish charm, but behavior that was charming in a boy was ridiculed in a man: "You lisp—your tongue's plaguey weak. My infant son could speak louder," followed by the greatest insult of all, "May I call you sister?"[23] Men who acted like women were so despised that by the time the Greek civilization passed to the Romans, there was no dishonor in raping them.

The Romans, unlike the Greeks, had few romantic pretensions, and to them sex was viewed as a means of humiliating enemies and unequals. Tiberius enjoyed witnessing the mutilation of the genitals of his enemies, and Nero castrated the boy Sporus, married him in a mock wedding, dressed him as a woman, and exhibited him as a plaything to the populace of Rome.[24] And in the eighteenth century, the notorious rake Lord Rochester also found pleasure in dehumanizing and brutalizing either his whore or his page:

> *I send for my whore and for fear of*
> *the clap*
> *I fuck in her hand and spew in her lap*
> *Then we quarrel and scold 'til I fall*
> *asleep*
> *When the bitch growing bold to my*
> *pocket does creep*
> *Then slyly she leaves me and*
> *to revenge the affront*
> *At once she bereaves me of money and cunt.*
> *If by chance when I awake, hot-headed*
> *and drunk*
> *What a coil do I make for loss of my punk?*

> *I storm and I roar and I fall in a rage*
> *And missing my whore, I bugger my page.* [25]

Lord Rochester, like Lord Chesterfield, saw women and children as the same and trifled with both.

# 5. A VICTORIAN CHILDHOOD

The honey of her infant lips
The bread and wine of her sweet smile
The wild Game of her roving eye
Does him to Infancy beguile.
William Blake, "The Mental Traveller"[1]

The nineteenth century was a time of unprecedented industrial advance and scientific achievement. It was also a century replete with gentlemen who had an overwhelming predilection for little girls. Marcel Proust said: "It is so short, that radiant morning time that one comes to like only the very youngest girls, those in whom the flesh, like precious leaven, is still at work."[2]

This attraction, or "the cult of the little girl," usually manifested itself in the deification of immature females, but when passion broke respectable bounds, the result was the molestation, rape, prostitution and pornographic degradation of Victorian children.

This contradiction is hardly surprising. For all their progress, Victorian Titans were unable to evaluate human sexuality. Scholars of the incipient schools of human behavior concurred that the female was naturally sexless and to imply that she had erotic feelings was to cast "vile aspersions" on the fair sex. The male sex drive, however, was the energy which enabled men to acquire wealth, property, a wife, a home and raise a family; in short, it was the source which advanced civilization. Given this monumental inflation of the male "creative instinct," some undesirable side effects such as the violation of children were tolerated. Even the most inadequate records indicated an alarming increase in sexual assaults upon children. In 1888, Krafft-Ebing, physician and sexologist, said:

*Criminal statistics prove the sad fact that sexual crimes are progressively increasing in our modern civilization. This is particularly the case with immoral acts with children under fourteen.*[3]

And, according to the socialist August Bebel:

*Still another gratification of the sexual instinct manifests itself in the violation of children, a practice that has increased greatly during the past thirty years.*[4]

Psychologist Theodore Stekel warned against grandfathers who enjoyed inserting their fingers into their granddaughters' vaginas, and told the story of a child who screamed when her surgeon, after a tonsillectomy, slipped his hands under the covers and handled her indecently. (She was forced to ask his forgiveness for raising such a fuss.)[5] Child molesters, particularly those of respectable families, were well protected. Lord Galloway, brother-in-law to the Prime Minister, Lord Salisbury, was accused of having his hand under the dress of ten-year-old Jane Gibson. Lord Galloway insisted that he and Jane were merely picking brambles, but one witness, Mrs. Moffat, attracted much attention when she shouted, "For shame, you old blackguard. What have you been doing?"[6] The court, nevertheless, held that since Jane was too young to understand a lewd motive, "if indeed lewdness was intended" (why else would his hand be under her dress?), no harm was done and the case was dismissed. Society breathed a sigh of relief. As long as a veneer of respectability was maintained, the watchful eye of Mrs. Grundy was quite ineffective and in the words of one writer, "The pretty, bright-eyed maidens who captivated the hearts of elderly gentlemen went through hell behind nursery and school shutters."[7]

## MEN OF LETTERS

The image of the innocent child emerged during the eighteenth century and continued throughout the nineteenth and early twentieth centuries in all media forms, but her virgin-whore demeanor created ambivalence in the noblest of men. Even the pious William Wordsworth, torn between reverence and desire, poetically subjected his "darling child" to an "overseeing power to kindle or restrain."[8] The lyric poet Ernest Dowson dedicated a series of sonnets to little girls, and to be assured of their constant purity occasionally condemned them to an early grave. In "The Dead Child" he ordered a young beloved to "Lie still and be forevermore a child."[9] Unlike Wordsworth, however, Dowson stepped beyond poetic fantasy and at age twenty-seven courted Adelaide, a twelve-year-old waitress. He proposed marriage to her before her fifteenth birthday but, under close parental control, she refused. Dowson, heartbroken, found gratification elsewhere. In a letter to a friend, he confided that he was compelled to give up underaged "tarts" because England had raised the age of consent from thirteen to sixteen and "le jeu ne valait," or "the game is not worth it."[10] Edgar Allen Poe also killed off his child love in verse when a wind came along, "chilling and killing my Annabel Lee."[11] But at age twenty-six, his marriage to his thirteen-year-old cousin Virginia was all too real.[12] Charles Dickens moved two continents to tears with accounts of the angelic, immaculate "Little Nell." He too prevented any possibility of corrupt maturity by sending her at fourteen to a pristine grave. After a marriage of twenty years, Dickens left his wife and eleven children and set up the eighteen-year-old Ellen Ternan as his mistress.[13] John Ruskin, the greatest art critic of his day, was positively foolish when it came to little girls. While appraising a Kate Greenaway illustration, he went into raptures over one child whom he said was "just three days and a minute too old for me" and mourned two other tiny ones because "I think they already have lovers."[14] At thirty-nine, Ruskin fell madly in love with his nine-year-old pupil, Rose la Touche. He never stopped pursuing (and tormenting) her until this sickly, deeply disturbed child died in her mid-twenties.[15]

## A DIFFERENT CASE

Lewis Carroll does not, in my opinion, belong in the category of men who sentimentalize little girls and then proceed to fall in love, pursue or marry them. But since so many have interpreted his active interest in female children as far from "innocent," I feel I cannot ignore him or the saga of his childhood friends. True, Carroll spent much of his time in the company of little girls, found little boys and infants unattractive, pressed for introductions to families where there were small daughters, went to the beach equipped with pins to accommodate children with long skirts who wished to go wading and, as an amateur photographer, preferred to pose his young models nude. In 1880 he suddenly abandoned photography, and there are those who speculate that he did so in order to avoid a scandal. After his death, his nephew, who did not wish to "lift the veil from dead sanctities," deleted portions of his diaries.[16]

Despite these implications, I fail to see Carroll as a "dirty old man"—in fantasy, perhaps, but not in fact. The photos he took of nude children were all returned to their models and the few that remain are, as were so many of his day, more sentimental than sexually provocative.* Carroll engaged his childhood friends in a variety of games, told them stories, took them on outings and to the theater. Wiser than his fellow idealists, he never made the mistake of falling in love with or marrying one of his dreams. When his companions matured, usually at age eleven or twelve, Carroll lost interest. These youngsters may have possibly been hurt by his sudden neglect but he did free them to grow up and never attempted to bind them to an eternal childhood.† Many of his child friends were child actresses (the child star was very much a part of the Victorian "cult of the little girl") who later became successful and sophisticated women. They would hardly have felt constrained to keep secret an "incident" had one occurred. Isa Bowman, Gertrude Chataway and Ellen Terry all found his "kindness to children wonderful"; some of their own children were later counted among his child friends and their high regard for him was unanimous. Enid Stevens, later Mrs. Shawayer, said, "My friendship with him was the most valuable experience in a long life . . . and wholly to the good." Alice Liddell, the real "Alice," remembered "an inexhaustible flow of the most delightful fairy tales as he went along accompanied by quaint drawings."[17]

What interests me in any analysis of Carroll's personality is the compulsion of his critics either to deprecate his apparent lack of sexual activity or to attribute salacious motives to his life and work. Some of his contemporaries saw him as a "spinster" or "maiden aunt" with limited interests who was absorbed in "girlish things."

---

*Sentimental photographs of nude or seminude innocent Victorian female children were quite the vogue. Mrs. Cameron, also an amateur photographer and contemporary of Carroll, was well-known for her photos of little girls in various states of dress and semi-dress. No one, as far as I know, ever attributed salacious motives to her work.

†He did continue a few of these friendships in later life and attempted to help some women achieve their goals as painters, writers, and such.

Later, those who admired his work and wished to rescue him from the stigma of "maiden aunt" assured us that underneath his shy exterior lurked a Humbert Humbert in search of his Lolita. Indeed, Leslie Fiedler says in an introduction to a collection of fairy tales, "*Alice In Wonderland* is one of the dirtiest and most delightful of all Victorian children's books."[18] As a professor of mathematics at Oxford, a writer, a devotee of the theater and fortunate enough to have many friends of all ages, Carroll cannot really be characterized as a man of limited interests, nor "Alice," with all its subtleties, as a dark or dirty book. Yet because Carroll never married, had a mistress or molested little girls, many wondered how he *did* handle his sex drive. What form of expression he used does not strike me as relevant. What *is* worth our consideration is that he never expected his child friends to accommodate themselves to *his* fantasies (erotic or otherwise); he enjoyed and responded to them on *their* level, gave as much as he got in mutual companionship and was essentially a kind man. In the words of his biographer, Florence Brecher Lennon, "he never drew blood."[19]

## COMMERCIAL SEX

The Victorian male's interest in female children, combined with the technological inventiveness of the nineteenth century, helped spur the wide production and distribution of child pornography. As soon as the camera was invented, Hollywell Street, London's pornographic center, was flooded with pictures of female children, naked and seminaked, posed in explicitly lewd positions. For those with literary rather than graphic interests, poetry such as "What I Saw in the Garrett" provided an introduction to children "unhid by clustering curls."[20] "The Three Chums" depicted a man entertaining himself with "an elder's grot as well as the hairless slit of her little sister," and in the continuing saga of "My Grandmother's Tale," or "May's Account of Her Introduction to the Art of Love," the barely pubescent Kate described the "heaves and thrusts" of her papa until "the crisis came and my womb was deluged with paternal sperm."[21]

   This was also a time when man had triumphed over nature, and since woman was "nature" and man her conqueror, what could better assure man of mastery than his ability to inflict pain? Pain became an essential ingredient for pleasurable sex. Honoré de Balzac advised men to ignore the cries of women during the sex act

because "nature has ordained her for your use,"[22] and even the mild
Havelock Ellis agreed that the infliction of pain was necessary for
man's sexual gratification. And since the defloration of very young
virgins can be excruciating, Victorians were obsessed with a "defloration mania." The screams of children became indispensable,
shrill torture was the "essence of delight" and many gentlemen
"would not silence a single note."[23] Later, Walter, the anonymous
author of the now authenticated sex biography *My Secret Life*,
illustrated the pleasure a gentleman obtained from deflowering a
fourteen-year-old virgin:

*She trembled. I pressed her and gave a tremendous thrust, and was on the right
road . . . she screamed "You hurt—get off—I won't let you!" She screeched
loudly and struggled violently.*

   *I rose on my knees and looked at the girl who lay quiet with her thighs
wide open and her hand over her face . . . I was delighted beyond measure, she
bled more than any virgin of her age which I ever yet have had I think.*[24]

Walter, as did so many other middle-class men, paid his way as he
availed himself of women and children in the London slums. By the
mid-nineteenth century, prostitution in Europe had reached alarming proportions. *The Lancet*, an English medical journal, estimated
that in London alone one house in sixty was a brothel and one
woman in sixteen a whore. There were 6,000 brothels and 80,000
prostitutes, and twenty years later this number, if anything, increased. Dr. William Acton, renowned British physician, authority
on venereal disease, prostitution and human sexuality, declared that
women were happily sexless but it was impossible to exaggerate the
force of the male sex drive; any suppression of this drive would
reduce a man to a pitiable condition.[25] If society found it necessary
to delay matrimony until a man was financially established, why,
then, the use of prostitutes was better than virtue. Acton fought for
the legalization and government regulation of prostitution, and to
counter any opposition attempted to raise the status of the prostitute. He claimed that she enjoys better health than married women,
does not rot in ditches or expire in work houses, and since she plies
her trade briefly, she soon re-enters respectable ranks, often marrying above her class. Despite his arguments, it was all too obvious
that prostitutes suffered from brutal treatment, disease and ill-
health, and were rarely able to extricate themselves from their trade.

With so much existing evidence of misery and poverty suffered by prostitutes, Acton set about to denigrate those who, as living examples, refuted his theory: Prostitutes who became ill, died and never freed themselves were, he said, unnaturally erotic, sinful and indolent.[26] His contempt is apparent from the acrimony he heaped upon the child prostitute.

*The extreme youth of the junior portion of the "street walker" is a remarkable feature of London prostitution and has been the subject of much comment by foreign travellers who have published their impressions of social London. Certain quarters of the town are positively infested with junior offenders whose effrontery is more intolerable and disgusting than that of their elder sisters. It is true these young things spring from the lowest dregs of the population and from what I can learn of their habits, their seduction—if seduction it can be called—has been with their own consent, by boys no older than themselves and is all but a natural consequence of promiscuous herding, that mainspring of corruption among the lower orders. That such are generally the victims of panderers and old debauchees is as untrue as many of these wretched fallacies set about by some who write fictions about social matters in the guise of fact.*[27]

## CHILD PROSTITUTION

Children who must depend on two poor struggling parents are generally vulnerable to life's hardships, but when they are also subjected to an unstable society, they can expect little protection. The shift during the nineteenth century from an agricultural to an urban economy, from farm to factory, resulted in many broken families and homeless children. In 1876 more than twenty thousand "street arabs" lived and died of disease and starvation in London. If these children survived, the boys did so by thievery and the girls by prostitution.[28]

Some very young girls who managed to find employment in factories, flower shops or as housemaids often fell prey to the "gay blades" of the period. Some learned that submission plus a fee augmented their meager income; others were seduced by the promise of love and marriage and then abandoned; and others were simply raped. All, however, became "fallen women," and the only door of respectability, marriage, was closed to them. Of necessity they became prostitutes. Very few, however, "went wrong" after age twenty-one:

*The majority of prostitutes are thrown into the arms of this occupation at a time when they can hardly be said to have arrived at this age of discretion. Of 2,582 girls arrested in Paris for the secret practice of prostitution, 1,500 were minors. . . . In September, 1894, a scandal of the first rank took the stage in Buda-Pest. It appeared that about 400 girls from 12 to 15 fell prey to a band of rich rakes. The sons of our "property and cultured classes" generally consider it an attribute to seduce the daughters of people whom they then leave in the lurch.*[29]

One study estimated that 58 percent of the nonregistered prostitutes in Vienna were minors and another study claimed that more than half of the prostitutes in Stuttgart, Germany, had been "deflowered" before they were seventeen.[30] During the first part of the century, half the reported prostitutes in Paris were minors, some no more than age ten.

America told much the same story. During the colonial period, young indentured servants were used for sexual gratification; Southern slave owners exploited eleven-, twelve- and thirteen-year-olds for breeding by having them indiscriminately impregnated by other slaves, overseers and their masters. Others were more carefully selected for personal use or to be hired out to brothels. America also had "street arabs" who at ages ten and eleven became featured attractions in bordellos. West Coast traders did a lucrative business in purchasing little Chinese girls and then selling them at a profit. A young healthy American child could bring sixty or seventy dollars for one evening, but a Chinese girl purchased at $1,500 to $3,500 could yield the owner who hired her out a 25 to 35 percent net return.[31]

In 1889, during an international conference on prostitution in Brussels, several experts agreed that close to 70 percent of all prostitutes suffered from syphilis before twenty-one. "Deflowered at sixteen, prostitute at seventeen, and syphilitic at eighteen,"[32] became an accepted formula. I think that these age estimates are an understatement. One English brothel-keeper explained that "our business is in maidenheads,"[33] and since girls tended to lose their virginity before fourteen, especially if they are poor, it was necessary to catch them young. Only the youngest were eligible for membership in the world's oldest profession.

## WHITE SLAVERY

There were never enough "voluntary" prostitutes to meet the voracious Victorian demand. Consequently, enterprising entrepreneurs established a system of obtaining "involuntary prostitutes," or "white slaves." (The term "white slavery," unrelated to skin color, merely distinguishes the traffic in women and children from the black slave trade.) Men who wanted sex with little girls were prepared to pay a good price, and a standard pricing system brought twenty pounds for a healthy working-class girl between the ages of fourteen and eighteen; a hundred pounds for a middle-class girl of the same age; and as much as four hundred pounds for a child from the upper class under age twelve.[34] Some merchants bred their own child prostitutes by using the children of adult prostitutes. One brothel owner told a reporter from the *Pall Mall Gazette* that "when they get to be twelve or thirteen they become merchantable and can get as much as twenty to forty pounds."[35]

Sex merchants moved from local, national, to international markets. England, Germany, France, Scandinavia and East European countries engaged in a lively trade, but routes also crossed continents. Malay Street in Singapore, the "Babylon hell of the East," housed Japanese, Chinese, Austrian, French and German preteen and teenagers in their brothels. American children were found in Hong Kong, Siam and Calcutta. School-aged English girls were transported through the United States to Buenos Aires. German preadolescents and adolescents were sent to Argentina and Uruguay, while others moved overland to Prussia, Poland and Russia. This extensive transportation of bodies could never have operated without official sanction and protection. The police and higher officials who took bribes never feared recrimination. Why should they? Even the king of Belgium increased his annual income by personally trading in English girls.[36]

White slavers developed a huge network of employees, and most vital were those who actually obtained the merchandise. In mid-century London it was roughly estimated that some 400 persons earned a living by "trenpanning" (ensnaring) girls between ages eleven and fifteen.[37] Managers and owners of employment agencies, factories and shops, persons advertising for "beautiful girls between twelve and fifteen suitable for adoption," enticed jobless, homeless, hungry youngsters and decoyed them to brothels around the world. Agents, pimps, procurers and "cadets" (slang for pimps) stalked every city, town and country for marks. In England and America, they found easy pickings among the steady flow of immigrants from Scotland, Ireland and the Continent, and yearly two thousand girls who arrived in New York disappeared like cattle. Agents and procurers haunted playgrounds, schools, recreation centers; later, movie houses proved fertile territory; and still later, a curious child could be easily seduced by the offer of a ride in the newly invented automobile.

Victorian modesty, which prevented the discussion of sexual matters, also kept children ignorant of the dangers of white slavery, and an uninformed, homeless child could with little effort be lured by the offer of food, money, shelter or a job. Even an adolescent with a devoted family could be flattered by a declaration of love, a promise of marriage and fine clothes, and follow a handsome young man to a strange city or country only to find herself penniless and stranded. One agent described the skills required of his profession:

*The getting of fresh girls takes time, but it is simple and easy enough when once you are in it. I have gone and courted girls in the country under all kinds of disguises, occasionally assuming the dress of a parson, and made them believe that I intended to marry them, and so got them in my power to please a good customer. How is it done? Why, after courting my girl for a time, I propose to bring her to London to see the sights. I bring her up, take her here and there, giving her plenty to eat and drink—especially drink. I take her to the theatre, and then I contrive it so that she loses her last train. By that time she is very tired, a little dazed with the drink and excitement, and very frightened at being left in town with no friends. I offer her nice lodgings for the night; she goes to bed in my house, and then the affair is managed. My client gets his maid, I get my ten pounds or twenty pounds commission, and in the morning the girl, who has lost her character, and dare not go home, in all probability will do as the others do, and become one of my "marks"—that is, she will make her living in the streets, to the advantage of my house.*[38]

If a captive became troublesome she was given a "drowse" such as chloroform or laudanum and would lie as dead while some gentleman raped her. A child who kicked and screamed had to be held down. When it was over she was told there was no use her crying or struggling, she had now lost her character and no one would take her in. Even if she ran away, friendless, under fifteen and alone in a strange city, she usually returned in a week. Charles Howard Vincent, former director of the Criminal Investigation Department (CID) of Scotland Yard, described the "breaking in" process during an interview with William Stead of the *Pall Mall Gazette:*

*"But," I said in amazement, "then do you mean to tell me that in very truth actual rapes, in the legal sense of the word, are constantly being perpetrated in London on unwilling virgins, purveyed and procured to rich men at so much a head by keepers of brothels?"*

*"Certainly," he said, "there is not a doubt of it." "Why," I exclaimed, "the very thought is enough to raise hell."*

*"It is true," he said, "and although it ought to raise hell, it does not even raise the neighbors."*

*"But do the girls cry out?" "Of course they do. But what avails screaming in a quiet bedroom? Suppose a girl is being outraged in a room next to your house? You hear her screaming, just as you are dozing to sleep. Do you get up, dress, rush downstairs, and insist on admittance? Hardly. But suppose the screams continue and you get uneasy, you begin to think whether you should not do something? Before you have made up your mind and got dressed the screams cease, and you think you are a fool for your pains."*

*"But the policemen on the beat?" "He has no right to interfere, even if he heard anything. Suppose that a constable had a right to force his way into any house where a woman screamed fearfully, policemen would be almost as regular attendants at childbed as doctors. Once a girl gets into a house she is helpless and may be ravished with comparative safety."*

*"But surely rape is a felony punishable with penal servitude. Can she not prosecute?"*

*"Whom is she to prosecute? She does not know her assailant's name. She might not even be able to recognize him if she met him outside. Even if she did, who would believe her?"*[39]

An American, Reginald Wright Kauffman, wrote *The House of Bondage* (1910) and detailed the social attitudes which trapped the seduced or abducted child into prostitution. Mary, age sixteen, after a year of slavery, attempted to return home. She pleaded with her mother for understanding:

Mother: *Don't tell me anymore, you coulda gone to work.*

Mary:     *I tried that, nobody would have me.*
Mother: *You coulda gone to church folk.*
Mary:     *I did but they couldn't give me a job.*
Mother: *You coulda gone to some institution already.*
Mary:     *How'd I lived after I come out?*
           *Her mother relented but then remembered: "It'd be all over town by*
*evening . . . think of your pop . . . he'll kill you . . . he'd beat you up and throw*
*you onto the street."*[40]

Mary went back to the brothel. Kauffman summed up the process
which guaranteed slavery:

*. . . to return home even if she had the money, would be impossible because to do*
*so would incur her father's anger and her mother's shame with no hope of either*
*pardon or justification. To go out to the cheerless street . . . would be . . . to*
*deliver herself to arrest or starvation. She was ignorant and young. Without,*
*there was hunger, jail, starvation and death. Within . . . a tolerable democracy*
*of disrepute, an equality of degradation, where food, at any rate and shelter and*
*raiment were certain and where old scars and fresh bruises were hidden from the*
*world. The price was no more than supine acquiescence.* *[41]

The society which defined prostitution as a "necessary evil" convinced itself that sexual exploitation was justified because "fallen"
females no matter how young were nymphomaniacs, sinners and
beyond all restoration. They deserved nothing better than the life
they so willingly walked into.


## THE REVOLT OF THE WOMEN AND SOCIAL PURITY

Woman was previously seen as the source of sin and man the embodiment of virtue, but when the exploding industrial economy
required undisguised aggression and conquest, this order was conveniently reversed. Men appropriated sin, sexual lust and ambition
as inherent positive masculine traits and assigned women, now

---

*Seventy years later, Kathy Barry, after examining current systems of sexual slavery,
confirmed Kauffman's estimation of this foolproof system:
     The sense of judgments being made upon her from the outside completely cuts her off
     from the possibility of return, if she could escape. There is no turning back. While she
     may have thought initially that she was being brutalized by her abductors, she now
     sees them as the ones who are keeping her alive. In that way she becomes a slave.*[42]

defined as innately pure, passive and asexual, as the guardians of religion and morality. Wifehood and motherhood were glorified and it became a man's duty to protect (or exclude) "the angel in the house" from the nasty business of money making, politics and world affairs. Man's excessive sexual needs were to be syphoned off by prostitutes, for without the prostitute the "unchallenged purity of countless homes would be polluted."[43] Captains of industry, political and religious leaders who created ethical standards were horrified however to find that those they charged with "guarding virtue" took their responsibilities so seriously that they condemned the entire male sex for their addiction to vice, lust, prostitution and sex crimes. After discovering "men's incapacity to deal with social problems,"[44] and assured that morality was their forte, women began to take matters into their own hands.

## JOSEPHINE BUTLER

One of the first woman Victorian crusaders was the deeply pious Josephine Butler. Born in England in 1828 and married to educator George Butler, her most ardent supporter, Josephine boldly identified and exposed the sexual practices of her day, devoting herself to the eradication of sexual exploitation.

Though Josephine Butler's cause was named "social purity," she was interested less in purity than in man's inhumanity to woman and the sexual double standard. She toured, lectured and wrote over 100 books, pamphlets and articles on these subjects. So many women were attracted to her cause that their clubs, associations and leagues multiplied into an "army" and their work was known as the revolt of the women.

In the sacred hall of Parliament, Butler claimed: *"For the purposes of seduction and seduction only our law declares every female child a woman at the age of twelve."*[45] She saw the traffic in female flesh as an economic enterprise, condoned and encouraged by upper and middle-class men, and said: *"I have seen girls bought and sold just as young girls in the time of the slave traffic."*[46] She likened this traffic to the commerce in blacks and called for an abolition of sexual slavery. She announced that the very men she was addressing were prepared to pay twenty-five guineas for the pleasure of raping a twelve-year-old virgin, and she cried: *"I will set a flood light on your doings."*[47] Her threat was not an idle one. Although maligned, ridiculed, rejected by men on the left and right, and branded as no better than a prostitute, Josephine was to decry sexism throughout her life.

Butler never advocated uplifting "fallen women" but suggested instead that it was "fallen men" who were in need of reform; her lack of condemnation and her compassion gave her the support of working class as well as women of her own class. Butler discovered that prostitution was rarely a chosen vocation. Whether abducted by a pimp or raped or seduced by her father, a farm gang master, a factory foreman, or as a junior domestic by her master and his sons; whether a daughter of the impoverished gentry or simply homeless and hungry—young girls and children from seven to seventeen, at the mercy of a society which deprived them of food, shelter, employment, respectability or even pity, were driven to sell themselves. In the year 1870 Josephine Butler engaged in her first public battle and openly attacked the Contagious Disease Acts.

Since a third of the British Army and Navy were infected with venereal disease, members of Parliament were persuaded by William Acton in 1864 and 1866 to pass the Contagious Disease Acts. To protect the health of soldiers and sailors and, incidentally, all males serviced by commercial sex, the Acts called for enforced medical examination of prostitutes. The legislation, which purported to protect men from disease, deprived women of their freedom. It gave police unlimited power to detain and arrest women without stating a cause. They could and did pick up girls who were out for a walk or seen talking or walking with a soldier or sailor. A girl could be reported by a spiteful neighbor or rejected lover and the police, in the employ of the slavers, could and did stop innocent girls and turn them over to brothels. Any female, under threat of imprisonment and hard labor, was forced to submit to painful, humiliating physical examinations and once detained, a girl's reputation was ruined; automatic recruitment into "the life" was thus assured.

Butler opposed all legislation which granted the police summary power to arrest and imprison without trial or conviction. She asked why infected men who spread venereal disease to their families were not subject to the same restrictions. (Thirty percent of women and children infected were not prostitutes.) She was appalled by a government which condoned and regulated "vice," yet divested itself of the responsibility of investigating the social and moral cause of that vice. She believed that the Acts, more than any other legislation, represented "an enshrinement in the statute books of the iniquitous double standard."

The attempts to repeal the Acts evoked cruel reprisals and women who organized against them were threatened, obscenely insulted and harassed by police, and brothel keepers hired roughs and rioters to assault them. During one tour, Butler was "covered with flour, excrement, her clothes had been torn from her body, her face discolored with dried blood and she was so bruised that she could hardly move." But persistence, courage and the urgency of her message rallied support. One meeting alone attracted 4,000 women who chanted "shame" while Josephine Butler scathingly asked, "What will the Acts do for fallen men?" As the revolt accelerated, defenders of the Acts insisted that the legislation curtailed VD and juvenile prostitution. Women retaliated with evidence that, if anything, VD was on the rise in countries where prostitution was government-regulated and their denial of any decline in juvenile prostitution brought about a public investigation. In 1871 a Royal Commission submitted the following report and recommendations:

*The traffic in children for infamous purposes is notoriously considerable in London and other large towns. We think that a child of twelve can hardly be deemed capable of giving consent and should not have the power of yielding up her person. We therefore recommend the absolute protection of children to the age of fourteen years making the age of consent to commerce at fourteen instead of twelve as under existing law.* [48]

THE ABOLITIONISTS

The report and recommendations brought few concrete legal results but the efforts of the women resulted in public sympathy. John Stuart Mill spoke out against the violation of personal liberty. Annie Besant wrote *The Legislation of Female Slavery in England* (1876), and books such as *The Europe Slave Trade in English Girls,* by Alfred Dyer (1880), *Moral, Constitutional and Sanitary Objections to the Contagious Disease Acts,* by Berbeck Nevins, (1873), *Is London More Immoral Than Paris or Brussels?,* by Benjamin Scott (1881), were widely circulated. Josephine Butler, now an international figure, addressed a women's conference in Geneva, wrote an appeal to the "mothers of England" and sent out a "Call for Action." Her crusade reverberated to America, where Lucy Stone, Elizabeth Cady Stanton, Mary Livermore, William Lloyd Garrison, Wendell Philips and Susan B. Anthony united in the struggle for the abolition of the "social evil." In America the abolitionists asked why a child of ten who could not sell her handkerchief or her doll could legitimately sell her "virtue."[49]

In England a distinguished member of Parliament, Sir James Stansfield, joined the abolitionists: "I have marked these women hounded down, hooted at with unseemingly language, gestures and even threats . . . and never will I desist and never will they desist until these degrading laws are blotted from our statute books forever." Stansfield was editorially smeared in *The Times:*

*It is to be sincerely regretted that a statesman of Mr. Stansfield's eminence should identify himself with such a hysterical crusade in which it is impossible to take part without herding with prurient and cynical fanatics.*[50]

Nevertheless, support continued.

Alfred Dyer, publisher; Benjamin Waugh, founder of the National Society for the Prevention of Cruelty to Children; and Benjamin Scott, Chamberlain of the City of London, formed the Committee for the Exposure and Suppression of Traffic in English Girls for Purposes of Continental Prostitution. This trio toured England and the Continent. In Paris they saw little girls from five to eleven housed in brothels and found that when homeless children in public shelters went unclaimed they were "apprenticed to brothels." Throughout Europe, children of all countries were raped and brutalized. Many begged the investigators to free them from their captors. These findings were published. One story was told of a father who, after requesting the sexual use of a twelve-year-old, found his own daughter, whom he had earlier sent off to school, bound, gagged and stripped awaiting him on a bed. His horror was sufficient to send at least one penitent father into the arms of the abolitionists. The Salvation Army, under the leadership of Florence and Bramwell Booth, joined the crusade, and their zeal resulted in open warfare. Salvation Army "troops" were attacked by organized gangs and brothel keepers. Hallelujah "lassies" were roped and pelted with hot coals. At Worthington one unit, led by twenty-three-year-old Ada Smith, brought such an onslaught that the British Cavalry was summoned to quell the riot. This attention encouraged even greater support.

WILLIAM STEAD

Victory, which finally came in the form of the repeal of the Contagious Disease Acts by Parliament in 1883, did not stop the revolt; white slavery was still rampant and the age of consent still only thirteen. The abolitionists were joined by William Stead, editor of the *Pall Mall Gazette,* and his articles created a sensation. His publication of *The Maiden Tribute to Modern Babylon,* with headings such as "The Violation of Virgins" and "Confessions of a Brothel Keeper," plus testimony from officials, ex-officials, members of the police, rescue workers and actual victims, exposed and verified the daily violation of children. Stories of the arrest and quick release of Mrs. Jeffries, who ran a house specializing in torturing children, the ridiculous argument that the children were "willing" victims, the exposure of a legal system which protected slavers and their customers rather than children, made a mockery of English morals and law. To obtain incontrovertible legal proof that children could be bought and sold, Stead arranged for the purchase of thirteen-year-old Eliza Armstrong. Stead's enemies produced Eliza's father, who charged that Stead had obtained the child without paternal permission (she was sold by her mother). Stead's friends, however, discovered that Eliza's father had never married her mother, thereby nullifying his paternal rights; after three months' imprisonment, Stead was freed. The circumstances of his arrest created such a furor and brought so much pressure that Parliament finally voted to raise the age of consent in England to sixteen.[51]

Josephine Butler died in 1907 and William Stead drowned in the *Titanic* disaster of 1912, but by then the cause moved on its own momentum. Several countries organized to intervene in the white slave trade; later the League of Nations and then the United Nations took measures against the international traffic in women and children; and in America, in 1912, the Mann Act was passed, exacting penalty for the interstate transportation of women and children for immoral purposes. But the days of the staunch determination of Butler, Stead and the Salvation Army soon passed, making way for an "enlightened" group of experts who affirmed that little girls have sexual feelings and therefore consent to sex with adults. Thus original sin was replaced with specious, misogynist sexology.

Although hundreds of international agreements have been

signed since the days of the abolitionist movement, the concept of childhood consent to sex has continually intruded to create confusion and ambivalence and hinder the effective enforcement of these agreements. Today as in the past, our society which affirms that a minor has not the discretion to vote, leave home, enter a contract, take a job or even legally sell her doll or handkerchief, paradoxically sees the female child as responsible enough to sell her body. Now as before, we have no difficulty condemning a man who will take a child's bicycle (with or without her consent, because an adult is expected to discriminate right from wrong), but will wonder whether a man is to be held responsible for sexually using a nonresisting child. It is only in sexual matters that a child is held accountable as an adult and man permitted to be as irresponsible as a child. Consequently, the sexual abuse of children by adults has never been established as an irrefutable legal and moral violation and to this day remains a debatable polemic.

# 6. CHILD MARRIAGE IN INDIA

Reprehensible is the father who gives not his daughter in marriage at the proper time; reprehensible is the husband who approaches not his wife in due season.
From the "Hindu Laws of Manu"[1]

Until 1955 child marriage was legal in India.* This chronological proximity to our own period illustrates how close we are in time to the integration of the sexual use of female children in national and religious institutions.

It takes considerable energy to push youngsters into proper sex-role behavior, and child marriage is perhaps the simplest and in some places the most widely used structure for training the female before she develops strength, experience and judgment, into accepting a lifetime subordinate role. Experts tell us that until about seven, children do not have the ability to associate masculine behavior with being a boy and feminine behavior with being a girl. But, since the masculine image is more desirable, female children resist their gender identity and girls more than boys are likely to express ambivalence toward their own sex. Wherever the male image is the desired image, girls wish to be boys more than boys wish to be girls. Boys may begin to take on a masculine stance at age five, whereas girls usually do not display "feminine" behavior until age nine, ten and often not until they are well into adolescence. And females who have not been severely disciplined into sex roles may behave aggressively and independently into adulthood.[2] It is hardly surprising then that the ancient Greek poet Hesiod instructed men of thirty to marry virgins "so that you can teach her good habits,"[3] that the Romans gave their daughters of twelve and under to marriage so that "their minds and bodies alike would be delivered

---

*In 1955, fifteen for the female and eighteen for the male became the legal marital age.

to their future husbands unsullied,"[4] and that Hinduism declares that the female child who is not married before age ten must needs go wrong.

As late as 1928 one Indian leader claimed that if a girl was not married before puberty "there was danger of her becoming a bad character,"[5] and another emphasized that marriage of girls before puberty "is a religious custom obtaining in practice from time immemorial."[6]

Hindu law and religion has decreed that the marriage of a female child before puberty is not only a virtue but a religious and social obligation. If a daughter is not bound in matrimony before her first menses her family is doomed to a fearful afterlife:

*A damsel should be given in marriage before her breasts swell. But if she has menstruated before marriage, both the giver and the taker fall into an abyss of hell; her father, grandfather and great grandfather are born insects in ordure. There is no atonement for a man who has had intercourse with a woman who has had her courses before marriage. . . .The father, mother and elder brother who tolerate a girl in her courses before marriage go to hell. A Brahmin who will marry such a girl is not to be spoken of or admitted into society.*[7]

And should a husband hesitate to copulate with his child bride, he was guilty of the crime of "brunahaty" or the "killing of the womb" and he too would suffer earthly and spiritual condemnation.*

Followers of Hinduism also saw child marriage as the only salvation for the lowly female who was said to be born without a soul. She existed only materially, but if she had been married and penetrated before her first menses and had been a devoted and obedient wife, she could attain a spiritual identity and a peaceful afterlife. To save both themselves and their child, parents gave their daughters in marriage before they were old or strong enough to resist a mature, even aging, diseased or cruel husband. In fact, the Kama Sutra, the official Indian sex guide book, instructs men in the art of child seduction:

*If she is a very young girl he should first seize her breasts which she will probably*

---

*Some Indian male children were also married at an early age (Gandhi was wed at age thirteen), but the disproportionately large number of child brides as compared to child grooms points to the female as the prime victim of this ancient custom.*

*protect from his onslaught by covering them with her hands—then he should slip his arm under her armpits and clasp her around the neck.*[8]

For the gentleman who prefers guile to force, other techniques are suggested:

*If she refuses he must plead with her and try to convince her by flattery and vows of fidelity . . . or try to capture her affection by childish games.*[9]

Attempts to eradicate premature nuptials have, for the most part, failed. Ram Mohan Ray in 1828 unsuccessfully organized a society to purge India of child marriage,[10] and legislation which appeared in the nineteenth century ordering the minimum marital age to be ten and then fourteen was never enforced. By 1921 more than 80 percent of the Indian population practiced child marriage; one out of ten females between five and ten and one in every four between five and fifteen were married. In 1929 the government-authorized Joshi Committee reported that consummation soon after marriage was universal, resulting in an extremely high rate of infant and maternal mortality. On the Committee's recommendation the legal age of marriage was raised to fourteen; the law was to be enforced six months after it was announced. Within this six-month period, marriage of female children under fourteen swelled from eight to twelve million and marriage of infants under five quadrupled. Two years later, 437 adults who participated in child marriage were prosecuted and of this number seventeen were imprisoned. Indian officials were obviously not determined to prevent child marriage.[11]

In 1927 Katherine Mayo, an American writer, published her book *Mother India.* She presented a scathing indictment against the lower status of Indian women, their lack of education, the custom of "sutee" (whereby a widow is expected to throw herself upon her husband's funeral pyre and die with him), but her accounts of atrocities resulting from child mariage attracted the most attention. She told of children from five to twelve years old who were married to men aged twenty-five to fifty. She interviewed medical personnel, investigated hospital records, and described the hemorrhaging, ruptured vaginas and uteruses, lacerated and mutilated bodies, peritonitis, venereal disease and even death suffered by child brides. One badly injured twelve-year-old managed to find her way to a hospital but her husband, an educated official of fifty, sued for restitution of his conjugal rights and it was understood he won the case. And if a child bride managed to survive sexual abuse, she did not always sustain pregnancy and childbirth. These small girls sometimes labored up to six days and unable to withstand the process, their bodies were torn apart and they died.[12]

Mayo's book created an uproar. *Mother India* appeared at a time when India was struggling for its independence from England and proved an embarrassment to the leaders of Indian emancipation. Ms. Mayo's work was answered with *My Mother India, Sister India, Father India, Understanding India, A Son of India Answers*, etc. She was accused of exaggeration, lies, manipulation of facts, white supremacy, racism,* and because she never married many suggested that her book represented her personal sexual expression and bitterness. The esteemed poet, Nobel prize-winner and friend to Gandhi, Rabindranath Tagore, wrote an essay condoning child marriage:

*There is a particular age ... at which attraction between the sexes reaches its height, so if marriage is to be regulated according to social will, it must be finished before such an age.*[13]

One Indian correspondent said by Mayo to be a man of "high position in society" and a friend of Gandhi, said:

*I think it improper to say that those who insist on child marriage are steeped in vice ... (it) is practically a universal practice in India. ...It appears probable that early marriage does not cause as much physical deterioration as some people believe.*[14]

Although Gandhi verbally objected to the "cruel custom of child marriage," he never opposed those who supported it nor took a firm, strong position on the issue. The problem of the child-widow who never knew sex and could not remarry, bothered him more. Hindu parents could marry their baby daughters to an old man but should the husband die, Hindu law forbade a widow (child or adult)

---

*Unfortunately, in a later work,* The Face of Mother India, *it was revealed that her criticism of child marriage was not directed at the problem itself but at India. She erroneously claimed that Christians, Jews and Moslems were never guilty of subjecting female children to marriage.*

to remarry. As a result, India was filled with widows from age five on and Gandhi protested:

*The existence of girl widows is a blot on Hinduism . . . I consider the remarriage of virgin widows not only desirable but the bounded duty of all parents who happen to have such daughters.*[15]

Gandhi reasoned that widow virgins were "never married at all" and therefore were, as he said, "strangers to love." Gandhi must have confused love with sex. He did not recommend that these children be protected from the brutalization of premature sex and child-bearing; it was their virginal state which troubled him.

Despite the opposition, Mayo had supporters. One member of the Indian Legislative Assembly pointed to maternal deaths and sickly babies and argued that child marriage was "sapping the vitals of our race."[16] The first woman member of the Bangladore District Council pleaded that unless child marriage is eradicated "there is no hope for the advancement of womankind or regeneration of the nation as a whole.[17] Later Sir John Megaw, an official medical advisor, estimated that one in every ten child brides was doomed to die, and Eleanor Rathbone in her work on child marriage in India said: "Such deaths are nothing less than deaths on the rack due to straining of the muscles and sinews, nerves and tendons in the body's effort to perform a function for which it is too weak, immature and ill-formed." A 1931 census indicated that child marriage had much to do with the high death rate among Indian females:

*The female is better equipped by nature for survival than the male; but in India the advantage she has at birth is probably neutralized in infancy by comparative neglect and in adolescence by the strain of childbearing too often.*[18]

India finally won her independence, but the issue of child marriage created more controversy than actual social change. In 1935 Mayo noted that despite all the furor the practice continues:

*Now that the panic and confusion are over, now that the dust has settled and eyes see clearly again, the age old scene reappears—the Hindu in his millions sitting undisturbed in his ancient way. Today as of old he marries his girl-child when he sees fit—always remembering that the younger she is, the greater the sanctity of marriage and the higher his own reward in heaven.*[19]

And though the legal age of marriage has been raised, Rhoda L. Goldstein, in an article entitled "Indian Women in Transition," said that in 1961 it was reported that 28.8 percent of the girls between ten and fourteen were married.[20]

The United Nations Commission on the Status of Women submitted the following resolution on the elimination of child marriage to the General Assembly:

*Child marriages and engagements made on behalf of girls before puberty shall be prohibited and effective measures including legal provisions shall be adopted to establish a minimum age for marriage and to make obligatory the official registration of marriage.*[21]

This resolution was adopted in November 1967 but it was not binding. Even so, India weakened the resolution further by adding "insofar as possible." According to the 1971 Indian census, 17.5 percent of girls between ages ten and fourteen were married.[22] On April 14, 1973, *The New York Times* carried a feature story entitled "Married at Ten, Deserted at Fifteen, She Lives in the Delhi Streets." Radha, who grew up in poverty, was married at ten to an older boy equally poor and although "such child marriages are officially banned they are still common among the poor."[23] In March 1975, "Youth Times" (an Indian publication) announced that marriage of female children in India is still common.[24]

It is not surprising that although the female is better equipped for survival than the male, India remains the only country where the female population (930 to 1000) is less than the male.[25]

# 7. A FREUDIAN COVER-UP

It is my thesis . . . that both cultural and personal
factors combined to cause everyone, including Freud
himself at times, to welcome the idea that reports of
childhood sexual victimization could be regarded as
fantasies. This position relieved the guilt of adults. In
my opinion both Freud and his followers oversubscribed
to the theory of childhood fantasy and overlooked
incidents of the actual sexual victimization in childhood.

Sexual assault upon children is ignored or
discounted at the expense of the psychological well-being
of the child victim.

Joseph J. Peters, *American Journal of Psychotherapy*[1]

In 1905 Dr. Sigmund Freud presented the world with his theory on
infant sexuality. He informed a society still deep in Victorian
prudery that very small children had strong erotic drives. His theory
shocked middle-class sensibilities at first, but eventually this same
middle-class society came to find Freud to be quite right. Today it is
almost universally agreed that children have erogenous zones and
sexual feelings, but, since Freud's interest focused on the psychosexual aspects of human development, he gave little attention to
other infantile endowments. He chose not to notice, for instance,
that just as children are sexually aware, so are all their other faculties
intact, and therefore they know when they have been humiliated and
exploited. Therefore Freud's claim that children who reported
sexual abuse by adults had imagined or fantasized the experience is
highly questionable. Children perceive the difference between reality and fantasy, often with more accuracy than adults, and sexual

advances are in fact made to children in the course of everyday life. To insist that these advances are imagined is to underestimate a child's perceptive capacity, create doubt and confusion, undermine self-confidence, and provide the food upon which nightmares are nourished.

I remember that as a child I struggled with a recurrent dream in which I pleaded desperately with uninterested adults to acknowledge my fears. Considering that I had been told that my tonsillectomy was "not that bad" or that the dentist whose hands were between my legs was really "fixing my teeth," my fantasy was not unfounded. Somehow I knew even then that if one is ignored or disbelieved too long and too often, one can lose one's bearings, panic and even go mad. As I grew older it was some consolation to learn that I had no monopoly over the theme of my anxiety-producing nightmare; that many others were so intimate with its horror that it was a favorite motif in literature and art. Franz Kafka was a master at communicating the anxiety resulting from general disregard of personal fear and sense of danger. Ralph Ellison's "Invisible Man" found the lack of recognition of his feelings so unbearable that he installed countless electric light bulbs in his room to illuminate and verify his existence. The world of science and suspense fiction is permeated with the eerie loneliness of distorted reality, and the theme has captivated a coast-to-coast television audience with such perennial crowd-pleasers as "Twilight Zone," "Star Trek" and "Chiller Theater." My own favorite embodiment of this horror, still enjoyed by late-show insomniacs, is the 1944 film *Gaslight*, a tale which so impressed the public imagination that even today the word "gaslight" is used to describe an attempt to destroy another's perceptions of reality and, ultimately, sanity itself.

In summary the plot, set in the Victorian era, has Charles Boyer marrying Ingrid Bergman, not for love, but to gain access to her home, where precious jewels are hidden. Once ensconced in her house and impatient to embark on his treasure hunt, Boyer plans to get rid of his wife. He calculates to unnerve her so that eventually she would agree to be institutionalized. To accomplish this, he simply alters the world in which she lives and trusts. When she sends a servant on an errand, he assures her that the order has never been given; a pair of scissors she placed on a table turns up elsewhere; and when the gaslight flickers, he convinces her that it is not the light but her perceptions that are failing. Gradually she becomes unsure and unsteady, and soon is so shaken that she can barely function. Boyer pretends concern, suggests a doctor, a rest cure, but just as she is on the brink of total collapse Joseph Cotten (always vaguely in the background) arrives to expose the scoundrel and rescue the wife's reality, confidence and sanity.

Because so many identified with the victim, this movie enjoyed great popularity. Like others, I know I have been "gaslighted" frequently in my lifetime, not the least traumatic instance being the denial of my own molestation. I recognize, however, that the gaslighting procedure, as it applies to the subject of sexual abuse, is far more serious than a Victorian suspense story and more effective than one man's treachery. It evolves from widespread indoctrination. Sigmund Freud, whose theories have had such enormous influence on modern thinking, knew that the sexual abuse of children existed, but he could not reconcile the implications of that abuse with either his self-image or his identification with other men of his class, and thus he altered his telling of reality. Eventually he succeeded in gaslighting an age into ignoring a devastating childhood reality and a very serious social problem.

## A FREUDIAN DISCRETION

Early in his career Freud believed his patients, who were predominantly women, when they consistently reported childhood instances of sexual molestation. Many of them suffered from hysteria, a common Victorian ailment affecting middle-class women. The symptoms could include loss of voice or appetite, compulsive vomiting, sneezing, coughing, temporary blindness, deafness, paralysis or epilepsy, and these symptoms, with no discernible organic base, were resistant to medical treatment.* Since his hysterical patients repeatedly reported sexual abuse, most often naming their fathers as the abusers, Freud, in his early theorizing, drew a casual connection between sexual abuse and neurosis,† maintaining that

---

*Hysteria is different from organ neurosis or psychosomatic illness. Though both are derived from psychological causes, in psychosomatic illness there is an actual physiological change in the affected organ. In hysteria or "conversion hysteria," function is impaired but the organ is unaffected.

†The term "neurosis" is used to describe all disturbances arising from psychological rather than physical cause.

hysteria was a neurosis caused by sexual assault. But exposure to repeated and persistent incrimination of fathers by his patients made him uneasy and, never quite comfortable with the seduction theory, he mentioned it publicly only in the year 1896 and not again until much later (1933), when he was able to reassign the abuse to female fantasy and disavow it as erroneous:

*Almost all my women patients told me that they had been seduced by their fathers. I was driven to recognize in the end that these reports were untrue and so came to understand that the hysterical symptoms are derived from phantasies and not from real occurrences.*[2]

More at ease with the fantasy rather than reality of sexual abuse, Freud was even more comfortable when he could name the mother rather than the father as the seducer. When he implicated the mother, however, he assured us that maternal seduction was based on reality:

*It was only later that I was able to recognize in this phantasy of being seduced by the father the expression of the typical Oedipus complex in women. And now we find the phantasy of seduction once more in the pre-Oedipus pre-history\* of girls; but the seducer is regularly the mother.*[3]

Here, however, the fantasy touches on the reality, he said:

*For it was really the mother who by her activities over the child's bodily hygiene inevitably stimulated and perhaps even aroused for the first time, pleasurable sensations in her genitals.*[4]

Before Freud could conclude that seduction by fathers was a fantasy, he had to be rid of his earlier theory. Since men did not complain of maternal seduction, Freud limited the "imagined" abuse to a specific female problem: "I was able to recognize in this phantasy of being seduced by the father the *typical Oedipus complex in women.*" To remove the onus from fathers, Freud found it necessary to under-mine the perceptions of his female patients. Unable to accept the father as seducer, he exchanged female veracity for female fantasy. Perhaps this shift can be better understood if we look at Freud the

---

\**That is, before the age of three.*

man, who, endowed with his share of human imperfection, had a history of withholding or altering information that did not suit him.

In the process of exploring the human psyche, Freud courageously exposed his own weakness, conflicts, anxieties and neurosis, but he withheld personal facts and feelings in two major areas—areas he established as vital to the understanding of the human personality: childhood and sex. At age twenty-nine, in anticipation of an interested posterity, he destroyed all his early work, notes and diaries because he said he "couldn't have matured or died without worrying about who would get hold of those old papers."[5] Even in later life, fortified by success and prestige, he was unable to reveal himself publicly, and so the story of Freud's childhood remains unknown to us. And if little is known about his childhood, less is known about his sex life.

We know, of course, that Freud formulated the Oedipus complex, the theory of innate erotic attraction of children to parents of the opposite sex, and that he gave us the "libido theory," or depiction of sexual energy as a vital life force. Yet this man who saw the sex drive as a dominant factor in personality development and the struggle to sublimate sexual gratification as essential to practical survival, to the mature psyche and to all of civilization, for that matter, told us nothing of his own sexual impulses, conflicts or experiences.* What makes this concealment even more surprising is the fact that Freud used his own life, his conscious and unconscious being, as a prime tool for understanding and explaining all of human sexuality. His theories evolved from self-analysis and the interpretation of his own dreams, yet he never once revealed a masturbatory fantasy or a sexual passion, nor did he ever associate one of his dreams with an erotic desire or a woman.

André Breton, French poet and essayist, criticized Freud for the stubborn and illogical silence that surrounded his own sex life, and even ventured to call him dishonest, but Freud never took up the challenge nor addressed himself to this issue. It should come as no surprise, then, that Freud also saw fit to censor what he thought was other ill-advised information. In a footnote to the 1924 edition

---

*In his private letters to his friend Wilhelm Fliess, published after his death (1950), Freud did reveal some sexual desires, dreams and feelings. He did not intend, however, that these letters be brought to public attention.

of his *Studies on Hysteria* (1895), he confessed that he had altered some studies for reasons of discretion. In two cases he had substituted an uncle for a father as sexual abuser:

*I venture after the lapse of so many years to lift the veil of discretion and reveal the fact that Katharina was not the niece but the daughter of the landlady. The girl fell ill, therefore, as a result of sexual attempts on the part of her own father.*[6]

And he added a similar footnote to the case of Fraülein Rosalia H.: "In this instance, too, it was in fact the girl's father, not her uncle," who was the seducer.[7]

It is customary in all professional relationships to protect a client or patient by disguising individual identity in a public presentation, and Freud adhered to this practice meticulously. He carefully changed names, places and other revealing clues, but to camouflage an entire group such as parents or "fathers" was not required or necessary, and such alteration could change the essential dynamics of the case history. In evaluating a case, whether it is the father or uncle who molests a child is of utmost importance, since a child's relationship with her father has much different meaning than that with an uncle; by altering this fact, Freud altered the case itself. Freud claimed to have made this significant change in the name of discretion, to protect fathers from unfair bias, but he was not moved to exercise the same discretion for the honor of daughters. In an age in which the sexual feelings of women were considered unseemly if not revolting, Freud freely exposed the sexual emotions of his female patients. In his presentation of "Dora" (1905), he did not hesitate to examine, in print, the reaction of a fourteen-year-old girl to the "erect member" of the married man who accosted her. Freud described a detailed discussion of Dora's experience of oral sex at eighteen and even recorded his suggestion that she enter into a relationship with the man, who also happened to be the husband of her father's mistress. In the light of Freud's rather arbitrary employment of discretion, his conclusions regarding female fantasy or the female personality can reasonably be questioned.[8] And were it not for the accidental recovery of Freud's correspondence with his one-time friend and colleague, Wilhelm Fliess, the story of his very subjective need to cover for the sins of the fathers and renounce the seduction theory would have been lost to us.

## THE FLIESS CAPER

The account of the Fliess letters is a lively and exciting tale in itself. From 1888 to 1902, when they quarreled, Sigmund Freud and his good friend W. Fliess, a Berlin nose-and-throat specialist, engaged in prolific correspondence. Central to their friendship was a mutual interest in the sexual aspects of the human condition, and Fliess had developed his own sex theory, which he felt would explain the phenomena of life and death. Freud admired Fliess tremendously and found his friend a man of supreme intellect and impeccable judgment. He welcomed his comments and criticisms regarding his theories, findings and even his writing style. But as Freud became more secure in his work, he looked to Fliess less, and finally the men separated over scientific differences.

Freud destroyed all his correspondence from Fliess, but his own letters, which included elaborate and detailed drafts and notes, were retained by Fliess. After Fliess's death in 1929, his widow sold a packet of 284 pieces of correspondence to a Berlin bookseller, Reinhold Stahl. Knowing that Freud would destroy the letters if given the chance, Frau Fliess gave Stahl instructions that they were not to fall into Freud's hands. Later, when the Nazi regime forced Stahl to flee to France, he offered the letters to Mme. Marie Bonaparte, a student and disciple of Freud, who perceived their value and happily purchased them for 100 pounds. She took the packet to Vienna and apprised Freud of the letters' existence and of the transaction. Indignant that they had been brought to light, he ordered them destroyed, and even after Bonaparte read portions to him to convince him of their scientific importance, he was adamant. "I don't want any of them to become known to so-called posterity," he said.[9] Bonaparte defied this order and deposited the correspondence in a safe-deposit box at the Rothschild bank in Vienna during the winter of 1937–1938. When Hitler invaded Austria, she used her status as a Greek princess and was permitted, under Nazi guard, to remove the contents of the box. She then placed the documents with the Danish legation in Paris, but when their security was again threatened by Nazi invasion, the letters, wrapped in waterproof, buoyant material (in case of a mine explosion), finally crossed the channel and reached England in safety. There they were transcribed and edited by Marie Bonaparte, Anna Freud and Ernst Kris, and finally a volume of 168 letters and notes, selected from the total of

284 pieces of correspondence, was published in 1950 under the title *The Origins of Psycho-analysis*—eleven years after Freud's death.

As a result of access to the Fliess letters, Ernest Jones, Freud's biographer, described the "Fliess period" as the most extraordinary experience in Freud's life, and others have thought it to be his most creative time. The editors of *Origins* felt that the documents amplified the early history of the psychoanalytic movement and offered insight into Freud's intellectual process, but to justify his reluctance to have them revealed, they explained that it was Freud's habit to publish personal material only to demonstrate unconscious connections.[10]

I found the correspondence, more than any history or intellectual process, the work of an extremely complicated, imaginative and talented human being. Nowhere does a novel reveal as artistically the ambivalence, ambition, courage of a man in a personal struggle. These letters, more than any information officially released by Freud, precisely demonstrated *his* unconscious connections, and from beginning to end tell why he could no longer abide his own seduction theory.

During the early years when he published *Studies on Hysteria* in collaboration with Joseph Breuer, Freud was already well into the exploration of the human consciousness in search of the secrets of neurosis. Having discovered "free association," a method whereby both he and his patients could explore hidden emotions in an atmosphere free of judgment and censure, Freud listened carefully and intently to his patients. But however clearly he recognized the existence of repressed thought and feeling, he did not, at that time, doubt that a real experience was the cause of hysteria. "I have come to the opinion that anxiety is to be connected, not with a mental, but with a physical consequence of sexual abuse," he wrote to his friend Fliess.[11] Freud later pinpointed vulnerability to sexual trauma as occurring during "primary sexual experience [before puberty] accompanied by revulsion and fright."[12]

In the year 1896 Freud presented his seduction theory in a group of three papers broadly titled "The Aetiology of Hysteria." This work was a public challenge to heredity as the cause of hysteria, and, in bold opposition to general medical opinion, Freud named social rather than biological causes of neurosis. *He identified the specific excitement of the genitals resulting from sexual abuse in childhood as the trauma that brought on hysteria* and cited eighteen cases, not one lacking in a sexual experience, to support his theory.[13] Moreover, in addition to this case evidence, Freud certainly realized that his Victorian world was notorious for its sexual license, particularly the sexual abuse of children. He could not have avoided journalistic exposures of the existence of large numbers of children in the brothels of Europe, the active international sex-slave traffic in children or the available statistics on increased sex crimes against children. Hardly ignorant of the social climate; Freud cautioned, "It seems to me certain that our children are far oftener exposed to sexual aggression than we should suppose."[14]

To Fliess, Freud continued to present case material to further substantiate his hypothesis. He named seduction by fathers as the "essential point" in hysteria,* and in one particular case uncovered a veritable nest of incestuous abuse. After persuading one patient to speak, he related his story to Fliess:

*Then it came out that when she was between the ages of 8 and 12 her allegedly otherwise admirable and high-principled father used regularly to take her to his bed and practice external ejaculation (making wet) with her. Even at the time she felt anxiety. A six-year-old sister to whom she talked about it later admitted that she had had the same experience with her father. A cousin told her that at the age of 15 she had had to resist the advances of her grandfather. Naturally she did not find it incredible when I told her that similar and worse things must have happened to her in infancy. In other respects hers is a quite ordinary hysteria with usual symptoms.[15]*

Despite continued evidence, Freud never again, after the 1896 presentation, publicly promoted his seduction theory. True, his theory was poorly received, and Krafft-Ebing ridiculed it, but Freud's reticence was hardly the result of adverse opinion; even then he was prepared to create a disturbance.[16] It was Freud's own faltering conviction that prevented risk of further exposure. Though staunch on sexual trauma as the cause of neurosis, he was extremely unhappy

---

*Freud sent Fliess elaborate drafts, diagrams and theses in which his theories on infant sexuality, repression, the unconscious and libido were developing. For example, he suspected that "hysteria is conditioned by a primary sexual experience [before puberty] accompanied by revulsion and fright; that obsessional neurosis is conditioned by the same accompanied by pleasure." However, for the purpose of this discussion, the simple relationship between early sexual abuse and neurosis is sufficient.*

with the idea of father as seducer, and though able to name him in the privacy of the Fliess correspondence, he was unable to do so publicly. Consequently, his 1896 papers were weak on identifying the perpetrators of the sexual trauma; he cited almost as many categories of sexual abusers as he cited actual cases, and created a series of unlikely contradictions. The grownup stranger as sexual abuser was the most infrequent offender, he said; nurses, maids, governesses, teachers and near relations were more often responsible. But children of the same age (or very close) and of the opposite sex, such as brother and sister, most frequently created sexual trauma.[17] This large category of predominantly female offenders did not fit the illness in question. Hysteria* was primarily a female affliction (a "male hysteric" was hard to find), and the sexual assaults Freud mentioned were heterosexual. Furthermore, in general discussion of sexual assault and hysteria, he always referred to the abuse of children by adults. Suddenly to claim that the largest number of offenders came from among children of the same age was a contradiction. The only credible abuser was the "real relation," whom Freud mentioned in passing but did venture to say "initiated sexual intercourse" more often than one thinks.[18] That Freud's inconsistencies reflected his need to protect fathers was substantiated as more than a possibility by the editors of the Standard Edition (a collection of Freud's work). They noted that in his 1896 papers on hysteria, Freud intentionally omitted and suppressed the role of fathers just as he had in the earlier *Studies on Hysteria*.

*In his early discussion of the aetiology of hysteria Freud often mentioned seduction as among its commonest causes... But nowhere in these early publications did he specifically inculpate the girl's father. Indeed, in some additional footnotes written in 1924 for the...Studies on Hysteria, he admitted to having on two occasions suppressed the fact of the father's responsibility.[19]*

The subjective reason for Freud's cover-up was revealed to him (and us) when he began to explore his own disturbing and complex reactions to his father's death.

---

*Hysteria, derived from the Greek word meaning uterus, was then a strictly female disorder. Freud did manage to come up with an example of a "male hysteric," but medical opinion of the day related this disease only to women.*

## FATHER FREUD AND OEDIPUS REX

The period of the 1890s was for Freud a troubled time. He was afflicted with what he termed "anxiety neurosis." He was worried about his heart and about dying; he endured painful migraine, urinary tract irritation, a spastic colon and gastronomical symptoms, plus agoraphobia and a neurotic fear of missing trains. But his father's death brought his anxieties to a climax. When Jacob Freud died in October 1896, Sigmund Freud wrote to Fliess:

*My dear Wilhelm,*

*I find it so difficult to put pen to paper at the moment that I have even put off writing to you to thank you for the moving things you said in your letter. By one of the obscure routes behind the official consciousness the old man's death affected me deeply. I valued him highly and understood him very well indeed, and with the peculiar mixture of deep wisdom and imaginative lightheartedness he meant a great deal in my life. By the time he died, his life had long been over, but at a death a whole past stirs within one. I feel now as if I had been torn out by the roots.* [20]

His father's death evoked in Freud such intense conflict and suffering that he felt compelled to examine himself—to search inward for the cause of his extreme reaction. This journey resulted in self-analysis, interpretation of his dreams and the beginning of the psychoanalytic process. It brought him to his own unconscious motives and drives by taking him back to memories of childhood experiences. It was these memories that made him aware of his own early sexual feelings. He told Fliess that at age two he had seen his mother naked and recalled that his "libido towards matrem was aroused." [21] The knowledge of his own youthful sexual feelings destroyed for him forever the myth that children were sexless; children, he now knew, had erotic feelings.

As he traveled further into his past, he found that his desire for his mother had stirred hostility toward his father, and when he looked at this complex of infantile sexuality—desire for his mother and hatred for his father—he understood his own extreme anxiety as guilt resulting from an unconscious paternal death wish. Conscious now that he harbored deep paternal aggression, Freud confided to Fliess in an unpublished letter (dated February 11, 1897) that *the number of fathers named by his patients as sexual molesters had truly alarmed him*; with the father as prime abuser he had "inferred from the existence of some hysterical features in his brother and several sisters that even his father had been thus incriminated."[22] But when it was later revealed to him in a dream that he was feeling overly affectionate toward Mathilda, his daughter, he wrote to Fliess:

*May 31, 1897*

*I do not want to do any more work. I have laid even dreams aside. Not long ago I dreamt that I was feeling over-affectionately towards Mathilda, but her name was "Hella," and then I saw the word "Hella" in heavy type before me. The solution is that Hella is the name of an American niece whose photograph we have been sent. Mathilda may have been called Hella because she had been weeping so bitterly recently over the Greek defeats. She had a passion for the mythology of ancient Hellas and naturally regards all Hellenes as heroes. The dream of course fulfills my wish to pin down a father as the originator of neurosis and put an end to my persistent doubts.*

And in some notes included in this letter, he added:

*Hostile impulses against parents (a wish that they should die) are also an integral part of neurosis . . . It seems as though in sons this death-wish is directed against their father and the daughters against their mothers.*[23]

Freud was becoming convinced that the suspicion he directed against his own father and himself and his acceptance of his patients' stories of seduction were prompted by his need to pin down the father as seducer. Based on personal inclination, he presumed that all his patients had the same need and therefore came to suspect that their stories of fathers as seducers were "defensive fictions." Freud continued to delve, and with the discovery of his death wish toward his father and the ensuing guilt he quite assured himself that he had reached the roots of his own "neurotica." As he solved his own problems, however, he simultaneously relegated his patients' testimony to fantasy, discarded his seduction theory and replaced it with the incipient Oedipus complex. He was not at all unhappy to make these changes and, in October 1897, one year after his father's death, he wrote to Fliess that his conviction of his patients' seduction as fantasy left him feeling triumphant:

*September 21, 1897*

*Let me tell you straight away the great secret which has been slowly drawn on me in recent months. I no longer believe in my neurotica. That is hardly intelligible without an explanation ... So I shall start at the beginning and tell you the whole story of how the reasons for rejecting it arose. The first group of factors were the continual disappointment of my attempts to bring my analyses to a real conclusion, the running away of people who for a time had seemed my most favorably inclined patients, the lack of the complete success on which I had counted, and the possibility of explaining my partial success in other, familiar ways. Then there was the astonishing thing that in every case ... blame was laid on perverse acts by the father, and the realization of the unexpected frequency of hysteria, in every case of which the same thing applied, though it was hardly credible that prevented acts against children were so general ... Thirdly, there was the definite realization that there is no "indication of reality" in the unconscious, so that it is impossible to distinguish between truth and emotionally-charged fiction. (This leaves open the possible explanation that sexual phantasy regularly makes use of the theme of parents) ...*

*It is curious that I feel not in the least disgraced, though the occasion might seem to require it. Certainly I shall not tell it in Gath or publish it in the streets of Askalon, in the land of the Philistines—but between ourselves I have a feeling more of triumph than of defeat (which cannot be right).*[24]

As he approached the source of the neurosis and evolved the now-famous Oedipal complex, Freud freely applied his particular personal discovery to everybody, to all cultures, and to females as well as males. He said to Fliess:

*October 15, 1897*

*I have found love of the mother and jealousy of the father in my own case too and now believe it to be a general phenomenon of early childhood ... If that is the case the gripping power of Oedipus Rex, in spite of all the rational objections to the inexorable fate that the story presupposes, becomes intelligible, and one can understand why later dramas were such failures ... The Greek myth seizes on a compulsion which everyone recognizes because he has felt traces of it in himself. Every member of the audience was once a budding Oedipus in phantasy, and his dream-fulfillment played out in reality causes everyone to recoil in horror, with the full measure of repression which separates his infantile from his present state.*[25]

So, as the son loved the mother and hated the father, so did the daughter love the father and hate the mother, he said. But he found the daughter's desire and need for the father so much more powerful than that of the son for his mother *that the daughter's wish to be seduced found its fulfillment in fantasy and fictitious seduction stories.*

Today "Oedipus complex" is a household term; however, the Oedipal myth as representative of a universal pattern of family interaction was a rather capricious selection. Though Freud associated the story with his own experience and that of some of his Viennese patients, its interest as a specifically Greek experience is surprisingly slight. Oedipus killed his father and married his mother quite by accident, and there is no suggestion, even in the play by Sophocles, that he was responding to some unconscious desire or reflecting a universal pattern.

The answer to the question of whether Oedipus suffered deep pangs of guilt depends on the version of the tale. In the earliest rendition by Homer, Oedipus, though upset by his unwitting behavior, neither blinded nor exiled himself and continued to rule over Thebes until the end of his days. His wife/mother, Jocasta, did however, hang herself. Considering the prevalence of brother-sister marriage, the early Greeks did not regard incest with much horror.* The family curse did not arise from the crime of Oedipus, but rather from the crime of his father, Laius, who abducted and raped the beautiful youth, Chrysippus, son of Pelops. Pelops cursed Laius for his deed, and this curse "descended gloomily from generation to generation, dominating the son and the grandchildren of Laius until it found its end in the death of Oedipus, who, after a long life full of sorrow, was cleared of sin by the powers of heaven."[26]

A far more dominant theme in Greek mythology is parental fear, hatred and slaughter of children. Ouranos, the cosmic sky god, imprisoned his children in a cave until his son Kronos castrated and supplanted him. Kronos, fearful of competition from his children, ate them all as soon as they were born. Rhea, unhappy mother, rescued Zeus; Zeus conquered and supplanted Kronos, but took the same precautions as his father and swallowed Metis, whom he had

---

*In one case of father-daughter incest, the daughter of Thyestes killed herself after her father ravished her. Herodotus tells the tale of an Egyptian king who also raped his daughter, and she too committed suicide. The shame and suicide always seemed to fall to the female rather than the male.*

impregnated. Laius pierced the feet of his son Oedipus and left him exposed to die; Agamemnon sacrificed his daughter Iphigenia to the gods; Medea slew her children to avenge her husband's infidelity; and the daughters of Cadmus, founder of Thebes, also violently destroyed their children.

If Freud had been inclined to view neurosis as the result of fear of the unconscious wish of parents to eliminate their offspring, he might have suggested the "Hercules complex." Hercules, famed Greek hero, in a period of temporary madness, killed his beloved wife and their six children. When he regained his sanity, he took upon himself the "Herculean" challenges of the Twelve Labors in repentance. Although I hardly advocate this story as an example of universal parent-child relationship, it would seem that anxiety growing out of childhood dependency and fear of adult authority and destructive powers is a much more plausible cause of neurosis than guilt from the questionable unconscious wishes imputed to children by Freud.

As long as Freud held to his own experience and unconscious motives, his discoveries were credible. That he desired his mother, competed with his father and found that conflict at the root of his neurosis, I believe. But to suppose from these personal insights that the testimony of his patients was fictitious requires mental acrobatics. It is much more reasonable to attribute Freud's denial of the reality of female sexual abuse to his own subjectivity, which he projected into a universal infantile-parental hostility. Freud never actually incriminated fathers; he never mentioned them publicly as sexual abusers and even took upon himself, as we have seen in the cases cited, to alter information in order to protect them. His conflicts about his own father may have caused him anguish and guilt, but does this exonerate other fathers?

It is unfortunate indeed that Freud was so resistant to the possibility of female childhood seduction, for, had he followed through, he might have come to believe—as many others do—that there were, in addition to sexual assault, other causes of female neurosis. He might have come to see that the middle-class Victorian woman afflicted by hysteria suffered from many abuses that frustrated and repressed normal growth and achievement. Freud's patients were talented, bright and ambitious women who, in addition to being sexually exploited, were discouraged from activity and deprived of rewards or recognition commensurate with their energy, interests, intelligence and skills. Though influential in removing hysteria from the sphere of physiological disturbance, Freud was unable to admit that women could contribute beyond the role of passive wives and mothers, and held along with others that they were inherently defective. As a result, he could not acknowledge that they suffered from sexual abuse and social inequality and discrimination. At the risk of belaboring Freud's misogyny, it must be noted that his theories on sexual abuse of children and female deficiency are so closely allied that his bias cannot be avoided.

The female, having no penis, was biologically inferior, Freud contended, and therefore she could only achieve an approximation of human completion by the "acquisition" of the penis through sexual intercourse and by eventually bearing a child (preferably male). When the male child matured, no matter how severe his castration anxiety, with his penis still intact he could manage to overcome castration fears, but the female, forever penisless, must always look to a man to achieve any degree of human status; her fantasy of being seduced therefore represented an actual biological need to make up for her natural deficiency. This fantasy represented her everlasting desire for the coveted penis and was implicit in her biology. Therefore, Freud found that the incestuous wish of little girls for their fathers was a "predisposition into traumas giving rise to excitation and fixation."[27] As the child was biologically ready, any external stimulation such as masturbation, sex play with other children, a dream, or a wish could trigger the seduction fantasy, or the wish for a penis.

With the elimination of the seduction theory and the adoption of the Oedipal complex in females, Freud had come full circle. The seduction theory incriminated incestuous fathers, while the Oedipal theory insisted that seduction was a fantasy, an invention, not a fact—and it incriminated daughters. When Freud replaced the seduction theory with the Oedipus complex he relieved himself of his "neurotica" and, as we have seen, vindicated fathers but implicated daughters. However, one must remember that when Freud arrived at the seduction theory, he did so by listening carefully and intently to his female patients; when he arrived at his Oedipal theory, he did so by listening carefully and intently to himself. His monumental *Interpretation of Dreams* (1900), the result of self-analysis and the basis for all his later theories, came from *his* memories, *his* dreams and *his* experiences, and, unfortunately, his theories strongly bear the stamp of *his* personality and *his* time, sex and class. The value of certain Freudian insights is not here denied, but in his attempt to shape a particular personal conflict into a universal mold, he reverted from a cultural to a biological determination of neurosis. This shift was damaging to the female, for it was she, not the abuser, who bore the brunt of her own seduction. This so-called "seduction fantasy," this myth of incestuous wish for the father, became integral and inevitable to the woman's nature, and therefore, even if she had been actually assaulted, the problem was not the assault but the result of her innate compulsion to possess a penis.

If a female child developed normally (that is, had faith that someday she would grow up, be married, get the penis, baby and all), Freud assured us, she would not be overwhelmed by the flood of anxiety and guilt coming from the incestuous desire for her father, and an external stimulus—an actual seduction—would be harmless. Freud therefore cautioned the world never to overestimate the importance of seduction and the world listened to Freud and paid little heed to the sexual abuse of the young.[28]

## A FREUDIAN GASLIGHT

Disciples of Freud who accepted penis envy as axiomatic soon surpassed their master and firmly established female "organ inferiority" as the crucial problem of molested children. Melanie Klein, known for her psychoanalytic work with the very young, held that little girls, even under ages two and three, were governed by the primacy of the penis and were desperately driven to possess the coveted male genital.[29] Helene Deutsch told us that the organless female child was endowed with an "erotic-passive attitude toward the father" and so saw him as her seducer.[30] While Karl Abraham, one of Freud's earliest followers, readily conceded the reality of sexual abuse, he argued that since *not all* little girls were molested, there must be something very wrong with those who were. The abused child, he assured us, was preinclined toward her own violation. Sexual assault could not be regarded as the "cause of the disease" for the woman who suffers from hysteria. As a child she "yields to the trauma"[31] of sexual assault, and "already has a disposition to neurosis or psychosis in later life."[32] This particular contribution by Abraham was applauded by Freud and has since become the rationale identifying the peculiar personality needs of sexually abused little girls.[33]

What can be the consequences of such thinking? Only confusion, resulting in a distortion of reality, total misunderstanding of female sexuality, and extensive damage to the confidence, pride and dignity of children. The reasoning is illogical. It categorically assigns a real experience to fantasy, or a harmless reality at best, while the known offender—the one concrete reality—is ignored. With reality sacrificed to a nebulous unconscious, the little girl has no recourse. She is trapped within a web of adult conjecture and is offered not protection but treatment for some speculative ailment, while the offender—Uncle Willie, the grocery clerk, the dentist or her own father—is permitted further to indulge his predilection for little girls. The child's experience is as terrifying as the worst horror of a Kafkaesque nightmare: Her story is not believed, she is declared ill, and, worse, she is left to the mercy and the "benevolence" of psychiatrically oriented "child experts."

The extent of Freudian influence can hardly be ignored, nor can the length to which some followers will go to vindicate the Master. Consider the following small deception by one of Freud's devoted disciples.

Freud, of course, attracted a coterie of notables. In his circle was one Dr. Hermine Hug-Helmuth, who in 1915 anonymously published *A Young Girl's Diary*, which the master enthusiastically endorsed. "This diary is a gem," he wrote to her publisher.

*Never before, I believe, has anything been written enabling us to see so clearly into the soul of a young girl . . . We have a description at once so charming, so serious, and so artless, that it cannot fail to be a supreme interest to educationists and psychologists. It is currently incumbent on you to publish the diary. All students of my own writings will be grateful to you.*[34]

Indeed his students and Freud were appreciative, for the work substantiated every detail of Freudian theory. Dr. Hug-Helmuth had reworked her own childhood memories in the light of psychoanalytic theories on female sexuality. The child in the diary, Greta, between the ages of eleven and fourteen, assures us on almost every page that she was far from innocent; that the behavior of a lecherous uncle was more "giggly" than disturbing; that she very deeply loved her father; that she was conveniently jealous of her mother and sister (charmingly, of course); and that at the proper time she was obsessed with getting married and having babies. The book, such an obvious accommodation of Freudian concepts, was later declared a fraud, created an embarrassing scandal, and was soon removed from German publication.[35]

When I point to this story as an example of a mechanical adaptation to Freudian thinking, I am often reminded by today's experts in the new psychologies that Freud's theories are now outdated. With the advent of ego, group and reality therapies and the miracle of weekend marathons, we are told that Freud is passé, the Oedipal complex is a period piece, the idea of penis envy is long out of date. But though the words may have changed, the melody lingers on and Freudian concepts are more popular today than ever. Just as loyal as his pupil Dr. Hug-Helmuth, students of the human services today—doctors, nurses, educators and social workers—and parents who perhaps have never heard of "infant sexuality" or "penis envy" readily accept Freud's theorizing that children are sexy; that they participate in, and even instigate, their own molestation; and that, in the famous words of every child molester, "the kid really asked for it." From a 1970 book on sex education, we have a variation on the main Freudian theme:

*There is the incontrovertible fact, very hard for some of us to accept, that in certain cases it is not the man who inaugurates the trouble. The novel* Lolita... *describes what may well happen. A girl of twelve or so, is already endowed with a good deal of sexual desire and also can take pride in her "conquests." Perhaps, in all innocence, she is the temptress and not the man.*[36]

In 1968 a book entitled *Vulnerable Children*, by Lindy Burton, discussed some thirty-odd studies on the sexually assaulted child from the mid-1930s to the mid-1960s. The analyses of the cases quoted seem to me to contend that the molester was the real victim while the young girls were juvenile delinquents acting out their pathology. The danger here is that classification of the sexually abused child as delinquent causes her victimization to appear to be the natural result of her deviant and anti-social behavior.[37]

Take for example the statement by Peter Blos, authority on adolescent behavior:

*Every therapist is aware of emotional reactions that work against spontaneous sympathy with the delinquent girl. Her behavior is seductive, impulsive, fickle, insincere, vengeful and capricious, hard to take, difficult to understand, impossible to predict and frustrating. This behavior fits the American delinquent girl. In contrast, the boy's aggression, his negativism and offenses are tolerated by the therapist with far greater equanimity . . .*

*We must never lose sight of the fact, clinically borne out, that female delinquency is far more profoundly self-destructive and irreversible in its corrosive consequences than is male delinquency. With the aggressive and retaliatory use of her body and her reproductive functions, the delinquent girl deeply violates the protective and caring attributes of her maternal role.* [38]

It is curious indeed how psychology can be used not to help, but to trap and ensnare the female. The myth of consent—that is, that the female desires to get a man, to have a penis—is freely cited to explain victim participation and therefore accepts as inevitable the sexual abuse of children. The tragedy is that this myth is believed and that so often it is the victim who is punished. Once a child has been raped or molested, no matter how impressive the psychological nomenclature described by her caretakers, the little girl is an outcast, a nymphomaniac, a whore.

During my years as a social worker with children, many cases involving dependent and neglected girls were brought to my attention. A large number had been victims of sexual abuse. If a child showed no visible scars, it was assumed that the experience had been harmless, but if she had problems, was difficult, angry, failed in school, attracted boys or became pregnant, she was diagnosed as acting out her incestuous wish for her father or other sexual fantasies. Here, in very condensed form, is a case history, cited from my records, of a girl who was sexually violated throughout her young life but, because she was abused, was presumed to be sexually promiscuous and finally, for absolutely no fault of her own, was sent to a reformatory.

*Mary, sixteen, was raped at eight by her stepfather. Later, her mother—who never believed the story—abandoned her, and Mary was placed in a foster home. She did fairly well until adolescence triggered repressed hostility and sexual acting out. She got the reputation for being "easy"; it was also rumored that she had been "had" by five boys (gang-bang). Mary denied the story, but a local physician found that she had been penetrated more than once. The foster parents could not tolerate local gossip, and at age fifteen Mary was sent to a home for dependent girls.*

*At first Mary was sullen and nasty, but later she relaxed, became friendly and trusting, and brought in dream material. Her fantasies revealed confused sexual identity, so it was not surprising when the cottage mother reported that Mary had not menstruated for two months. She was tested for pregnancy, was found positive, and despite her insistence that she could not be pregnant, was sent to Brown Memorial to have her baby.*

*One month later, Brown Memorial called to say that Mary was not pregnant and sent her back. Although everyone apologized, Mary was angry, fought, broke a chair, and became otherwise physically destructive.*

Diagnosis: *Adjustment reaction of adolescence with tendency to act out hostility and repressed sexual fantasies.*

Recommendation: *As a result of increased negative behavior, hostility, and sexual aggression, Mary must be moved to a closed institutional setting where she can be controlled—an institution for delinquent girls.*

What was Mary's offense? She was raped, sexually assaulted, suspected of a nonexistent pregnancy, and despite the crimes perpetrated against her, it was Mary—not her assailant—who was branded with the "tendency to act out sexual fantasies." This story is repeated constantly.

Despite the enormous importance psychotherapy places on sexual experience, I was taught as a social worker never to deal directly with the sexual abuse of a child in treatment. Annie, age twelve, had been in an incestuous relationship with her father for two years before she came to the Bloomington Home. The father was in prison, not for incest, but for robbery, and Annie's mother, in deep depression, was hospitalized. The children knew that the social worker had access to case records, and I made it a point not to pretend I knew nothing of their past. I told Annie that I was aware of her relationship with her father. She hung her head, but when I suggested she talk about it or not, as she wished, she moved on to other things. I reported the interview to my supervisor, a psychiatrist, who was appalled. "She can't talk about it. She's too guilty and ashamed," he explained. I had thought I might help her to understand that her father was the guilty one, and he was the one to be ashamed. But my supervisor would have none of that. The actual event did not shame her, he continued. It was her deep, unconscious, incestuous wish for her father that made her feel guilty. One must listen carefully, he went on, be sensitive to the nuances of the child's fantasies, and at the right moment help her to understand that her shame evolved from her own deep sexual desires.

Although women—young women and even children—do not talk freely about their molestation, there are few who consciously, or otherwise, consistently avoid the subject. For women who have not been believed or had the opportunity to confront their molester (with adult support), there is always a sense of unfinished business; there is always humiliation and rage. When the subject of sexual abuse of children received some media exposure as a result of feminist discussions on the radio, in lectures and in articles, many women approached me and finally found an opportunity to ventilate their long-festering secret. In their stories, the psychiatric practice of avoidance or distortion of the sexual-abuse problem has been prevalent. One young woman, fifteen years old, gives the following account:

*From 9 to 14 I was constantly "felt up" by my orthodontist during my weekly visits. He tried to be sneaky and pretend that he was wiping the instruments off—but I knew. The day of the last visit, after five years, I told my mother. She didn't call the orthodontist, but sent me to a therapist. I told my therapist, but he hardly talked about it, and finally said I was disturbed because deep down I really enjoyed it. I didn't talk about it anymore.*

I discovered that women were as shocked and disturbed by the lack of sympathy and acknowledgment of the problem as by the incident of sexual abuse itself. When Sigmund Freud ventured to explore the cause of his neurosis, and uncomfortably suspected his father to be his seducer, he took great pains to ferret out the reality of something he vaguely remembered. He checked into his past and was relieved to discover that "my father played no active role," but that an elderly, ugly nursemaid "was my instructress in sexual matters." This supposedly took place when Freud was under age two, but Max Schur, in his study of Freud, found the possibility of any actual seduction very unlikely.[39] Freud's effort to verify the cause of his own anxieties has been hailed as courageous, whereas a similar investigation by a child or a woman is today discouraged.

Alice B., with the same driving curiosity as Freud, and with much greater cause and anguish, tried to reach the roots of her "neurosis" and anxiety, but her psychiatrist would have none of it. By the age of twenty-five, without the ego or status of a Dr. Freud, she was rebuffed. As she told us:

*I don't remember when it started. I was so little. My father was always putting his hand under my dress and messing around, and he would come into my bed at night and fondle me. He never had an erection, but I could feel his wetness. He was gentle and he never lied. I mean if it hadn't been for him I wouldn't have survived, but I suppose if it hadn't been for him I wouldn't have had to worry so much about surviving. Everything was destroyed because of him. I didn't know what he was trying to do. School was destroyed because I couldn't learn. When I was thirteen I actually had an orgasm, but at first I thought he was trying to kill me.*

*I'm sure my mother knew. Since I've grown up, my aunts have told me he was always feeling them, and my cousin had an experience with him too. I used to try to scare him away, make noises and stuff. I felt dirty and my mother didn't like me; she liked my brother better.*

*My father is now dead. Before he died I wrote him a letter about what happened. I wanted to confront him with it, to talk to him and ask him why he did it. And he wrote me this incredible letter. He said he didn't know what I was talking about and that it wasn't nice for a girl to write a letter like that to her father.*

*I really feel that this thing with my father destroyed my life. I have no confidence, I never did. At twenty-four I went to a psychiatrist, but you know they don't talk. But I was upset and talked about it so very much that he finally said that what happened to me was very common, but he said, "I think your most important problem is your mother. Your father didn't have anything to do with your unhappiness."*

With no less courage than Freud, and brave enough to confront her father-molester, Alice tried to rescue herself and her sanity. But, with the exception of her aunts, she was engulfed in a world bent on covering up for fathers, no matter what the cost to human reason and dignity.

In another testimony, told in the third person in an attempt to keep distance from the trauma, another child actually groping for protection also found only insult and frustration at the hands of her psychiatrist and family.

*A girl of ten is alone in a quonset hut. The front door slams and her father enters—a handsome man with a ready smile. She runs to hug him. He sheds soggy gloves and a flight suit, and they talk of trivial things. How nice to have a warm, affectionate father.*

*Later he stops her in the narrow hallway and hugs her again. It feels different. But why? This happens several times, always when they are alone.*

*One morning he kisses her on the mouth. Why does it seem so different than the kiss on the cheek? He tells her not to mention this to her mother. She can't understand why it must be a secret.*

*Late one night she is sleepily aware of him slipping into her bed. His large warm hand gently rubs her stomach, caressing her beneath the flannel nightgown . . . her chest, her thighs, her genitals. Something is wrong. Would he do her harm? Not daddy! She wakes alone. Was he there?*

*This recurs regularly for two years. She wants to tell her mother but cannot. It has been going on for so long, and she is ashamed. She does not know why. She tries to avoid her father. She is twelve now. When he touches her it makes her sick.*

*She is thirteen. She is taking a bath. When she comes out her father corners her. She is very frightened. She hates him, she loathes him. She runs and hides under the house. When her mother returns she tells her. She tells her her father had sexually molested her for three years. Her mother turns quite pale.*

*"Do you realize what you are saying?"*

*"Yes."*

*"Don't tell your grandmother."*

*A week later, the girl is sent to the Navy psychiatrist. He puts his hand on her leg and tells her that all little girls attempt to seduce their daddies. The next morning she is sent to live with her grandmother in Alabama.*

## IS FREUD TO BLAME?

To hold Freud responsible for a seventy-year "gaslighting" episode is pointless. He lived in an age in which logic, reason and science supposedly supplanted religious mysticism—an era which required scientific rather than religious authority to justify brutal social injustice and inequities. Freud filled the bill. His theories, surrounded by scientific aura, allowed for the suppression and concealment of the sexual exploitation of the female child.

Bronislaw Malinowski, the noted anthropologist, discovered that among the Trobriand Islanders sex relationships between members of the same kin and clan were regarded with horror. But he was surprised to learn that despite the incest taboo, affairs that were carried on *sub rosa* and with decorum might provoke gossip but did not demand punishment. However, should the affair be exposed (by a jealous lover, perhaps), the public disgrace was answered by the suicide of those who broke the taboo.[40] Just as in Trobriand custom, the Freudian cover-up—the refusal to name the offender—was more than one man's attempt to hide illegal or immoral sex practices. Victorian men were permitted to indulge in forbidden sex provided they managed to keep their activities hidden. Adultery, practiced with impunity, was kept under wraps, and prostitution, which operated with police sanction, had simply to avoid public exposure and scandal. Within Freud's own circle, his biographer Ernest Jones was implicated in sexual adventures with his patients and little girls, but he managed—at some financial cost and the resignation of a job—to avoid public scandal.[41] The excesses of the loving and exuberant Ferenczi, known to be intimate with his patients and his wife's daughter, were tolerated by Freud and his circle.[42] Freud, who regarded the incest taboo as vital to the advance of civilization, appeared to demand only that forbidden sex be practiced with tact and discretion so that surface Victorian respectability was in no way disturbed.

The little girl, then, with her innate passion for a penis, is—as in Christian doctrine—the temptress Eve, and if she is violated, the nature of her sexuality renders her culpable. Any attempt on the part of the child or her family to expose the violator also exposes her own alleged innate sexual motives and shames her rather than the offender; concealment is her only recourse. The dilemma of the sexual abuse of children has provided a system of foolproof emotional blackmail: If the victim incriminates the abuser, she also incriminates herself. The sexual abuse of the child is therefore the best kept secret in the world.

# 8. MYTHS, FAIRY TALES AND FILMS

My appetite for reading was omnivorous. . . . One result of my infantile reading was that I did not like to look at my own face in a mirror because it was so unlike that of heroines always pictured with "high white foreheads" and "cheeks of perfect oval." Mine was round, ruddy and laughing with good health; and though I practiced in the glass a good deal, I could not lengthen it by pucking down my lips. I quite envied the girls who were pale and pensive, as that was the only ladyfied standard in the romances. Of course the chief pleasure of reading them was that of identifying myself with each new heroine.

Lucy Larcom, *A New England Girlhood*[1]

Since it is the function of a society to shape the motives and energies of its members, each social structure leaves as little to conscious behavior and thinking as possible, but tries to direct individuals to comply with and even find gratification from the standards established by each society. And since our Western society wishes females to conform to sex roles and stereotypic symbols of femininity, Simone de Beauvoir comments on the unnoticed but nevertheless powerful effects of legends, songs and stories upon the impressionable female child:

*The songs and legends with which she is lulled to sleep, are one long exhalation of man . . . children's books, mythology, stories, tales all reflect the myths born of pride and desires of men; thus it is that through the eyes of men the little girl discovers the world and therein her destiny.*[2]

Snow White, in order to merit her Prince Charming, had to cook, clean and care for seven dwarfs. Rapunzel suffered the pain of providing access to the tower by her long hair; the miller's daughter was challenged to spin straw into gold; and Cinderella, maid of all work, hardly idled in luxury before she was matched to her glass slipper and her prized prince. Some fairy tale heroines put up with loathsome dragons and animals before being granted their reward. Beauty catered to a beast, the sisters Snow White and Rose Red took care of a huge bear and the King's daughter ate and slept with a repulsive frog.

Unlike Sleeping Beauty, who lay passively until activated by a kiss or the obedient, hard-working Cinderella, some more spirited heroines rebelled; but each familiar tale tells us that rebellion is improper and must be punished, whereas obedience is rewarded. In the tales of *King Thrushbeard and the Swineherd,* for example, a haughty daughter who spurned all suitors was finally given in marriage by her exasperated father and taken in hand by a seemingly cruel and repellent husband. After the husband had labored, abused, insulted and humbled the proud daughter, he revealed himself as a rich, handsome, kindly king and, grateful and subdued, the daughter finally realized that both husband and father had acted in her own best interest.[3] "The Frog King" is a variant of this theme.

While playing outdoors, the story goes, the King's daughter became exceedingly distressed when her golden ball rolled to the bottom of the fountain. A frog offered to retrieve it if she would in turn agree to feed, sleep with him and become his companion. She agreed but never intended to keep her promise. "How silly the frog does talk! He lives in the water with other frogs and croaks and can be no companion to any human being." So as soon as she received her ball, she ran off. During dinner that night there was a loud knock at the castle door. "King's daughter, youngest! Open the door," the frog ordered. The King wanted to know the cause of the commotion, and when the Princess told him of her venture with the "disgusting frog," he commanded, "That which you have promised you must perform. Let him in."[4] The Princess obeyed and the frog insisted she keep her word. He enjoyed eating from her plate but, repelled, she almost choked on each mouthful; and at bedtime, she carried him with two fingers at arm's length to her bed. Her father scolded, "He who helped you in trouble ought afterward not be despised."[5] It can be argued that eating and sleeping with a frog is a high price to pay for a retrieved ball, promise or no promise, but the

King's daughter, caught between father and frog, nevertheless performed her hateful tasks. Just as it all seemed most unbearable she was happily surprised when the frog, who was really under a spell, changed into a handsome king with "kind eyes," and because she had heeded her father the Frog King became her dear companion and husband.

Several theories have evolved to explain this popular tale. Some students of folklore suggest that a frog wooing a maid exemplifies the ancient belief in kinship between humans and animals; others, that the girl who resists the frog is filled with anxiety at the thought of separation from her mother; and those under Freudian influence see the frog as "a penis," with the resisting maiden as overcoming her initial aversion to sex as she finally "transcends her anxiety and hatred changes to love." Bruno Bettelheim, of the last school, has said:

*The fairy tale by agreeing with the child that the frog [or whatever animal it might be] is disgusting, gains the child's confidence and thus can create in him [sic] the firm belief that . . . in due time the disgusting frog will reveal himself as life's most charming companion. And this message is delivered without ever directly mentioning anything sexual.*[6]

The assumption that the female initially resists sex and must be persuaded to relinquish her aversion is one man's conjecture. Little girls do not have a natural aversion to sex and do not need to be persuaded into sexual activity with their peers; they do understandably fear the coercion implicit in a relationship with a male adult (or a frog). And since coercion, no matter how seductively employed, can never magically transform a frog (or a man) into "life's most charming companion," it only reinforces rather than eliminates sexual anxiety.

The popular fairy tale, in fact, rarely advances the welfare of the female child. It instructs, rather, that each little girl suppress any healthy manifestation of individuality, strength and independence and urges her to blindly and humbly deliver herself to a man no matter how old, repulsive or unsuitable he may be.

## HANS CHRISTIAN ANDERSEN

Unlike his sunny, charming screen impersonator, Danny Kaye, Andersen relished the sadistic torture which he, as author, imposed upon little girls who committed the mildest offense. Little Inger ("The Girl Who Trod on a Loaf") had a "proud and arrogant nature" and was made to suffer thirst, hunger and her skin crawling with insects because she wiped her feet on a loaf of bread. Karen ("Red Shoes") was possessed of an uncontrollable need to dance because she vainly wore her red shoes to church. Her perpetual motion was finally halted by the amputation of both her legs. On crutches she finally repented for her sins and found salvation in death and heaven:

*The organ sounded and the children's voices echoed so sweetly through the choir. The warm sunshine streamed brightly through the window, right up to the bench where Karen sat. Her heart was so overfilled with sunshine, with peace and with joy that it broke. Her soul flew with the sunshine to heaven and no one asked her about the red shoes.*[7]

Even good little girls were better off dead and in heaven. Andersen celebrated the virtue of the obedient, noncomplaining, poverty-stricken Little Match Girl by having her freeze to death.

But no matter how much Andersen allocated suffering and heavenly reward to female children, he never extended the same treatment to their male counterparts. Little Claus and Hans Clodhopper, the soldier of "The Tinder Box," were each rewarded for their crimes and chicanery with wealth, a bride and a kingdom. No one was more vain than the Emperor of "The Emperor's New Clothes"; he incessantly primped, bedecked and gazed at himself in the mirror. However, with no mention of pain, God or the church, Andersen was satisfied to have him endure little more than the embarrassment of exposing his foolishness and nakedness as he walked in a public procession.[8]

## FAIRY TALES ARE MADE, NOT BORN

I do not see that the traditional tales from which most of our current fairy stories are derived represent collective unconscious or universal truths. Their implication and meanings stem from a particular geography, history, economy and place in time. They lack uniformity, consistency and logic, and any overall theory implying one credible interpretation can be extremely misleading. Norse mythology, for example, claimed that only ice existed before there was life, while in America the Ottawan Indians believed that first there was only earth, but the Navaho decided that originally all was fire.[9] Myths, the traditional tales of gods, kings and creation, not only vary from one society, but from one generation to the other, and in this process the sex of deities and other mythical characters changed over time. In the Assyrian-Babylonian accounts, Tiamat, the female creator of all life, was replaced by the God Marduck, who was later hailed as the sole progenitor. The Goddess Ishtar, embodiment of all creation, was ousted when the "theologians of ancient Israel came to see Yahweh as the creator of all fertility."[10]

And since so many of these tales were orally transmitted, details depended also upon the personality and inclinations of the storyteller. In the seventeenth century, Charles Perrault refined the peasant tale for the amusement of the French court. The classical renditions of "Bluebeard," "Beauty and the Beast," "Puss in Boots," "Hop O' My Thumb," "Little Red Riding Hood" and "Cinderella" came to us from his editorial pen. As Susan Brownmiller has noted, "Bluebeard," patterned after the fifteenth-century Giles de Rais sex murders of countless little boys, was converted into a more pleasing version:

*It is almost as if the truth of Bluebeard's atrocities was too frightening to men to survive in the popular imagination, but turned about so that Bluebeard's victims were acceptably female, the horror was sufficiently diminished (not of course to women). Charles Perrault who included the heterosexual version of Bluebeard in his tales of Mother Goose, deserves credit for the turnabout of the Bluebeard legend, which had its most recent incarnation in the form of a Richard Burton movie, widely advertised with pictures of seven pretty young women, each in the throes of a different and terrible violent death.*[11]

During the Christmas season of 1812, German booksellers presented their customers with *Kinder und Hausmarchen*, later known in English as *Grimms' Fairy Tales*. The brothers Wilhelm and Jacob Grimm, founders of the science of folklore, scoured the countryside for thirteen years to gather authentic peasant tales. Some modern folklorists, however, have been critical of their Germanic "chauvinism" and the undue liberties taken in transposing the stories from their oral to written form:

*In their methods the luster of the brothers has dimmed. Through the successive editions of the Marchen, Wilhelm steadily veered from the concept of fidelity to the spoken text toward a synthetic tale adapted from the available variants and refined with his editorial hand. Consequently he abandoned the* Volksmarchen *or true folktale collected exactly from the lips of the storyteller for the* Buchsmarchen *or literary version shaped by the editor.*[12]

Subsequently others who transposed the *Buchsmarchen* imposed further changes. One editor who could not bear to have Gretel (of Hansel and Gretel) push the wicked witch into the fire disposed of her less aggressively by having her simply disappear. And by the time Cinderella, Snow White and Sleeping Beauty reached the Disney studios their docility and passivity were reduced to a state of semiconsciousness. And nothing could better illustrate manipulation than the current selection of "fairy tales" for popular consumption.

The Grimm brothers gathered about two hundred and ten tales, and of this number about twenty-five are popularized in American and European markets and these are limited to stories with passive heroines. Those who make the selection do have a much wider choice. For example, in "Rumpelstiltskin," a miller gives his daughter to a king with the pledge that she can spin straw. She accomplishes the task with the aid of a mysterious little man and promises him her first-born child in return for his help. The King marries the miller's daughter and a year later a child is born. When the little man comes to collect, the Queen cries and pleads to be permitted to keep her child. The little man allows that if she can guess his name he will release her from her word. Fortunately, the Queen obtains the answer from a bird and when she announces it as "Rumpelstiltskin" the little man, furious, dies of excessive rage. Excluded from common editions, however, is another version, entitled "The Three Spinners." Here a widow turns her lazy daughter over to a Queen with the assurance that she is a prolific spinner. The Queen's son is offered in marriage if she can produce, but the daughter is miserable because she cannot spin. Three elderly "spinsters" hear of her plight and come to her assistance; they do the job for her. The daughter insists that her three friends remain in the royal household after her marriage, and at dinner one night the prince asks one spinner why her thumb is so thick:

*She answered, "It comes from picking" [picking the flax]. The second one had a thick nose. When he asked about it, she said that it came from the dust. The third one had thick lips. He asked her too and she said that it came from licking. Now he called out, "My wife has been spinning so much! She must never do it again! I do not want her to have a thick thumb, thick lips and thick nose." So she was relieved.*[13]

And so the story ended.

If we consider the influence of sex stereotyping, moralizing and values featured in children's literature, the disparity of these tales is of great significance. One gets a totally different impression regarding the relationships, character, capabilities and cleverness of women if rescue comes from other women, and certainly if a female by her own wit exposes an occupational hazard while simultaneously relieving herself of a damaging and hateful task.

What is more, many tales from around the world illustrate female heroism, positive mother-daughter relationships and evil fathers, but these are kept from public view. According to Kay Stone in her contribution to the *Journal of American Folklore*:

*Among the Ozarks tales collected by Vance Randolph we find women who destroy the threatening male villains and also a girl who does not need her father to convince her that frogs make interesting bedfellows . . . In "The Little Girl and the Giant" a mother and daughter cooperate in escaping from a giant and destroying him, etc.*[14]

From other parts of the world we have "Cantenella," where a father-king forces Cantenella to marry a vile husband. She flees from him and finally the wicked man is killed by her loyal friends. There is no suggestion here that blind obedience to her father is a virtue or that a hateful spouse will be transformed into a Prince Charming.[15] The moral is, rather, that a wicked man, husband or not, should be punished. And in contrast to the many wicked mother stories, in "Sunchild" a brave and clever twelve-year-old girl, without any male assistance, escapes an evil spirit and returns to her mother, where they both live in "happiness and contentment" ever after.[16] "Nix Nothing and Naught" is a sex reversal of both "Jack and the Beanstalk" and "Sleeping Beauty." A giant's daughter rescues a prince from her father and later, when the young man, under a spell, cannot be stirred out of a trance, she awakens him with a kiss.[17] But most surprising is the little-known English tale of "The Marriage of Sir Gawaine."

One day as King Arthur was walking in the forest, he was

overtaken by a wicked knight who would free him only if he could answer the riddle: "What is it every woman desires?" Permitted to search for the answer, the King consulted with his knights. Some suggested that what a woman most desires is "jewels" or a "rich husband," but Arthur somehow knew they were incorrect. He sadly returned to the wicked knight without an answer, but on the way he met the "ugliest lady he had ever seen," who offered the answer if he would grant her wish. He agreed. She whispered the answer in his ear and Arthur quickly whispered it into the ear of the wicked knight. Since it was correct, the wicked knight was compelled to release him.

Later, however, the King was horrified to learn that the ugly woman wished for a hand in marriage to one of his young knights. Arthur was prepared to die rather than subject one of his loyal men to such a union, but Sir Gawaine, handsomest and bravest of all, stepped forward and offered himself as the groom. After the wedding it was all Gawaine could do not to turn from his bride's ugliness but when he saw tears in her eyes he pitied her. He took her in his arms and kissed her, and suddenly, to his amazement, he held a beautiful young girl. But his kiss did not entirely free his wife from her ugliness, for she was under a spell cast by the wicked knight. She explained that she would continue to be ugly for half a day. The young bride asked her husband to choose which half, night or day, he would prefer her to be beautiful. Gawaine thought for a moment and then answered, "Choose for yourself, my dear. I give you your own way." Whereupon:

*The fair young girl laughed with joy and threw her arms around the handsome knight. "You have broken the spell! Now I shall always be as you see me at this moment. By both day and night I shall be fair to look upon for you have answered the riddle which the wicked knight asks for all strangers, "What is it a woman most desires?" It is her own way.*

*And from that day forward Sir Gawaine and his lovely lady rejoiced in happiness forever after.*[18]

This story must have escaped the attention of Sigmund Freud, I think, for he too asked, "What does a woman want?" Had he been exposed to tales such as these, rather than the *Frog King* variety, he might have avoided much confusion.

## THE MANUFACTURED IMAGE

Media experts today have a much wider influence than those who displayed the works of the Grimm brothers during the Christmas of 1812. Current technology can evoke such vivid images that they are often substituted for reality.

Helene Deutsch, well-known Freudian analyst and author, has determined that for reasons innately female, the young girl will renounce "intensification of her activity, most particularly her aggression," to win her father's approval. Deutsch chose Judy Graves, heroine of *Junior Miss* (1939), a popular novel by Sally Benson and later a radio serial, Broadway play and movie, as an example of prepubertal behavior:

*No clinical or statistical studies can tell us as much about psychology or prepuberty as the little episodes in Judy's life . . . for instance, after having seen a play in which the heroine is a self-sacrificing daughter [*The Little Princess with Shirley Temple*] she plays the role of a young girl who loves her daddy more than she cares for anything in this world and is quite disillusioned by her father's prosaic response.*[19]

Judy of *Junior Miss* moved from a direct, humorous, pudgy child to curves, makeup and boys; from a funny, aggressive child to a poised "junior miss"; from an ugly duckling to a swan. She became the forerunner of the *Gidget* and *Tammy* epidemic. Judy, however, is a media invention, a stereotype, and even so the intelligent Helene Deutsch would have us believe that by relinquishing her individuality and acquiring the stance of a well-attired sex object, she will win her father's approval and thereby self-confidence and maturity.

In another rather maudlin example Deutsch offered as "a poet's intuitive insight into the psychological process of a young girl"[20] Andrea, from the Danish story "The Child." Andrea, age sixteen (emotionally if not chronologically, pre-adolescent), is dying and finds solace in no one but her father:

*The sick Andrea is blissful in the arms of her father; "Kiss me Daddy my magnificent, splendid father, put your hand on my forehead then we will be silent together." In the face of imminent blindness she says, "Father if I really become blind, it won't matter much . . . couldn't we both do with one pair of eyes?"*[21]

Funny Judy and tragic Andrea, far from offering "insight into the psychological process of a young girl," reveal a rather banal fantasy of what a girl *should*, rather than what she *does*, feel. What is proposed is not insight but propaganda, and the power of this propaganda cannot be ignored.

During much of my own childhood I was an avid reader and, along with my friends, sobbed and thrilled to the bittersweet suffering of Heidi, Sara Crewe and Elsie Dinsmore. We were able to immerse ourselves in their agonies because we knew that somewhere, somehow, a father, brother, grandfather, uncle, stepfather or other male adult would magically appear, enfold each little girl in strong masculine arms and protect her forever from life's cruelties. Every page promised that if a little girl abandoned herself to suffering and self-sacrifice, a man would appear and transport her in an ecstasy of love. Rather than reflect, these stories *created* a girl's dreams, and since anguish was the path to pleasure, self-abnegation, self-sacrifice and pain were the prerequisites to happiness.

Martha Finley, American writer of juvenile novels, produced among the one hundred or more of her works the very successful *Elsie Dinsmore* books, which spanned the late nineteenth and early twentieth centuries. Each book told pretty much the same story. Eight-year-old Elsie, pious, brave and misunderstood, was in constant torment. Her mother died in childbirth and her father, young, handsome and rich, was cruelly severe. Wanting her father's love above all else, Elsie, through twenty-eight volumes, sobbed, "Oh Papa, don't be angry with me, dear Papa." When Papa punished her unjustly (I'm ashamed of you, go to your room and bed immediately), Elsie, bursting with grief and mortification, obeyed, but her pillow was wet with many bitter tears before the weary eyes closed in slumber. Elsie's protracted suffering was mercifully interrupted from time to time by the longed-for affection, and when it arrived the preliminary torture was worth every moment:

*Then for the first time he folded her in his arms and kissed her tenderly saying in a moved tone, "I do love you my darling, my own little daughter."*

*Oh the words were sweeter to Elsie's ears than the most delicious music! Her joy was too great for words, for anything but tears.*

*"Why do you cry so my darling?" he asked soothing her, stroking her hair and kissing her again and again.*

*"Oh Papa! because I am so happy, so very happy," she sobbed.*

*"Do you indeed care so much for me my love?" he asked, "then my*

*daughter you must not tremble and turn pale whenever I speak to you as though
I were a cruel tyrant."*

     *"O Papa! I cannot help it, when you look and speak sternly. I love you
so dearly Papa I cannot bear to have you angry with me; but I am not afraid
now."*

And later:

*He now and then bestowed a kind look upon his little girl and attended carefully
to all her wants and Elsie was very happy.*[22]

In Frances Hodgson Burnett's *The Little Princess,* Sara Crewe is the
unspoiled seven-year-old daughter of a wealthy, handsome, kind,
tender, adoring father. When Mr. Crewe leaves for India, Sara,
seated upon her father's knee, looks hard and long into his face as
they say their last good-bye.

*"Are you learning me by heart, little Sara?" he said, stroking her hair.*
     *"No," she answered. "I know you by heart. You are inside my heart"
and they put their arms around each other and kissed as though they would
never let go.*[23]

But when her father dies, Sara is left penniless at the mercy of a cruel
schoolmistress. After two years of menial labor, deprivation and near
starvation, Sara by her continued courage, dignity and generosity
proves herself to be a true aristocrat, a "princess." She is then
rewarded with a carbon copy of her father. Mr. Crewe's partner, who
has been searching for Sara, finally finds her and she sees him,

*with the look she remembered in her father's eyes—the look of loving her and
wanting to take her in his arms. It made her kneel slowly by him just as she used
to kneel down by her father when they were the dearest friends and lovers in the
world.*[24]

Johanna Spyri's Heidi and George Eliot's Eppie of *Silas Marner* each
became the companions and saviors of bitter, cynical men. Heidi's
sunny disposition, kindness and piety teach her grandfather humil-
ity and love.

*Her hands were still folded as if she had fallen asleep saying her prayers, an expression of peace and of trust lay in her little face, and something in it seemed to appeal to the grandfather, for he stood for a long time gazing down at her without speaking. At last he too folded his hands and with a bowed head he said in a low voice: "Father I have sinned against heaven before thee and am not worthy to be called thy son." And two large tears rolled down the old man's cheeks.*[25]

When Silas Marner's gold was stolen, a child appeared to replace the hoard. Eppie humanized the eccentric recluse and miser, and returned Silas to human dignity, companionship and to life:

*No child was afraid of approaching Silas when Eppie was near him; there was no repulsion around him now, with young or old, for the little child had come to link him once more with the whole world. There was love between him and the child that blent them into one, and there was love between the child and the world—from men and women with parental looks and tones to the red lady birds and the round pebbles.*[26]

These images are seductive and it is extremely difficult for a child (or woman) to resist the promise of reward for self-sacrifice to an old man.* The Victorian idealization of the female child as so trusting and pure that she could rescue the most degenerate reprobate continued into the early twentieth century and then the booming movie industry.

THE WALKING, TALKING IMAGE

Over an expanse of seventy-odd years, from Mary Pickford and Shirley Temple to Tatum O' Neal, the little girl of the silver screen may have changed her costume, cut her curls, straightened her hair and learned to smoke, but her relationship with men remained unaltered. Whether she was a woman made into a child or a child

---

*The child as man's savior sometimes included male as well as female children. Eventually, however, the male child was rescued, if not from exploitation in factories and the mines, at least from eternal victimization in literature. The pens of Robert Louis Stevenson, Mark Twain, Sir Walter Scott and others freed the boy to become a hero, indulge in amusing mischief, adventure and spirited independence, but the little girl remained doomed to eternal suffering, sacrifice and father love.*

made into a woman, or no matter how updated, she still sacrificed for, pursued or reformed a father figure. The little girl/grown man combination proved so successful that *Daddy Long Legs*, in which an orphaned child grows up and actually marries her rich, middle-aged benefactor, was adapted for film four times and successfully performed by Mary Pickford, Janet Gaynor, Shirley Temple (in a film renamed *Curly Top*) and Leslie Caron. Whether thirty-five-year-old Mary Pickford was reduced to infancy or five-year-old Shirley Temple was propelled beyond her years, the welfare of the celluloid child-woman, who never associated with peers or female adults, rested with men only.

Hollywood found the combination of childishness and sex extremely popular and lucrative. The independent screen female (as the assertive fairy tale heroine) was reduced in roles played by Richard Burton (*The Taming of the Shrew*), John Wayne (*The Quiet Man*) or Clark Gable (*It Happened One Night*) to proper infantile status. Any man worth his salt could bring the "little girl" out in any uppity woman. The popular Hollywood sex goddess, however, did not have to be cut down to size. Her neurotic anxiety, uncertainty, childishness and inability to cope as illustrated by Hollywood's image of Marilyn Monroe and Jayne Mansfield were satisfyingly synonymous with the helpless, needy woman-child. Monroe and Mansfield were appreciated not for their mature bosoms alone but because their childlike fragility in a well-developed body was exceedingly appealing. Innocence in a child or a woman is sexy not because it evinces the vigor of integrity but because it betrays the weakness of dependency. For the man who enjoys a sense of power over female companions, whether childishness emanates normally, from a little girl or abnormally, from a grown woman is a matter of personal taste.

And since yielding compliance is preferred, the strong screen woman is usually presented in her negative aspects. A woman with power is a shrike (June Allyson in *The Shrike*), a demented killer (Bette Davis in *Whatever Happened to Baby Jane?*), a rapacious, cruel mother (Shelley Winters in *A Patch of Blue*), or an obsessively possessive wife (Rosalind Russell in *Craig's Wife*). The witch and stepmother of the fairy tale became the shrike, the shrew and the destructive "Mom" of the silver screen. And since little girls, no matter how bossy, assertive and "fresh," are obviously powerless, these traits in them can be safely "cute" and nonthreatening.

## MARY PICKFORD AND SHIRLEY TEMPLE

In 1909 Mary Pickford, age sixteen, began her career under the tutelage of D. W. Griffith.* As America's Sweetheart her actual age increased as her screen age declined; at twenty-eight and thirty-two she played twelve-year-old Pollyanna and twelve-year-old Little Annie Rooney respectively. And since America did not want her to grow up, she cut her curls and retired at forty. We did not remain long, however, without a little girl; Shirley Temple, at age four, moved in to fill the vacuum. Although Pickford's career spanned twenty-five years and Temple's flashed and dimmed during six years between age four and ten, Temple and Pickford supplied the same dream: Both were seen in *Poor Little Rich Girl*, *Daddy Long Legs*, *Rebecca of Sunnybrook Farm*, *The Little Princess* and *Little Annie Rooney*. Whether the fantasy was filled by a woman who acted as a child, or a child who acted as a woman, mattered little; the result was equally satisfying.[27]

In 1932, four-year-old Shirley Temple strutted seductively in several shorts entitled "Baby Burleskes," and by 1934 she had completed small parts in five feature films, with a notable role in *Stand Up and Cheer*. From 1934 to 1938 she outranked most adults and starred in nineteen record-breaking box-office hits. In addition to her talent for mimicry, her confidence and poise, her success was also due to an extremely reliable story format: A child whose mother died or otherwise disappeared was rescued by a father, grandfather or other male benefactor and in this process the child often saved or reformed her rescuer, who was most often a grumpy old man, tycoon, gangster or even a simpleton. Rarely veering from this formula, Temple hugged, kissed, sang to, danced with, admonished and scolded (when necessary) an impressive number of male adults.†

---

*Griffith collected other teenagers such as Lillian and Dorothy Gish, Blanche Sweet and Mae Marsh, but Mary Pickford climbed the highest cinematic peak as the eternal little girl.

†Among others were Adolph Menjou (Little Miss Marker, *1934*), James Dunn (Baby Take a Bow *and* Bright Eyes, *1934*), Gary Cooper (Now and Forever, *1934*), Lionel Barrymore (The Little Colonel), John Boles (The Littlest Rebel *and* Curly Top), Guy Kibbee (Captain January), Victor McLaglen, C. Aubrey Smith and Cesar Romero (Wee Willie Winkle), Jean Hersholt (Heidi), George Murphy (Little Miss Broadway), Ian Hunter, Arthur Treacher and Cesar Romero (The Little Princess), Randolph Scott (Susannah of the Mounties) and Michael Whalen, Henry Armetta and Jack Haley (Poor Little Rich Girl).

In *Curly Top,* Shirley, at seven, was too young to decently supply the love interest, so a big sister was created for the job. With romance properly allocated to Rochelle Hudson (the big sister) and John Boles (rich, middle-aged benefactor), Hudson, who served her purpose, was made as insignificant as Lolita's mother. With Hudson out of the way (until she married Boles at the end) the film freely focused upon exquisitely dressed little Shirley Temple and John Boles, who was the recipient of her hugs, kisses and fondling. Motherless, eight-year-old Shirley in *Poor Little Rich Girl,* whose governess was struck dead by a car, lavished her sunshine on Henry Armetta, grumpy Claude Gillingwater and "puddinhead" Jack Haley, in addition to her daddy, Michael Whalen. Both Armetta and Haley had perfectly fine film wives, but Shirley's attention was riveted upon the male adults only. Carole Lombard and Gary Cooper were equally billed in *Now and Forever* but Lombard had scarcely a chance as Temple and Cooper mutually indulged in sorrow, joy and other such attention-getting pastimes.[28]

This persistent little girl/grown man combination exclusive of women cannot be dismissed as harmless entertainment. With a regular weekly movie audience of over sixty million people, Hollywood set the styles in clothes, hairdos, morals and daydreams. The Shirley Temple model was so successful that parents invested in Temple hair permanents so that their little daughters could acquire those coveted corkscrew curls; they arranged for dancing, elocution and acting lessons so that they could learn to charm men and skip along the same road to fame and fortune. The image was further perpetuated by other attractive young performers. Edith Fellows was paired with screen father Richard Dix, who kidnapped her from the clutches of a demanding mother in *His Greatest Gamble* (1934); five-year-old Sybil Jason in the *Little Big Shot* (1935) sported with ne'er-do-well Edward Everett Horton and Robert Armstrong; and Jane Withers joined her disreputable uncle in *Keep Smiling* (1938). Before Baby Sandy could walk, she was protected by singing taxi driver Bing Crosby in *East Side of Heaven* (1939); later in *Sandy Gets Her Man* she shared Stu Erwin and Jack Carson; she was in the company of Billy Gilbert and Mischa Auer in *Sandy Is a Lady* (1940), and in *Bachelor Daddy* (1941) was adopted by Edward Everett Horton, Donald Woods and Raymond Walburn.[29]

Occasionally this precise formula varied, but no matter how it altered, Hollywood almost never focused upon children in a positive relationship to women.* When little girls were occasionally involved with women they were usually used as foils to a sacrificing mother´as in *Imitation of Life* and *Stella Dallas*. Eight-year-old Patty McCormack was cast primarily with women in the film *The Bad Seed* (1956), but as a psychopathic child murderer, her relationship to her mother was, to say the least, terrifying. And though male children were prominent enough in films, the girl/man formula was not balanced by a boy/woman counterpart. Little boys, just as little girls, ignored women and related positively to men only. Long before Shirley Temple, young Jackie Coogan and Charlie Chaplin (silent films) and later Jackie Cooper and Wallace Beery were unbeatable teams. Subsequently, other popular child actors were paired with men† but unless some subtle homosexual message escapes me, mature and immature males were always friends and comrades. Furthermore, boys, given a wider berth, also performed in many tales of heroism, adventure‡ and animal stories.§ But little girls never strayed from the straight and narrow. Shirley Temple performed in Rudyard Kipling's *Wee Willie Winkle*, a tale which focused on the rebellion-torn Khyber Pass and was written for a boy. And though she saved a regiment and prevented a war, eternally feminine, she was made to thaw out C. Aubrey Smith, Cesar Romero and Victor McLaglen. Graham Greene, who reviewed the film in England, found Shirley so seductive that his review inspired a lawsuit for libel. His comments cannot be reprinted but he did say of Temple that "some of her popularity seems to rest on coquetry quite as mature as

---

*There are, of course, always exceptions, such as* I Remember Mama.

†*Bob Watson with Lionel Barrymore in* On Borrowed Time *(1939) and with Wallace Beery in* Wyoming *(1940); Dean Stockwell with Dana Andrews in* Deep Waters *(1948) and Wallace Beery in* The Mighty McGurk *(1947); Brandon de Wilde and Alan Ladd in* Shane *(1953); Kevin Corcoran and Ernest Borgnine in* Rabbit Trap *(1959); Tommy Rettig and Richard Widmark in* Panic in the Streets *(1950); Peter Miles with Robert Cummings and Brian Donlevy in* Heaven Only Knows *(1947); Tim Hovey and Jeff Chandler in* Toy Tiger *(1956) and others.*

‡*Adventure films such as* Captains Courageous, Treasure Island, Kidnapped, Tom Sawyer, Huckleberry Finn, The Prince and the Pauper, Kim, *etc.*

§*Animal stories such as* Old Yeller, The Shaggy Dog, Sign of the Wolf, Dog of Flanders, The Sad Horse, Misty, My Friend Flicka, Lassie Come Home, Goodbye My Lady, Buena Vista, Once Upon a Time, The Red Pony, *etc.*[30]

[Claudette] Colbert's and on an oddly precocious body as voluptuous in grey flannel trousers as Dietrich's."[31]

Though Temple's early precociousness cannot be denied, I think her "coquetry" could be better understood in terms of her ability to imitate and take direction (before capable of mature discretion) rather than as an innate sexual characteristic. Shirley Temple's body was clearly that of a sturdy, healthy, chubby little girl. If her behavior was mature, her body was not. Looking younger rather than older, the description "voluptuous" is oddly inappropriate; at an age before she could establish an independent perspective she clearly mimicked the current styles in sex appeal.

But Shirley's strong personality, if not her imitative capacity, persisted beyond childhood and, unable to "act" or be other than herself, she lost her appeal. The assertiveness and independence so attractive in the child was unattractive in the woman. Shirley Temple, however, was not alone. Irrepressible Deanna Durbin and cantankerous Jane Withers, also child stars, were similarly afflicted and met with the same fate, whereas the unchanged quivering uncertainty, timidity and high-strung sensitivity of child-stars Judy Garland and Elizabeth Taylor carried them to adult screen success.

In 1973 *Paper Moon,* advertised as a far cry from the sugared sentimental Temple productions, starred Tatum O'Neal and essentially followed the same formula as the Shirley Temple movies. It is the story of an itinerant con man, Long Boy, who is saddled with an illegitimate orphan, Addie Pray (her prostitute mother is dead). Making their way through the Depression-ridden flatlands of Kansas, they steal from widows and small storekeepers, with wised-up little Addie Pray used to soften prospective victims. Addie, smarter and more practical than Long Boy, takes care of him, loves the scoundrel and even ruthlessly rids herself of an adult rival. After a series of shabby thefts and close brushes with the law, she has the opportunity to live in a comfortable stable household with an aunt (whom we never see), and though she yearns for "a home and piano," she chooses instead a transient, police-dodging twilight existence in order to be with Long Boy.* Here again the mother and all other females are eliminated. The message, loud and clear, is that for a girl a man, any man, is better than any woman. In *Bad News Bears*

---

*Though many of the films mentioned in this chapter are adapted from novels and stories, all references are to the screen versions.*

preteen Tatum O'Neal (with mother mentioned but never seen) is at first tough and feisty. She stands up to and resists Walter Matthau's attempts to use her as a pitcher on a Little League team. Eventually, however, she not only acquiesces but dissolves into complete compliancy toward this decidedly unattractive, unreliable alcoholic screen character as portrayed by Matthau. Just as the King's Daughter, who is at first assertive and strong, she yields to the repulsive frog.

Unfortunately these images and messages affect us beyond story and screen fantasy. Their pervasive projections have such powerful influence that persons of the stature of Helene Deutsch and Bruno Bettelheim confuse contrivance with reality. The painfully realistic poet Anne Sexton was singularly impressed by the influence of the fairy tale and in her collection of poems, *Transformations*, reminds us that the Princess who submits to a frog may soon learn that he never becomes a prince and is not so charming after all:

> *It's not the prince at all,*
> *but my father*
> *drunkenly bent over my bed*
> *circling the abyss like a shark,*
> *my father thick upon me*
> *like some jellyfish.* [32]

When the Princess finally awakens, what awaits her may be more terrifying than any nightmare.

# 9. THE DEMON NYMPHETTE

What I had madly possessed was not she, but my own creation, another fanciful Lolita—perhaps more real than Lolita; overlapping, encasing her, floating between me and her and having no will, no consciousness, indeed no life of her own.

Humbert Humbert describing the chimerical nature of his conquest in Vladimir Nabokov's *Lolita*[1]

Media images are synthetic. Designed to produce particular impressions and elicit particular feelings, they befog actual knowledge, experience and reality. The image of the little girl which is today expertly packaged and distributed was, however, befogged before the advent of modern technology. In the seventeenth century, for example, the American Indian princess Pocahontas, who saved the life of John Smith, converted to Christianity, became the respectable bride of colonist John Rolfe and was royally received in England, was nonetheless in a bit of early American ribaldry described as "a well featured wanton girlie who at age 11 or 12 did get boyes forth with her in the market place and wheele herself naked as he was, all the forte over."[2]

## THE ARTISTS

Each century has contributed to artistic images of the carnal child. John Dryden, seventeenth-century English poet, assumed the voice of an under-fifteen-year-old who impatiently pleaded, "Take me; take me some of you."[3] In the eighteenth century, Robert Burns did the same for a virgin who begged to be relieved of her "maidenhead."[4] The prominent nineteenth-century photographer O. D. Rejlander posed his eleven-year-old model Charlotte Baker in the nude and seminude so that her immature body communicated incongruous sexuality.[5] During the same period, Dostoyevsky fashioned his female children as strangely depraved and harlotlike. In *The Possessed* the downtrodden twelve-year-old Matroysha, first frightened when seduced by Stavrogin, soon became an unpleasant aggressor:

*Finally such a strange thing happened suddenly which I will never forget and which astonished me: the little girl grabbed me around the neck with her arms and suddenly began kissing me herself. Her face expressed complete delight. I got up almost in indignation—this was all so unpleasant for me, in such a little creature.[6]*

And in *Crime and Punishment* the fifty-year-old pedophile Svidgrigailov dreamed of a lustful five-year-old:

*There was something shameless and provocative in the quiet childlike face; it was depravity, it was the face of a harlot . . . now both eyes opened wide . . . they laughed . . . there was something infinitely hideous and shocking in that laugh, in those eyes . . . "What, at five years old" muttered Svidgrigailov in genuine horror. "What does it mean?" And now she turned to him, her little face aglow, holding out her arms.[7]*

At the inception of the movie industry, D. W. Griffith produced *Broken Blossoms*, in which a twelve-year-old evoked lust, murder and suicide in a religious, peace-loving Buddhist. Jules Pascin painted his female children as cheap and available (in his portrait "Girl Reading," he graces viewers with a preteen "spread shot"). The later Balthus discovered that one way of sharpening erotic reaction was to exhibit seductively the immature female body which was "not yet ready for sexual experience."[8] In the mid-fifties Arthur Miller attempted to parallel the 1692 Salem witch hunts with the dark days of McCarthyism in his play *The Crucible*. To make his point, he resurrected the historic eleven-year-old Abigail Williams as a seventeen-year-old nymphomaniac; in Miller's Salem it was a harlot's cry rather than the fanatic theocratic founding fathers who perpetrated the brutal witch hunts.[9] In *Gigi* an old roué, played by Maurice Chevalier, smirked and leered as he sang "Thank Heaven for Little Girls," and today the popular photographer David Hamilton has pubescent and prepubescent females pose vacant-faced, in a trance-like sexual involvement with themselves or each other. In admiration of Hamilton's work the novelist Alain Robbe-Grillet described the girls as follows:

*She is an idiot. She understands nothing, she sleeps like an overripe fruit. Then come back towards the bed and whisper lowly in her ear saying clearly: "you are nothing but a whore, a slut, a damp meadow, a half open shell."*[10]

## THE HUCKSTERS

Because so many men are attracted to children, advertisers wishing to capture this lucrative market transform the most nonsexual products into a garden of childish delights. Bell Telephone at one time circulated a picture of a twelve-year-old standing on a book reaching for something unseen. The caption, which read "Are you using your phone book properly," instructed that the phone book was for finding numbers rather than adding height. But by provocatively exposing the child's buttocks, the picture also made a direct appeal to male sexual interest in children.* In addition, Wilson Bryan Key, author of several books on media manipulation, notes that embedded in some advertising material featuring children, the words *sex* and *fuck* can be subliminally perceived.[11]

Today subliminal imprinting is hardly necessary. Tots and teens openly model "demure briefs" and "sensuous thongs" to sell underwear, while Caress soap pushes its product with a T-shirt on which the word *caress* invitingly covers an adolescent bosom. The alliance between sharply focused adult sexuality and childhood innocence is so appealing that women are offered the fantasy of achieving not only youth but infancy. Elaine Powers sells her beauty salons by displaying the naked rear of a toddler. Love's Baby Soft Cosmetics sports a full-page ad in most popular journals of a seven- or eight-year-old made up to look like Marilyn Monroe and holding a teddy bear in order to persuade potential consumers that "innocence is sexier than you think."†[12] Stax Records introduced ten-year-old Lena Zavorini as the bombshell who belts out "Ma, He's Making Eyes at Me" in the style of Midler, while Gilbert O'Sullivan, in the

---

*After protests by a group of women lawyers, this picture was removed from circulation.

†The teddy bear is frequently used to symbolize the sexy woman-child and in his day Elvis Presley gyrated as he sang "Let me be your teddy bear."

popular ballad "Claire" (put out by Atlantic), hints of a sexual attraction to his five-year-old niece.

During the liberated 1960s, the fashion industry made a very direct appeal to grown men by offering nymphettes as playmates. Fourteen-year-old Romaina Power (Tyrone's daughter) and seventeen-year-old Twiggy (who stood five feet six inches but weighed no more than ninety pounds) were models of high fashion. Small, childish and infantile was beautiful[13] and women who shopped in Bloomingdale's and Lord & Taylor could hardly find costumes long enough to cover their private parts. But in the 1970s, when Madison Avenue moved from the nursery to the bedroom, women followed, with daughters and little sisters trailing behind. Calvin Klein created a very soigné black satin and velvet tuxedo for his ten-year-old daughter, Marci, and designer Betsey Johnson boasted that her nine-month-old daughter loved ribbons, hats and "doesn't even own a pair of dungarees."[14] B. Altman & Company advised that daddy does not have to be "Daddy Warbucks" to keep his little girl attractive because "Jean Cacherel, France's finest fashion man, has created a couture collection for young ones . . . his designs have the same charm and delightful detailing that made him a favorite with grown-ups."[15] To complement kiddy fashions, beauty salons and charm schools will happily teach those from three and up how to look attractive, arrange their limbs and be charming even if they don't feel that way, and "Little Miss Half-Pint" beauty contests are springing up all over the country. During one contest, a five-year-old outcharmed fifty-three other contestants as she "planted her hands on her eighteen-inch hips, pivoted and tossed her head over her shoulder à la Betty Grable."[16] In 1977 Harper's Bazaar asked us to take a look at Hollywood, where twelve-year-old Tatum O'Neal and Jodi Foster were already "femmes fatales" and toddler Chastity Bono was sure to become the "tiny terrific of TV land."[17]

## THE THEATER, THE CINEMA AND TV

Ostensibly, the eroticization of children is frowned upon, but if the little girl is to be exhibited as a sexual commodity, the rift between decency, male interest and the profit motive must somehow be reconciled. Media experts are masters at harmonizing such blatant contradictions. One successful strategy used in advertising is to highlight a sexy little girl while her male admirers remain unseen.

When a writer or director wishes to focus upon a pedophile, the reverse tactic is used. In this case the little girl, who is never seen, is reduced to an inconsequential cliché whose suffering, humiliation and even death disturbs no one. For example, in the 1931 Fritz Lang film classic, *M*, a dramatization of child sex murders, actual sex and murder are never viewed, but they are symbolized by the bleak floating away of a child's balloon as she walks off with her murderer. In the later films *The Mark* and *Short Eyes*, sex offenders are featured but not their crimes. While discussing *The Mark*, film critic Pauline Kael wondered if compassion for the criminal would be diminished if "we had actually seen him attack a child."[18] The answer, I think, is obvious, but Sidney Buchman, writer and director of *The Mark*, answered her most adequately. *The Mark* was based upon the true story of a man who had indeed raped a child, but if he told the truth, Buchman said, "I wouldn't have a movie" because "I couldn't get people to have compassion for him."[19] Buchman was, of course, right. If we were to see an actual assault upon a child, *see* her fear, *hear* her screams and pleas for mercy, compassion for the offender would be impossible.

Another diversion is to shift the focus from the problem of sexual assault to that of mistaken or false accusation and unjust punishment. The authors of both *The Mark* and *Short Eyes* presented us with molesters who never even molested anyone. Buchman created a man who was attracted to children, abducted one, never laid a finger on her but, feeling decently guilty for his motives rather than his behavior, turned himself over to the police. In *Short Eyes* the accused child molester is badgered and finally murdered by his fellow prisoners, and only afterward do his murderers and the audience learn that he never committed the crime for which he was imprisoned and despised. On TV in one *Kojak* caper, a group of mothers so harass a suspected but innocent child molester that he kills himself; in another TV play a confused schoolgirl unjustly accuses an innocent teacher of molestation; and in the British film *Ten Rillington Street*, attention is shifted from a series of brutal sex murders (this time of women) to the problem of hanging the wrong man. We are obviously not permitted to have a negative reaction to the child sex offender, but since admiration for him is impossible, our media persuaders have exchanged admiration for sympathy, and so the image of the "sick" child molester emerges.

When we are finally confronted with the child sex murderer

in *M,* any possibility of harboring or expressing incipient rage is quelled by the vision of a terrified little man (Peter Lorre) pathetically screaming, "I couldn't help it." In case we did not immediately get the message, one member of the cast informs us that the murderer is sick and needs a doctor, not a policeman. One person I spoke to found that *M* helped her to understand the terrible suffering of the human being who murders. By the time we are introduced to the pedophile (played by Stuart Whitman), in *The Mark,* he has served three years in prison and is in treatment with a charming psychiatrist (Rod Steiger) who convinces both patient and audience that the man's interest in little girls was provoked by his monstrous mother. And as the molester is being tormented by his fellow prisoners in *Short Eyes,* a prison sage advises that this weak, confused man is sick.

Emotional illness is often used to explain male hostility and aggression against females. Steven Marcus in *The Other Victorians* described the pornographer as "an infant screaming for the mother's breast from which he has been torn"; his "misogynist creations reflect," Marcus writes, "revenge upon the world—and the women in it—in which such cosmic injustices could occur."[20] But if we can sympathize with "the terrible suffering of the human being who murders," hold child molesters blameless because they are "sick," and forgive pornographers because they seek revenge upon the world of women where "cosmic injustices occur," we can hold those who rape, assault and murder females as responsible for their behavior as much as we can an earthquake for the havoc it wreaks.* Hannah Arendt said, and I agree, "Nothing . . . can be more dangerous than the tradition of organic thought in political matters by which power and violence are interpreted in biological terms."[21]

## LITTLE FEMMES FATALES

Since the media can take the sting out of inequity, it can also create evil where none exists. A little girl who is made to appear sexy can

---

*The only film I know of which approached this problem with a modicum of insight was De Sica's* Two Women. *In this drama a thirteen-year-old and her mother painfully survive the perils of war-torn Italy with their capacity for human love and understanding intact. However, when mother and daughter are raped by soldiers, the child becomes embittered, cynical and sells herself to a soldier for a pair of nylons. De Sica affirmed that the sexual violation of the child came closer to her emotional destruction than the sum total of war's brutalities.*

also be portrayed as "la belle dame sans merci." The body of Regan in that enormous box-office success *The Exorcist* was invaded not only by the devil but by masters of engineering and special effects. By combining revolting behavior with obscene language, masturbation and genital exposure, evil was directly related to her sexuality. In the equally popular thriller *Carrie*, director Brian De Palma made a conscious connection between Carrie's first menstrual period and her destructive powers of telekinesis. She used telekinesis to destroy the population of half a town, and this power, according to De Palma, was "an extension of her emotions" and "an expression of her passions."[22] Frank de Felita, who wrote the book *Audrey Rose* (later also a movie), selected a "sensuous" nine-year-old girl to be invaded by an odious supernatural force even though it was his untalented six-year-old son who was found one day masterfully playing the piano, that inspired the story of reincarnation.[23] *Communion* by Frank Luria is the chilling novel of murder and rage frighteningly exhibited by a thirteen-year-old, and in *Suffer the Little Children*, a "seductive" eleven-year-old kills a cat and three children. *Ruby* is advertised as the sixteen-year-old daughter of Satan and of sin; the *Death Knell* is the retelling of the Nazi holocaust through the body of little Pamela; and the beautiful woman in *The Killing Gift* used her pernicious talent in childhood.*

In the films *Lolita*, *Taxi Driver* and *The Little Girl Who Lives Down the Lane*, prepubescent girls are grouped in a genre where evil and corruption emanates directly from themselves rather than an invading spirit. *Taxi Driver*, dripping with gratuitous violence, has been hailed as a metaphor for modern life. One example of this metaphor is a twelve-year-old prostitute who will happily gratify any male sexual desire in order to please her loathsome pimp. Jodi Foster was so well received in this role that she soon starred in *The Little Girl Who Lives Down the Lane*, where as a thirteen-year-old bundle of budding sexuality she kills her rapacious mother, a bigoted real estate woman and an unlikely child molester.

The "demon nymphette" has come to us from a long line of fanciful, nefarious young females, but eager for a modern

---

*There is also a smattering of deleterious male children such as* The Omen. *However, in the few examples where male children are used, the terror they invoke is never related to their sexuality.*

representation, society pounced upon the "Lolita Syndrome," and in the process carelessly misconstrued her creator's intentions.


## LOLITA

In 1954, before the sexy little girl became fashionable, the manuscript of *Lolita* was turned down by five publishing houses. It was dismissed as obscene, lewd and pornographic. Vladimir Nabokov suspected that his rejectors never got beyond the first one hundred and fifty pages because "their refusal to buy my book was based not on my treatment of the theme but the theme itself."[24] When Olympia Press published *Lolita* in 1955, some suspected that its readers were attracted to a salacious love affair between an aging European and a twelve-year-old American child. *Lolita* was banned in several public libraries and Nabokov was branded a dirty old man. A few years later, the book was republished by the more dignified Putnam and hailed as an honest, courageous, important literary and psychological contribution. But I suspect that those who hailed the work, no more than those who rejected it, also never got beyond the first one hundred and fifty pages. They too were more interested in sex with children than in Nabokov's treatment of the theme.

Nabokov obviously researched the psychiatric literature for descriptions of pedophiles and incestuous fathers. Humbert Humbert is almost a carbon copy of psychiatrist Benjamin Karpman's description of a "normal pervert"—that is, a man who functions well in all areas but is afflicted with "one unorthodox, unacceptable orientation."[25] As a case in point, Karpman described William K., an upstanding school principal whose one unorthodox orientation was manifested by sleeping with his fifteen-year-old daughter and her little sisters. Humbert Humbert, an English scholar with a few published essays to his credit, also had one unorthodox orientation: He was sexually attracted to little girls. Although Nabokov drew from acceptable psychiatric literature in presenting an incestuous father figure, his Humbert was a caricature, an invention, a humbug. It was Humbert Humbert the humbug, not Nabokov, who invented the "demon nymphette." This "normal pervert" kidnapped Lolita, drugged her and then, playing upon her childish need to brag, prodded her into boasting of a nonexistent sexual sophistication. (The extent of her sexual experience had been experimentation with her peers.) When Humbert finally succeeded in copulating with her, he admitted that Lolita "was not prepared for the discrepancies between a kid's life and mine."[26]

Most of us have been led to believe that Lolita seduced Humbert, but a mere four pages beyond the seduction scene, Humbert is shaken from bliss when his "darling" calls him a child rapist and wants her mother. When she learns that her mother is dead, she goes sobbing to Humbert, but he knows quite well that she came to him only because "she had absolutely no place else to go."[27] From page 144 on, Lolita is Humbert's prisoner in a tale of horror. For two years the fifty-year-old scholar pits himself against a very ordinary, gum-chewing, comic-book-reading twelve-year-old. As she connives to escape, he connives to hinder her escape. As she manages to save some money, he confiscates her meager hope. She threatens to report him as a child rapist. He threatens to send her to reform school. He watches her every move, constricts her life so severely that she does badly in school, develops a tic and becomes noticeably depressed. Humbert realizes that he has succeeded in "terrorizing Lo." When she does not lash out with "I despise you" (especially when he makes sexual demands), she pleads "Pulease, pulease leave me alone ... for Christ's sake leave me alone."[28] Finally when she becomes so ill that hospitalization is required, she uses this opportunity to escape and takes off with Quilty, another pedophile. She soon leaves him to marry a very ordinary gas jockey and chooses to lead a very ordinary life. In a more reflective moment Humbert concedes that "even the most miserable of family lives was better than the parody of incest which was the only life I could offer the waif."

Nabokov said that when he wrote Lolita he "had no moral in tow."[29] I believe him. I even suspect that he was not overly fond of either Humbert or Lolita. He took far greater delight in his own brand of humor, the sensuality of his words, and in painting both grotesque or romantic word pictures. His pleasure in art far surpassed anything as commonplace as "nice" people or morality. What Nabokov thought or meant mattered little, for the world would have their "Lolita": Lolita the baby pro who haunts conventions and who for a price will gratify men kinky for sex with kids; Lolita the tease, the seducer, corrupter, who ensnares decent daddies and old men who are tragically attracted to little girls.

The image of the demon nymphette is so pervasive today

that I have found some small comfort in the knowledge that I am not a lone dissenter. Film critic Molly Haskell said that "when there is pain and recognition of suffering as in Nabokov's *Lolita* . . . the pain turns out to have been inflicted by a child whose innocence is only an illusion, a veil behind which a malevolent minx is waiting to lure a man."[30] And from sociologist Edgar Z. Friedenberg we hear:

> *Lolita is every bit as much a tragic heroine of adolescence as Holden [Catcher in the Rye] is a hero . . . they are both victims of the same corruption in adult society and the same absence of any real opportunity to grow up to be themselves . . . but this is not the way Lolita—the character, not the book—is generally received. Unlike Holden she has no cult and is not vouchsafed any dignity. It is thought to be comical that, at fourteen, she is already a whore.*[31]

The concept of the child-whore has been so effectively internalized that when a fifteen-year-old boy raped a high school girl, the judge before whom he was brought did not castigate him for being a youthful lecher, but granted that he acted "normally" toward girls who entrap boys by wearing "revealing and provocative clothing." This is a popular opinion. When the number of rapes of very young girls increased alarmingly in Canada one man stated to the press:

> *Teenage girls in tight jeans and so on who importune passing motorists are probably looking for some kind of action that is likely to follow when a male pulls up. These girls know the score; some get raped, a few get murdered, generally they asked for it.*[32]

If the young girls are evil and can be judged as evil, then they can be justifiably loathed, raped and even murdered.

In the later 1970s the media graduated from projecting the image of the inherently evil female child and purified her in order to romanticize child-adult sex. The film *Bambina*, a love story between a grown man and an adolescent (slightly retarded, I think), was advertised as beautiful, guileless, simple, innocent and basic. Louis Malle, French film director, also dignified innocent sex between a man and child in the more popular *Pretty Baby*.

## PRETTY BABY

*Pretty Baby* is the story of a twelve-year-old prostitute who was born and raised in a New Orleans brothel in the early twentieth century.

On her twelfth birthday the child's virginity is auctioned off to the highest bidder in front of a group of obviously aroused men. Violet's reaction to her initiation into the "life," with the man who purchased her for $400, is portrayed as one of pleasure, poise and pride. When the brothel is closed by irate citizens she appears at the door of the bearded photographer Bellocq and proceeds to seduce him with an aggressive enthusiasm and finesse inappropriate for her age. Bellocq later is shown photographing her in painstaking detail, clothed and in the nude. Critic Vincent Canby saw the film as paralleling life and art. But despite his enthusiasm he managed to ignore the artistry (or lack of it) of Brooke Shields, the twelve-year-old actress who played the starring role. "I have no idea whether Brooke Shields can act in any real sense," he said. But to Canby, as to Malle, her skill was irrelevant. Shields was simply a sex object. "She has the face that transcends the need to act,"[33] said Canby. Critic Judith Crist found *Pretty Baby* to be visually beautiful but "pointless"—especially the gratuitous flashing of "the heroine's prepubescent nudity."[34] I found the film for all its artistic trappings to be no more than a pandering to pedophilic interests.

The film was patterned after the life of an actual child prostitute who lived in an actual brothel; but with hard evidence that these prostitutes suffered the ravages of venereal disease and bodily abuse, Malle seemed to prefer a sugar-coated fantasy to reality. He indicated that in the brothel world there was neither victim nor violator. But if a depiction of a child prostitute can be presented without a victim or a violator, then the statement, however artistic, can be no more than a legitimization of a man's right to purchase a child for sexual use. The poet Christina Rossetti said of the artist that he paints the female not as she really is but as she fills his dream.[35] If the creator of the female child refuses to acknowledge the power of one sex over the other and of the mature over the immature, then whether the little girl is fashioned by an artist or hack pornographer, as an objet d'art or a slut, her representation can be nothing more than an insulting reflection of the mind's eye of her creator.*

---

*John Gagnon and William Simon, in their book* Sexual Conduct, *stated this same concept in their discussion on sexual liberation. They said: "The rhetoric from Freud to Esalen Institute, from D. H. Lawrence to Norman Mailer, from Comstock to Spiro Agnew agrees on the same social significance: when one behaves sexually, one is acting out the metaphor of sex as power, sex as transgression, sex as reinforcing natural masculine and feminine roles."*[36]

# 10. FATHERS AND DAUGHTERS

According to one study, fathers confronted with
detection . . . often express surprise that incest is
punishable by law and frequently insist that they have
done nothing wrong. Some fathers believe sexual access
to be one of their parental rights.
*Sexual Assault: The Target Is You*[1]


Female children whose fathers rape them are seen as
"seductive"—or the mothers are blamed for not
preventing the rape-incest, or for secretly "wanting" it.
In any event, the tone is one of "no great harm has been
done anyway."
Phyllis Chesler, *Women and Madness*[2]


There have never been firm taboos against the sexual use and abuse
of children by adults, or against incest. The "horror" of sex or
marriage between blood relatives has never been a barrier to erotic
behavior. Marriage between kin is not a universal crime, and incest
taboos are simply codes designed to regulate mateships. In early
small communities when everyone was related to everyone else,
liaisons were controlled by specifying with whom one may or may
not have sex or marry. In some societies cousin, sibling and even
parent-child marriage was permitted; in others, persons without any
ancestors in common were forbidden to each other. The only
common denominator is that all known societies, to greater or lesser
degrees, control mateships and deem certain sexual liaisons
unlawful.[3]

  In the ancient Middle East, marriage between close kin was,
in fact, encouraged. In order that a tribal chief might be assured of
the support of his brothers and sons, he gave them to his daughters

in marriage. Nor was it unusual in pre-Islamic Arabia for a father who could afford not to sell a favorite daughter, for either money or allegiance, to marry her himself.[4] Mosaic law, derived from Middle Eastern legislation, also permitted marriages between brother and sister (same father only), cousins and uncle and niece.*[5] Men were even urged in the apocryphal Book of Tobit to "take a wife of thy father's tribe and not a strange wife which is not of thy father's seed"[6] in order to discourage them from straying from the Judaic faith.

Mosaic law was far more concerned with protecting a man's sexual property than preventing carnal knowledge between kin. The concept of illicitness, subsumed under the Biblical phrase "uncovering the nakedness of," concentrated upon hindering men, under penalty of death, from infringing upon one another's property rights. For example, a man was commanded not to "uncover the nakedness of his daughter-in-law" because "she is your son's wife."[7] And though men were generally advised not to "approach anyone near of kin,"[8] marriage between siblings with paternal permission was not uncommon. Abraham, our first patriarch, and his wife, Sarah, were half-brother and -sister, and before Ammnon raped his half-sister Tamar, she pleaded, "I pray you speak to the King [David, their father] for he will not hold you from me."[9] Obviously, their father's permission would have been forthcoming. Adultery, or taking another man's wife, was a capital crime, and taking a man's daughter without permission demanded monetary reparations and an obligation to marry the devalued daughter. Absalom killed his brother Ammnon not for the crime of incest, but because Ammnon took their sister without paternal permission and then refused to marry her.[10]

When, as in Middle Eastern and Judaic law, property rights were foremost and women were a property, a son who took his mother, stepmother, or wives or concubines who belonged to his father committed the gravest crime. Jacob deprived his first-born son, Reuben, of his inheritance because "you climbed into your father's bed"[11] and took his concubine Billah. And when the rebellious Absalom, son of King David, went to his father's concu-

---

*Aunt-nephew marriage was forbidden. Some scholars maintain that this taboo existed because in a patriarchal system, age discrepancy would probably lead to the dominance of the female partner.

bines "in the sight of all Israel,"[12] this defiance was an open challenge to David's kingship and resulted in war between the armies of Absalom and David; not until Absalom was killed and his armies defeated did David re-establish rule. For a man to take his father's women was a threat not only to one father but to the entire patriarchal system; mother-son incest therefore elicited "horror" and was the most stringently enforced taboo.

Considering the serious political implications, the prohibitions against mother-son or stepmother and stepson are understandable, but why should the same taboo apply to sex between a father and his daughter? A man might be forbidden to a married daughter because she belonged to her husband, or forbidden to his granddaughters because they belonged to their father, but an unmarried daughter belonged to her father alone! Logically, then, the same prohibitions and penalties should not apply to father-daughter sex. And logically the same prohibitions and penalties *did not* apply. *In fact, there is no specified taboo in the Bible forbidding father-daughter incest.*[13] When Lot's daughters, convinced that all humanity had been annihilated after the destruction of Sodom and Gomorrah, plied their father with drink and cohabited with him in order to continue his line, this cohabitation incurred not the slightest social or supernatural disapproval,[14] not even a small family curse. To the contrary, the issue of the first daughter, Mohab, became and is "to this day" the father of the Mohabites. The second daughter bore Benjamin, who is "to this day" father of the Ammonite tribe.[15] And to this day father-daughter incest is the relationship least affected by the incest taboo.

Though the behavior of an incestuous father has never been explicitly condoned, neither has it been condemned. The ancient historian Herodotus (5th century B.C.) told of the King of Egypt who "conceived a passion for his daughter and violated her." The shamed daughter killed herself and the mother amputated the hands of the servants for not "preventing the outrage," but no one punished the father.[16] Plutarch (A.D. 100) noted that the King of Persia married his daughter.[17] Pope Alexander VI (15th century) publicly announced that he was the father of his daughter's children.[18] Also in the fifteenth century, Beatrice Cenci contrived the death of her father, Francis Cenci, a notoriously vicious criminal who had raped her. Despite all the evidence that she gave in her own defense, and notwithstanding enormous popular support and sympathy on her behalf, Beatrice Cenci was beheaded.*[19] The popular folk tale of "Patient Griselda" told by both Chaucer[20] and Boccaccio[21] illustrates the cavalier attitude toward father-daughter incest in the Middle Ages. When the Marquis of Saluzzo decided to take a wife, the story goes, he chose the peasant girl Griselda. After several years he wanted to test her devotion. He falsely informed Griselda that he had killed their children, a son and daughter. Though heartbroken, Griselda acquiesced to his spousal and paternal authority. Still unsatisfied, the Marquis stated that he wished to remarry and the new bride was to be their daughter, now twelve years old, and the most beautiful thing ever seen. Griselda (it is never clear whether Griselda was aware that the bride was their daughter) humbly welcomed her, merely begging the Marquis to be kind to the child for, unlike herself, she was young and had been delicately brought up. Finally convinced of her fidelity, the Marquis informed "patient Griselda" that she had passed all tests and they lived happily ever after. The moral of this story is that a good wife will tolerate all her husband's outrages, including incest with their own daughter.

Today, the popular sexologist R.E.L. Masters finds the young female/older man combination so natural that the frequency of father-daughter as compared with mother-son incest "has nothing to do with avoiding the mothers," he explained. "It is simply a matter of esthetics."[22] Wardell Pomeroy, member of the Kinsey team and author of several works on human sexual behavior, advises that when a charming young daughter hugs, kisses and presses against her Dad, "it would be an extremely obtuse father who would not be aroused and continue the situation."[23] One "Dear Abby" correspondent discovered that her husband was making advances to their daughter but was placated by the family doctor, who persuaded her that the practice was quite common.[24] And the prestigious Margaret Mead found a father's attraction to his little daughters so commonplace that "society must" find the means of "protecting him from temptation."[25] Society, in this case, can be none other than the mother, who in many cultures is assigned the task of keeping her baby daughter covered, training her to be modest or else be held accountable for tempting an incestuous father.[26] And though currently all states carry penalties for incest (from six months' to fifty

---

*This tragedy was immortalized in literature by both Shelley and Stendahl.

years' imprisonment), judges and juries are very reluctant to punish an incestuous father.

During the early twentieth century, fifteen-year-old Lulu Roller, who was raped by her father, sued for damages. The Washington State Supreme Court dismissed the case on the grounds that "the rule of prohibiting suits between parent and child is based on the interest that society has in preserving harmony in domestic relations."[27] Harry Kalven and Hans Zeisel, in their study of *The American Jury,* described a case in which a defendant charged with the rape of his ten-year-old daughter was found guilty and sentenced to life imprisonment. On appeal, a new trial resulted in a hung jury. After the defendant had spent thirteen months in prison, he was tried again. This time the jury acquitted him after thirty minutes' deliberation, not because they found new evidence, but because they felt the man had "suffered enough." In sympathy, they collected sixty-eight dollars which they presented to the defendant when the case was over.[28]

Given these sanctions it is not surprising that father-daughter incest emerges as the most common form of incest. Dr. S. Kirson Weinberg, in his study of *Incest Behavior,* found that of 204 cases under investigation, 164 were father-daughter, 76 were brother-sister, and two were mother-son.[29] Herbert Maisch, in his work on the subject, identified a typical study in which 90 percent of the incest offenders were fathers or stepfathers,[30] and in the Kinsey investigation of imprisoned sex offenders, the few incarcerated for incest were either fathers or stepfathers.[31] But because the act is illegal, and on the surface at any rate incurs disapprobation, it is performed sub-rosa. *The New York Times* carried an account of three teen-age girls who ran away from home because their father forced sex upon them. The article recognized that this exposure was rare since "incest between fathers and daughters from every social and economic class is far more common than ever reported."[32] We may hear of more occurrences among the scrutinized poor, but when discovered and dealt with at all in middle-class homes, the problem is usually buried in the private files of a psychiatrist's office.

But despite furtiveness, sources do obtrude to apprise us of its prevalence. Ann Landers confessed that she was "chilled" by numerous letters from young girls who informed her that they had been sexually assaulted by their fathers,[33] and the columns of "Dear Abby" (Abigail van Buren) include a complaint about a "dad" who entered his daughter's bedroom and engaged in sex play with her and a letter from a mother who was horrified to learn that her husband had been "bothering" their young daughter.[34] There is scarcely a study of female prostitution, delinquency, drug addiction, battered wives and children, runaway girls and even conflicts over child custody which does not bring cases of father-daughter incest to light. Those currently in the struggle to allow minors the right to abortion without parental consent protest that any bill insisting upon parental consent *would force a teen-ager to seek consent from her father who is also the father of her unborn child.*[35]

Judith Herman and Lisa Hirshman, in their study of father-daughter incest, have justifiably asked:

*Why does incest between fathers and daughters occur so much more frequently than incest between mothers and sons? Why though this finding has been consistently documented in all available sources has no previous attempt been made to explain it? Why does the incest victim find so little attention or compassion in literature while she finds so many authorities who are willing to assert that the incest did not happen, that it did her no harm, or that she was to blame for it?*[36]

A backward glance clearly identifies the potent part played by culture in generally encouraging male sexual license and denial of a modicum of female sexual expression. Unchaste wives and daughters were stoned to death, and during the so-called repressive Victorian era, it was women, not men, who were expected to deny their sexual needs. In 1886 Richard von Krafft-Ebing asserted that sexual desire in the female "arouses suspicion of its pathological significance."[37] And less than 100 years later, a psychiatric text used by medical students informed that "the occurrence of mother-son incest bespeaks more severe pathology than does father-daughter incest."[38] When female sexual expression is not restrained by actual physical punishment, societal judgment will accomplish as much. It is perhaps this omnipresent double standard which prompted anthropologists Clelland Ford and Frank Beach to suggest that all incest taboos should be considered "within the famework provided by the general tendency of men to bring female sexual freedom to a minimum by social regulation."[39] Weighed by past and present adverse judgment, females have come to believe themselves that they are sexually dangerous and have developed an extremely punitive superego which, more than any threat of external punishment, will ensure restraint. Krafft-Ebing described one mother who, in despair of her "inordinate" sexual impulses, attempted suicide and when that failed, begged to be institutionalized.[40] And Wardell Pomeroy, who felt that a father who resisted his daughter's charms was "obtuse," could produce only this pathetic case as an example of mother-son incest. He told of a divorced woman whose insecure eight-year-old son asked to come into bed with her at night. One night she found him masturbating against her. To her horror, the woman found that she was sexually aroused and quickly removed the boy from her bed. Her arousal, however, so appalled her that she hurriedly consulted a therapist, convinced that she was "not normal."[41]

Not only do incest victims find little attention or compassion in literature, but they are usually blamed for the behavior of incestuous fathers. One "Dear Abby" correspondent complained that when mothers and daughters choose clothing that emphasizes "beautiful young bodies" some fathers cannot help but be aroused.[42] This opinion is not limited to the common man, but is repeated by men in the medical profession:

*In father-daughter incest . . . the father is aided and abetted by a conscious or unconscious seduction by his daughter and by his wife's collusion. The mother forces a heavy burden onto her daughter by causing her to assume the role of the wife and lover with her own father, thus absolving the mother of this unwanted role.*[43]

The above concept of the sexually guilty female is so pervasive that the few apprehended incestuous fathers often complain that they have been seduced by their daughters, even if the daughters are only nine, and were not able to resist because their wives "would not come across." Daughter victims are even convinced that they are responsible for sexual transgressions against them; they often assume the guilt which belongs to the fathers.

Father-daughter incest occurs more frequently than mother-son incest because it is tolerated and excused, whereas the latter is so unconditionally condemned that a mother at the slightest indication of arousal will punish herself rather than act out this impulse upon her child. I do not recommend that we impose the same general sexual cruelty upon men as that suffered by women, but rather than forgive and forget, it would help if the incestuous father were confronted and held responsible for his conduct. If he could be held accountable for the "horror" we say we feel, and if exposure would produce enough guilt to restrain him, this would be progress indeed.

# 11. SEX EDUCATION AND THE CHILD MOLESTER

And although she [Mary Calderone] deplored the exploitation of women inherent in the double standard she seemed to subscribe to the most Victorian notion that the male sex drive was generally more easily unleashed and more difficult to control than was the female's.

Mary Breasted, *Oh! Sex Education*[1]

Professional advice on child rearing is at best a hodgepodge of contradictions. On the one hand we are told that children need discipline, and on the other we are urged to be flexible and listen to their demands. But if instruction on general child rearing is perplexing, sex educators who refuse to deal with the prevailing sexual double standard contribute further to existing confusion and reinforce myths of male superiority and female inferiority. In *What to Tell Your Children About Sex,* prepared by the Child Study Association of America, the question "Why doesn't a girl have a penis?" was asked and answered as follows:

*You may find that your young one has difficulty accepting the basic bodily differences. No matter what you say, your girl—or boy—may decide that everyone should have a penis and that girls have somehow lost theirs. A girl may resent this imagined loss and feel that it is some kind of punishment. A boy may fear losing his. There is no predicting the notions a youngster may get and cling to.*

*Explain that having a vagina or penis is simply one of the things that makes a child a girl or boy and it is all right to be this way. Assure the child that he is as he was meant to be and will never change. (If the little girl seems upset because she doesn't have a penis it will probably help to reassure her that only women can have babies.)*[2]

Both question and answer presume that "penis envy" is an unchallenged natural female characteristic. One authority on the subject of sexual differences arrogantly stated that certainly every child knows that having something is preferable to not having it. Having something, like six fingers and two heads, is certainly not always preferable. When my daughter saw her infant brother's penis for the first time, rather than envy she thought something was wrong and asked in alarm, "What's all that stuff he has between his legs?" She had to be reassured that there was nothing wrong with him. But parents, clearly affected by the myth of male superiority and biological male advantage, prefer male to female children, the polls tell us. And female children, sensitive, observant and quick to catch discrepancies, no matter how much "reassured," eventually feel that they enter this world biologically disadvantaged.

It is small wonder, then, that in a culture which subtly or otherwise advances male superiority, the problem of child molestation, clearly an assertion of male power, is, if discussed at all, either minimized, distorted or interpreted to absolve the offender and fault the victim. Despite repeated news reports of successful and wealthy athletes, politicians, professional men, film stars and directors who have been sexually involved with children, Dr. Benjamin Spock, for example, America's foremost authority on child rearing, suggests that "the men who occasionally molest little girls are often (not always) lonely, unsuccessful people, middle-aged or beyond, who have been inadequate in most ways in dealing with adults." Dr. Spock, however, cautions boys who baby-sit that "a girl in the three-to-six year-old period can become very seductive if, for instance, she gets excited in roughhousing." "A youth with strong sexual feelings of his own," Spock continues, "may find it difficult to resist such a disarming temptation to sex play, unless he's somewhat prepared." "As a matter of fact," he concludes, "it's better for older boy-sitters to avoid exciting games with young children."[3] The image of the harmless pedophile and the sexually dangerous female child is promulgated by our most prestigious educators.

## IF SHE'S BIG ENOUGH, SHE'S OLD ENOUGH

Because the female matures physically before the male and can conceive with the onset of menstruation, there is agreement among lay people and professionals alike that when a girl reaches puberty she is ready for sex. In *Normal Adolescence,* prepared by the Committee on Adolescence, Group for the Advancement of Psychiatry (with an introduction by the Assistant Secretary of the United States Department of Health, Education and Welfare), we are told that:

*Physiologically, girls are older than boys from birth to maturity and their earlier pubescence is only the culmination of their generally more precocious development . . . On the onset of menstruation the girl signifies to her parents and her peers that she has become sexually mature.*[4]

And further:

*Girls usually express their new found maturity in styles of clothes and make-up which their parents are likely to consider "sexy" and inappropriate whereas boys demand the car for dating and stay out too late. In girls the ultimate act of defiance is sexual promiscuity whereas in boys it is more likely to be an aggressive act such as stealing.*[5]

This association between menstruation and sexual interest is extremely misleading, particularly since girls today begin to menstruate at a very early age. During the nineteenth century the average age of menarche was between fifteen and seventeen, whereas today (for reasons speculated but unknown) it has dropped to twelve, with a downward trend of about four months every decade.*[6] It is not uncommon, therefore, for a child to start menstruating at eight, nine, ten or eleven. This early capacity to reproduce hardly coincides with desire for coitus, but we are nevertheless advised that when a girl reaches puberty, no matter how young she may be, she is ready for carnal knowledge. As a result, a display of affection by a nine-year-old can be interpreted by a male adult who is attracted to little girls as an invitation to sexual activity. As noted earlier, a common defense of the rarely apprehended child molester is that "the kid asked for it."

The most amazing illustration of ambivalence and inconsistency on the subject by sex educators is offered by SIECUS, the Sex Information and Educational Council of the United States. Their comments are particularly disturbing because since its inception in 1964 this organization has, in the face of strong opposition, been

---

*This trend now seems to be somewhat stabilized.*

first in the struggle to dispense honest, forthright sex information to children, parents and teachers whether "beautiful or painful."[7] SIECUS has unflinchingly exposed the dangers of venereal disease, unwanted pregnancy, irresponsible sexual relationships, supported each individual's right to dignified sexual treatment, and has denounced any act of coercion, exploitation or sexual violation. But after granting that 20 to 40 percent of all girls between the ages of four and thirteen will be sexually victimized by an adult, that the majority of the offenses will be committed by family members, friends or acquaintances, and that children usually react negatively and fearfully to the experience, this weighty information is interpreted to the benefit of the offender and at the expense of the child victim. SIECUS assures us that children are rarely accurate reporters; that they sometimes participate in or precipitate the event, and that most incidents involving fondling and exhibitionism are "minimally harmful."[8] And since the molester strikes without warning, parents are advised that education for purposes of prevention in this area might only shake a child's confidence in adults and create "monsters." The greatest harm, SIECUS warns, may be caused not by the offender but from parents who tend to blow up a trivial incident, thereby exposing their own "unresolved sexual conflicts."[9] However, should a child be unduly disturbed because a man has touched her genitals or exposed his own, rather than make a fuss and confront the molester, parents are advised to look to the child for the problem. Since the child *should not be so bound up in sexual fears that an event of this kind becomes demoralizing,*[10] professional help for the child is recommended.

It is not that parents are uncaring; they are simply confused. First told that in sexual matters "honesty is less traumatic than deception," they are then advised that in case their child is molested, in order to avoid her associating sex with something "dirty" it is best not to mention sex at all. They are urged to help their child understand that her molester is lonely, emotionally deprived or, as one authority put it, friend-sick.

The issue is further muddled by a culture where parental status is enhanced by a sexually desirable daughter. Whether on the beach, playground or someone's living room, proud parents and even grandparents regularly boast, "she's only nine and we can't keep the boys away"; "wow, is that kid stacked, the phone never stops ringing, even men can't keep their eyes off her," and so on. If their daughter is molested, parents who have thus encouraged sexual precocity feel that they have contributed to the crime and that responsibility will be traced back to them. They therefore prefer not to believe their daughter when she reports an encounter. If they cannot help but believe her, they minimize the problem; and if it cannot be minimized or concealed, in guilt and desperation they may turn upon their daughter, who yesterday was just an adorable, sexy kid but is today suddenly transformed into a slut.

Parents have been blamed too much and too long for problems which they do not understand and over which they have no control. But blame them or not, where does this leave the molested child? Feeling unworthy of protection, she gets the message that her body and its most sensitive areas can be touched and manipulated for another's pleasure. And when the adults she looks toward to verify her own reality and self-worth fail her, she is convinced that she is indeed inferior and deserves no more than to be sexually used. A woman who was molested in a movie house as a child says:

*I was raised to think that men can't help it if they are aroused by women and it's our responsibility. We are sexy, fleshy things to tease poor men who are out of control. I just feel fleshy and dirty.*

A woman who was molested by her father's friend puts it this way:

*I wish I had been able to handle it. As I grew up I found myself submitting to men I didn't even like. Later I learned to say "no," but if I had someone to talk to earlier, maybe I would not have been so ashamed and unsure. I might have been able to say "no" sooner.*

If the experiences are repeated, and they usually are, by the time a girl is grown she is no longer sure that she has the right to demand decent sexual treatment. She may yield to sexual aggression because she has never learned that she has the right to freely choose a sex partner who will please, satisfy and treat her with dignity and respect.

Of what, then, are we afraid? Today discussions of the realities of death, war, pollution, atomic annihilation and even human extinction take place in schoolrooms and homes, but the dangers of sexual abuse are rarely talked about. Why this compulsion to ignore the problem? Why the need to forgive the molester and blame the child and her family? Is it possible that we still believe that children must be sacrificed to an overwhelming male sex drive? Are we fearful that the fact of child molestation will turn little girls against men, even their own fathers? If it were true that *all* men sexually molest children and this behavior was naturally inevitable, such concern might be reasonable. But if this is the thinking behind current paradoxical treatment of the problem, then feminists have more faith in the capacity of men to change than those chained to concepts of immutable, biologically determined sex roles. Women, who have for centuries struggled against their second-class status, have always insisted that the sexual exploitation of females by males is culturally acquired behavior and that since we all have the ability to reason, learn and change, then sexual exploitation and its detrimental consequences can be eliminated.

I have seen that when the sexual abuse and use of a child is acknowledged and the insult imposed upon her is recognized, the child's love for her parents and her feeling of self-worth are strengthened. When Cathy was sexually assaulted, her parents believed her and were outraged. The results were amazingly positive:

*It was around Christmas-time. I was ten years old and going to visit an aunt. As I was walking this man, about eighteen, said he wanted to show me something. I was pretty naïve and followed him. When we got to a basement he took down my pants. I got very frightened. He shoved me in a corner and went to pick up some rope. I pulled up my panties and ran. When I got home I was upset. At first I was embarrassed. I didn't want my parents to know that men did such things.\* But they insisted I tell them what happened and it all came out.*

*My father and I went to the police and reported what had happened. One day while my father and I were walking I saw the man. My father chased him but he got away. After that my father got me this big dog because there was a lot going on in the neighborhood. The next winter I was walking with the dog and I felt him get tense and start to growl, and for some reason I knew exactly what I was going to see—there was the same young man who took down my panties. I let go of the dog, who chased him, and ran home. My father asked which way they went, ran after them and when he returned he said, "That man will never bother you again."*

*I was very proud of my father. I always trusted him. Neither*

---

\**This reaction is not uncommon. Many children feel they must protect their parents from realities which they feel will disturb them.*

*my mother nor father ever asked, "Well why did you go with him?" They never blamed me. They were just angry with the man.*

*When I reached thirteen my uncle began to bother me. He was a man I had always liked a great deal but when he began rubbing up against me I got furious. I said immediately, "Don't do that again. I'll tell my father." And I added, "Don't tell me I imagined it because I didn't." My uncle got frightened and never did do it again. He knew I would never let him get away with it.*

The above is an account of parental intervention involving a stranger; however, when in the more difficult situation where the offender is a family relative, and the child is supported, the same positive results occur. Marie told her story:

*Because we had no money and my parents were ill, my brother and I were sent away to stay with an aunt and uncle. I was ten. When my aunt was not home my uncle played a game with me. He tickled me. Tickling soon meant being cornered on a couch and your pants are going to be pulled down and his penis was going to be pulled out. I tried to avoid him. I became tricky. Whenever he was home I'd maneuver to leave the house. I was constantly trying to figure out ways not to be alone with him. Every time I went home I was afraid.*

*One day my father came to visit. I was always able to rap with my father. Finally I told him about my uncle. He said "You're not going back there." He took me to my grandmother and soon the whole family knew the story. He went to the police. They asked if I hadn't imagined the whole thing, if I hated my uncle, what I was wearing and they acted like I tried to tempt him. I was only 10 years old.*

*I felt the police did not believe me but that my mother and father did. We went to court but my uncle got a suspended sentence. After the trial his wife called me a "little son of a bitch." My aunt turned on me but my mother and father were with me all the way. That helped. Later when a man tried to molest me on the street I said, "Keep your lousy hands off me." I knew then that only when you're sure of yourself that they will stop. If you are shy and don't want to face what is going on, then they've got you.*

*Two years later my aunt and uncle got a divorce. He molested two other children. They checked his record and he had a history of molestation. Finally he was sent away.*

If a father can accept that his daughter has been sexually used, then he is in a position to cope with this reality for himself, reinforce his daughter's right to protection from sexual abuse, her right to protect herself, no matter who the man may be, and thereby fortify her own self-estimation. With such a father, a growing girl will be able in later life to settle for nothing less than equality and mutual respect in a sexual relationship; with such a father a growing girl will approach the world with a more positive attitude toward men than the child who, abused and insulted, has no male model who will believe and understand her and whom she can trust.

Currently, thousands of books on sex education flood the market. By failing to differentiate between sexual expression and sexual oppression, they tend to foster polarization and antagonism between the sexes. If we could teach our children that the popular concepts of human sexuality have deployed sex for power purposes we could embark upon a program of sexual equality and teach that sex and coercion, violence and hostility are not synonymous. Once this is understood, we will be free boldly and unconditionally to condemn the behavior of child molesters and incestuous fathers.

Children gravitate toward sex play with themselves and their peers as automatically and naturally as they do toward food, water play, teddy bears, a fuzzy blanket or anything else that provides them with body and tactical pleasure. The job of sex education, in addition to teaching the physiological process of reproduction and the hazards of pregnancy and venereal disease is, in this world where sex can mean exploitation, to arm our young against real pitfalls and teach them that "by saying 'yes' to sex, one doesn't say 'no' to power."[11]

# 12. A HARD LOOK AT THE LAW

Laws pertaining to sexual behavior are for the most part not directed toward the "preservation of public order" as are most criminal laws. Rather, they embody a particular ethical point of view of sexual behavior.

H. A. Katchadourian and D. T. Lunde, *Fundamentals of Human Sexuality*[1]

Crime has no sex and yet today
I wear the brand of shame;
Whilst he amid the gay and proud
Still bears an honored name.

Can you blame me if I've learned to think
Your hate of vice a sham
When you so coldly crushed me down
And then excused the man?

From the poem "Double Standard" written by Frances E. W Harper, born 1825 of free Negro parents and died in 1911.[2]

Every state in this country has some legislation designed to protect children from sexual abuse. Impairing the morals of a minor, lewd acts, obscenity and indecent exposure are misdemeanors, and abduction of minors for sexual use, carnal abuse, genital contacts, forcible or statutory rape* are felonies.[3] But for the most part this legislation, as with all sex-biased legislation, offers little more than an academic theory of justice.

Sexual discrimination in the law is by no means a relic of the

---

*Sexual intercourse with a nonresisting or even willing child under statutory age. Statutory age varies in each state from approximately twelve to eighteen.*

past or a mere historic curiosity; it is a fact of everyday life. The mere suspicion of sexual promiscuity is all juvenile authorities need to throw a young girl in jail just as if she were a robber or murderer. More than one half of the girls who are referred to juvenile court are referred for running away, truancy, incorrigibility, or acts that would not be criminal if committed by adults, whereas one fifth of the boys who come to juvenile court are referred for such behavior; when boys are arrested it is for committing an actual crime. Although boys are given to sexual promiscuity far more than girls, they are less likely to be taken into custody than girls for a "sexual offense," and despite the fact that girls are less prone to delinquent behavior than boys (one girl is arrested for every five boys), the cut-off age for incarceration of males is sixteen, whereas it is eighteen for girls. There exists a great gulf between what constitutes delinquency in boys and girls. Bad behavior in a boy is understood as "normal rebellion," an attempt to gain freedom, independence and masculine identity, but the same behavior in a girl is regarded as "criminal" or as evidence of "deep emotional disturbance."[4] As one authority on juvenile delinquency put it:

*Male delinquency appears in boisterous, exuberant boys who have found satisfaction among more rebellious peers, but wayward girls are more often unhappy misfits.*[5]

And since it is men who sexually use and abuse children, the law, written and executed by men, tends to be extremely lenient with the sex offender. In the sixteenth century, the eminent jurist Sir Matthew Hale, addressing himself to the testimony of a fourteen-year-old complainant in a rape trial, advised the jury that "rape is an accusation easily made and hard to be proven and harder to be defended by the party accused who be ever so innocent."[6] He cautioned the jury never to be swept away "with so much conviction of a person accused thereof by testimony of sometimes malicious and false witness." This same Matthew Hale, however, was known to "manipulate court proceedings" and to "accept perjured hearsay evidence,"[7] in order to secure the conviction of witches. Today, Hale's "dishonourable" conduct is forgotten, while every courtroom rings with his assertion that "rape is an accusation easily made." And in England, in 1832, when the statutory rape age was ten, a man was acquitted of this crime because the child's baptismal certificate indicated that the rape took place after her tenth birthday.[8] The statutory

age in England is now sixteen; however, physical rather than chronological maturity is used today to justify leniency or acquittal. In 1976,
a twenty-two-year-old English carpenter admitted to having sex with
a consenting fifteen-year-old. Judge Neil McKinnon, who put the
carpenter on probation for twelve months, said;

*Some girls at sixteen are not mature, but some at thirteen or even twelve are
fully mature. Should he [a man] be branded a criminal not because of maturity,
but because of her age?*[9]

Whether a man is forgiven for technical reasons or one's concept of
female maturity depends not upon the law but quite arbitrarily upon
what, at any given time, pleases the court.

## STATUTORY RAPE

Statutory rape is one of the oldest crimes in the annals of Anglo-
American history. It is founded on the premise that the underaged
are neither experienced, responsible nor mature enough to give informed consent to sexual intercourse. Unable to comprehend the
risks of venereal disease, lost reputation and pregnancy, their consent is adjudged as immaterial and therefore it is the adult male
partner alone who must be held criminally responsible. Many
legalists today argue that chronological age is unimportant. What
matters is whether or not a girl knew what she was doing at the time
she acquiesced to sex, or, according to an opinion stated in a law
journal: "It requires no great imagination to picture a situation
where a relatively inexperienced male becomes involved with an
underaged female who is no better than a prostitute."[10]
          Technically, all that is required to convict a man of statutory
rape is proof of penetration and the age of the female. However, in
an atmosphere where the "Lolita complex" flourishes and an underaged female can be viewed as "no better than a prostitute," juries pay
less attention to the letter of the law than to a girl's reputation. If
reputation linked with consent is material, then the age of the child is
no longer a prime consideration. If members of a jury decide that
the female child is bad, brazen, uses offensive language, is not a
virgin, was previously pregnant, or even has an immoral mother,
they are prone to acquit.
          In many states, lack of chastity is admissible evidence. Proof
that a girl is a bawd, lewd, kept female, or has a bad reputation, can

result in either acquittal or a lesser charge. Today, where girls are pressed into early sexual activity, it is not surprising that Kalven and Zeisel in their study *The American Jury* could not find one "chaste" underaged female in their samples of statutory rape."[11]

It is ironic that the law which was established to protect the young from sexual exploitation manages to deprive the most vulnerable of this protection. The teen-ager who manages to remain "chaste," to say no, is fortified by an extraordinary strong personality, good sense, protective family or community and would probably never become involved in a statutory rape charge. It is the sexually used, once-pregnant, raped nonvirgin; the insecure girl, easily influenced by male pressure and unrealistic fantasies imposed by the ever-present media, who needs the legal protection defined in the statutory rape laws. But each time a man is acquitted of statutory rape because of a girl's "unchaste character," a flag goes up announcing that she is fair game for further sexual use.

Some legalists feel that our statutory rape laws deny the young the same sexual rights "normally granted to adults,"[12] interfere with sex between adolescents of like age and furthermore, "if intercourse is harmful to persons of tender years, then it should be equally harmful to young males as well as females."[13] In fact, sex is not equally harmful to both males and females of like age. It is far more harmful to females who can become pregnant or whose reputations can be damaged. This popular concept of equality, however, has prompted many states to grant immunity from a statutory rape charge to males under a certain age. In Maryland, statutory rape cannot be committed by anyone under eighteen. Alabama, Maine and Oklahoma have extended immunity to all males under twenty-five, and some states agree that a male who has sexual intercourse with a female under sixteen, if he is only four years older than the female, would not be guilty of a lesser offense such as "corrupting the morals of a minor."[14]

If the law were not biased in favor of the male and antagonistic to the female, adjustments regarding the age of the male might have merit. But the fact remains that the possibility of perpetrating injustice upon the male is almost negligible. According to the 1975 FBI Crime Report, arrests for statutory rape, no less convictions, appear to be almost nonexistent. Statutory rape is only a portion of a total of the 37,000 arrests made under the general category of "sex offenses." Sex offenses (which exclude forcible rape and commercial sex) are a potpourri of arrests made for offenses or attempts such as statutory rape, offenses against chastity, common decency and the like. There is no breakdown in this category identifying the number of arrests for statutory rape, but considering that each year one million females under statutory age—not including the 30,000 under fourteen—become pregnant, no matter which way one may slice the 37,000 arrests for "sex offenses," those for statutory rape are so small as to represent nothing more than an "academic theory."[15]

## FORENSIC PSYCHIATRY

In the early twentieth century, the distinguished German physician, psychotherapist and sexologist Albert Moll, who wrote *The Sexual Life of the Child,* strongly urged that every effort be made to legally apprehend and restrain child violators and that violators be denied any opportunity to plead "extenuating circumstances."[16] However, no sooner did Moll object to "extenuating circumstances" than he began to provide the child molester with a series of medical and psychological mitigating excuses. Ignorant men who believed that sexual intercourse with children cured venereal disease, unfortunates afflicted with alcoholism, epilepsy, syphilis and imbecility, those so insecure that they were unable to approach a mature woman, others so hungry for affection that anything warm such as an animal or small child would suffice, unhappily married men, or men inadvertently exposed to seductive, unsupervised, neglected little girls could not be blamed or held responsible for their behavior, nor could they be classified as true child violators, he maintained.[17]

And no sooner did Moll acknowledge that children, even infants, were subject to adult sexual misconduct than he set about to assure the public that child victims "completely fail to understand that it [they] had been made use of for perverse purposes,"[18] and therefore went unharmed. Furthermore, little girls who were infected with gonorrhea were "usually the instigators of intercourse,"[19] and what is more, for purposes of blackmail and extortion, pretty, smiling, charming little females managed to successfully deceive judges and magistrates with false accusations of sexual abuse.[20]

About forty years later, the American Bar Association, swayed by more entrenched psychiatric opinion, suggested that a woman or young girl complainant in a sex offense should be examined for moral delusions which might cause "distortion of imagination in sex cases."[21] In 1954 the Supreme Court passed the "Durham Rule," which held that "an accused is not responsible for his unlawful act if the act was produced by mental disease or defect."[22] Today, when alcoholism and emotional immaturity are classified as diseases, the alcoholic or emotionally immature child molester is viewed as an unfortunate victim of a "compulsion" rather than as a criminal. By 1959 the behavior of the child violator was so tolerated and the child victim so suspect that the Supreme Court ruled that the uncorroborated testimony of any child under twelve "was not sufficient evidence to sustain a conviction of indecent liberty."[23] The effect of psychiatry on the law has resulted in reinforcing prejudice against victims of sexual assault and reducing their protection.

## LYING CHILDREN

Those who have ever worked with children can attest to the fact that their perception of their environment and experience is far more concrete than fanciful. Among the volumes of literature on disturbed children, the problem of "lying" is almost never discussed. Any nursery or grade-school teacher will verify that children differentiate between "make-believe" and reality often more accurately than adults.

*From age three on . . . a child is well aware of the "make-believe" qualities of his fantasies. Even as he indulges in the most fantastic projections, he retains emotional contact with his actual environment [reality]. . . . This was shown in a study where children in free play sessions were approached by an observer . . . to whom they could reveal the "pretend" character. . . .* [24]

Kenneth S. Carpenter, Director of the United States Special Programs Division of Justice, Law Enforcement Assistance Administration, posed and answered the following question regarding the possibility of children inventing stories of molestation:

*Question: Are some children prone to imagining sexual molestation by an adult and unable to distinguish fact from fantasy—or is a statement of sexual abuse by a child almost invariably accurate?*

*Answer: There is no evidence in the literature or among the service providers that children are unable to distinguish fact from fantasy in these situations. Of course the younger the child the more unlikely it is that the child would or even could imagine such things, given the detail and accuracy with which children report these incidents.* [25]

When caught in behavior which might elicit adult disapproval, children might lie to protect themselves; "Johnny stole the cookie, not me!" Or to achieve status with their peers, some may boast "We have ten cars and six television sets." But children cannot and do not make up stories outside the realm of actual experience. If sex with adults were openly approved and encouraged, a child might tell a falsehood for self-aggrandizement, but the reverse is true. Little girls are shamed by a sexual encounter with an adult and tend to conceal rather than reveal an incident. Child therapists have uncovered a sexual encounter by exploring disturbed behavior rather than from direct information:

*One eight-year-old victim drew a picture of the assailant between her legs and his face on her genitals and another female in the room with a smile on her face. The child then took an eraser and erased the drawing of the man. In elaborating on the drawing, she explained that the other female was watching and laughing. This data provided an opportunity for the child to further describe how upsetting and embarrassing the incident had been to her and she "wished to erase it from her mind."*[26]

Criminologist Fred E. Inbau, professor of law at Northwestern University and former director of Chicago's Police Scientific Detective Laboratory, and his colleague, John E. Reid, found that "it is exceedingly rare for a child to falsify a sex report," and that "females generally are very reluctant to reveal the details of the offense."[27]

Because of a general reluctance to establish the sexual abuse of children as a serious offense and a tendency to forgive the molester and blame the victim, the law and its agencies have made prosecution of sexual offenders against children so difficult that they are almost never apprehended, convicted, sentenced or imprisoned. In a study of 256 known cases of sexual abuse of children involving 250 offenders conducted by the Brooklyn Society for the Prevention of Cruelty to Children, parents and family found the police process so trying and frightening to the children that 76 cases were dropped, leaving 174 cases eligible for prosecution. Once charges were officially made, the number of interrogations and court appearances resulted in such trauma to the children and their families that another 77 were so discouraged that they too dropped the charges. This left 97 cases. Of this number, 39 offenders either absconded, were acquitted or were left pending, leaving 58 to be tried. Of this number, 49 pleaded guilty in order to take a lesser charge such as assault rather than rape or incest; 4 were found guilty as charged, and 5 were committed to mental institutions. Of the 53 found guilty (excluding the 5 sent to mental institutions), 30 escaped jail sentence by suspension or fine, 18 were sentenced to jail from six months to a year, and 5 received indeterminate sentences.[28]

When Mr. Bumble, in Dickens' *Oliver Twist*, was told that he was responsible for his wife's behavior because "the law supposes that your wife acts under your direction," Mr. Bumble, who was convinced that his wife controlled him rather than the reverse, sputtered in indignation, "If the law supposes that then the law is a ass—a idiot."[29] But Mr. Bumble was wrong. The law is neither an ass nor an idiot. If the law supposes that women and children must act under male direction, no matter how strange or devious its ways, rather than an ass or idiot, the law accomplishes precisely what it has set out to achieve.

# 13. CHILD PROSTITUTION AND KIDDIE PORN

No girl . . . sets out to be a prostitute. Such stupidity would be incredible. Who wants to be a pariah, a social outcast . . . treated with contempt, jailed, beaten, robbed and finally kicked in the gutter when she is no longer salable? A prostitute can count on no more than ten money-making years. Then she is through. . . . No wonder people ask what propels a girl into this short and unhappy life.

No doubt there are as many answers to this question as there are sociologists, psychiatrists, philosophers and doctors of divinity. But in my opinion the greatest single factor—and the common denominator in an overwhelming majority of cases—is poverty.
Polly Adler, *A House Is Not a Home*[1]

During the early part of this century the irrepressible Emma Goldman wondered why reformers were suddenly appalled to discover the world's oldest profession[2]—prostitution. Ancient Greeks and Romans have amply documented its existence, the Bible is filled with references to "whores" and "harlots," and during the Middle Ages and after, licensed brothels provided both church and state with substantial revenue. I agree with Emma Goldman. It is rather naive to suddenly become alarmed by this unheard-of condition.

White slavery is supposedly a thing of the past; however, Tracers Inc., a private detective agency, has claimed that one million Americans are reported missing yearly, with a tenfold increase in the disappearances of children over five. Approximately fifty cases of white slavery are reported in the United States each year but these rarely result in conviction. Occasionally we get some "tip of the iceberg" information regarding national and international prostitution rings and hear of horror stories of kidnappings, torture and forced child prostitution. From time to time we read of agencies which advertise for models or dancers, and once teen-agers are lured from home, no job awaits them. Penniless and friendless, they are "encouraged" to go into prostitution. Organized operations are usually efficiently run and scrupulously concealed. Adults who sell sex are business people; they know whom to trust, bribe and control. But when a child becomes a prostitute, without money, experience, connections, know-how or social protection, she is prone to visibility, censure, arrest, incarceration, harassment and punishment.

## CHILD PROSTITUTION

Much like the "street arabs" of a hundred years ago, the child prostitute of today is a rejected, abandoned or neglected child (often by adults as helpless and powerless as herself) or is one who has fled from adult brutality. Children who leave a reasonably good environment due to a quarrel or in search of adventure usually return within a week. The more affluent flower children of the 1960s looking for love and freedom were in the eighteen-year-old age range, older than the nomads of the seventies, whose ages spanned from thirteen to sixteen. The runaways of today can't or won't return home because they were thrown out, starved, raped, beaten, and the street, miserable as is it, is better than what they left.³ One social worker told me of a thirteen-year-old who ran away to preserve her sanity. She was looking for a place to live, a home, "a place where people can't fuck you over," as she put it. In a letter to Ann Landers which sums up the problem, a mother said she had become pregnant out of wedlock at fifteen. The man she later married, who was not the baby's father, molested the child, Anna, when she was eleven. Anna finally ran away from home. Her mother later learned that the fourteen-year-old girl was "now a prostitute."⁴

But children are not equipped to cope with the street. Underage, without a legal guardian or a bona fide address, they are ineligible for programs which provide training, education and jobs for youths, or for welfare benefits. Without adult status, protection or a family, they are juvenile delinquents who are subject to arrest. Once picked up by the police they may be sent back home (only to run away again), sentenced to a reformatory, or remanded to an inadequate, overcrowded, understaffed, underfunded, punitive "rehabilitation" institution. The Runaway Youth Act, passed in 1973, allotted eight million dollars to establish shelters for street children, but with one million minors needing help each year, the sum provides for only a small number. Without food, shelter or protection, these youngsters soon fall prey to drug peddlers, pimps, pornographers and men kinky for sex with kids. Unlike previous years, today 70 percent of the total number of our street children are females. When a homeless girl is hungry, she panhandles or steals; when exhausted, she sleeps on a park bench or in a subway and, soon desperate, will sell herself to men on the prowl for preteen or teen-age girls.[5] The homeless female juvenile is barred from every occupation but prostitution.

Stephanie was a teen-age prostitute. She left home because her father was a man "who could play with my breasts one minute and be at the dinner table the next and show no signs of discomfort" and because her stepmother beat her so severely that "sometimes I thought she was going to kill me."

*I started running away when I was very young but got hauled back each time. Running away was my only sense of personal power. But I did it so often that when I was fourteen they said I was "incorrigible" and was to be sent to a reformatory. After that I ran away for good.*

*Life on the street was horrible. I had no food, tried to sleep on park benches and one cold night I wandered into a bar. A man came up to me and said he would give me $20.00 if I slept with him. I never slept with a man before. I didn't know if I'd like it or not but I could sure use that $20.00 so I went to bed with him. I hadn't the vaguest idea how to act but I learned. I wasn't a prostitute in the sense that I got dressed up and tried to seduce men. I just sat at a bar and got plenty of offers because I was so young.*

*Soon I could handle myself and say, "You've bought yourself a certain amount of time and if you can't get it off by then either you give me more money or forget it." Once I tried this on a guy but he pulled a gun on me and raped me. Once I got busted but I made a deal with the cops. It cost me $250.*

*I found other ways to make money. Word would get around that there was a "party" where we'd pose for porno pictures and movies and get paid $100.00. The younger the better.*

*A lot of runaways died. They all take drugs. I used to take bennies to stay awake, particularly if I had no place to sleep. I might have got hooked on heroin except a friend of mine, a nice guy, died of a hot-shot. None of us knew enough about drugs so as not to kill ourselves. But after he died I stayed away from drugs.*

*Some girls got pregnant. We had no birth control and some were butchered or killed by hack abortionists. I got pregnant but my Catholic upbringing stopped me from trying abortion. I didn't even know how a birth took place and when I went into labor I was terrified. I wanted to keep my baby but I was only fifteen. Everything was so crazy that I gave her up for adoption.*

*By the time I was eighteen, and the cops couldn't pick me up anymore, I got a job. I worked in a factory, then a dry cleaners and felt more settled. I didn't want the street life anymore. As I got older I could see that because I had no education or could not become a chemist or anything like that the best I could do was to become a prostitute.*

Stephanie was luckier than most. She did not get hooked on drugs, found a job as soon as she reached legal age and stayed alive. Karen Baxter who began prostituting at twelve, however, was found murdered at fifteen,[6] and Veronica Brunson, a prostitute at eleven, died after a mysterious plunge from the tenth floor of a shabby hotel frequented by prostitutes and pimps. Veronica's story, which appeared in the press after her death, presented a classic case of how a child can float through our police and legal system without the help that could be reasonably expected for a child. Arrested several times, she marched through arraignment, fingerprinting, and so on, and no one questioned her obvious immaturity. But had she tried to pass for eighteen in order to get a job, her baby face would have incurred enough suspicion to result in unemployment.[7] It's obviously easier to be an underaged prostitute than an underaged employee. Stephanie was very lucky indeed! She never even got involved with a pimp. The pimp is a businessman who can identify "hungry eyes." With a room for a night and a meal as a lure, a child will gratefully accept his kind offer. Once sheltered and fed she will learn that he is a pimp. He will tell her that she is a lawbreaker who can be turned in and the master-slave or pimp-prostitute relationship has been initiated.

Pimps, however, do not sit around and wait for hungry eyes to appear. With a reservoir of 700,000 homeless female runaways, they go after their merchandise. They scour the streets of San Francisco, Los Angeles, Boston, Chicago, New York, Minneapolis or the shabby areas in any big city where "young-bloods" huddle together. They find the troubled, hungry and homeless, promise them an income of one thousand dollars a week, put them through a training period for hustlers and, after they have earned their plane fare, arrange to meet them in another city. Pimps never travel with "jail bait"—transporting minors from one state to another for sexual purposes is a felony. However, so many have been successfully imported from Minneapolis, the runaway center for the Midwest, to New York, that the area between Fortieth and Fifty-ninth streets on Eighth Avenue is known as "Minnesota Strip."[8]

   Polly Adler was a Russian Jewish immigrant who ran a "house" from 1920 to 1945 and her description of the pimp-prostitute relationship holds today:

*A pimp seeks out a girl and seduces her into the life. Far from weaning her away from drugs, it is he who teaches her the habit. He makes no attempt to protect her from customers (since, for the pimp the customer is always right). He does everything in his power to keep her a prostitute for if she quit the racket, it would reduce his income. And instead of helping her to save money he takes every cent she's got and beats her into making more.*[9]

Girls never see their promised thousand dollars a week; all their earnings go to their pimp. One fourteen-year-old who made at least $150 per night said she gave her pimp close to $100,000 over an eighteen-month period. Most girls want to break away, but with no place to go and living examples of beatings, broken bones and even murder among those who tried, they are terrorized. One child pleaded with a customer for help. The customer was a spy for her pimp. She was beaten, scarred and turned out on her own. Unable to find a job or get on welfare, she returned. Now scarred, she was forced to work for less money.[10] And even if a girl were willing to reveal her state of slavery and identify her pimp, conviction, which requires corroboration, would be very unlikely and physical danger to herself a certainty. The street girl has no reason to trust the law. In 1977, much was made of the effort on the part of New York City police to apprehend the pimp who feeds off children. Judy Klemesrud, who covered the story for *The New York Times*, did not find their activity too encouraging:

*Despite the officers' tough talk about "smashing, squashing and stomping every* *pimp in town," apparently they too have their limits. . . . They stopped a pimp named Rufus and warned him that . . . a $15,000 contract had been put on his head because he failed to pay some gambling debts . . . . He thanked the officers and sped down 55th Street in his El Dorado . . . the sergeant said . . . the guy may do us a favor some day—he may turn in a pimp.*[11]

Regardless of concrete evidence that almost all prostitutes sell themselves to survive, authorities have found it necessary to assuage any potential public guilt by assuring us that in addition to the money motive, the prostitute also plies her trade because she is lazy, wants a good time, an easy life, is a nymphomaniac (or frigid, as the case may be), hates her mother, her father, all men, and gives vent to her hostility through her work. Even if the prostitute is nine or ten we are told that "for a few cents and some sweets she will endure immoral handling,"[12] while those who are more artful, the "baby-pros" or the "Lolitas of whoredom," aged ten to fifteen, "work expensive conventions and hotels," enjoy a very high tax-free income and indulge themselves in every material pleasure.[13] Simone de Beauvoir spoke of two girls under twelve who were picked up in a brothel. As they were about to identify their customers in a court, the judge cautioned them "not to befoul the names of respectable gentlemen." A man who deflowers a girl remains respectable, said de Beauvoir, whereas the child who is sexually used is "perverse, corrupt, vicious and fit only for a reformatory."[14]

## CHILD PORNOGRAPHY

Those who profit from child prostitution will also exploit the lucrative sideline of child pornography. Organized prostitution rings are usually well supplied with cameras and movie equipment. And once a child learns to survive by prostitution, earning a few extra dollars posing for porn pictures and films is not too difficult. Father Ritter, who runs Covenant House, a shelter for runaways, said that the first ten children who came to him had made money appearing in porno films. "These children cannot go home, cannot find jobs nor take care of themselves," he said. "First they are approached to pose in the nude and it is a quick progression to engage in sexual acts for movies or in strip joints along Eighth Avenue for one hundred dollars for four performances."[15] But entrepreneurs primarily profit from this $2.4 billion industry. A man and his wife, who lived in a fashionable

Long Island suburb, put an ad in *Screw* magazine offering $200 for girl models between the ages of eight and fourteen for a one-day session of nude shots. Mothers and fathers together or singly brought their daughters. The money is easy, good and, just as in any other business, pornography soon becomes quite routine. Ron Sproat, a writer who did a short stint in a "porno factory," described the formula he was instructed to use for kiddy porn:

> *I was given a guideline. It said: "Emphasis on the innocence of children, lechery of adults. Boys from six to thirteen; girls six to fifteen. Emphasize hairlessness, tiny privates, lack of tits,"etc.*[16]

The more we are exposed to pornography, as to all forms of brutality, the more we become desensitized to its dehumanizing influence. The Victorian era, which was inundated with pornographic material, introduced the collecting of "erotica" (sometimes dignified as "anthropology") as a respectable pastime for men of leisure.[17] An example of such a collector was James Campbell Reddie, whose knowledge in this domain was so thorough that scarcely any obscene book in any language escaped his notice. He wrote *The Amatory Experiences of a Surgeon*, in which a surgeon finds among his patients a lovely thirteen-year-old girl suffering from a spinal affliction, "to caress, to lie with, to suck."[18] William S. Potter, possessor of an impressive collection of erotic books, engravings and photographs, authored (anonymously) *The Romance of Lust*, in which, after 600 pages, a sexual adventurer finally settles into a happy incestuous family life with his ten-year-old daughter.[19]

Some recognized writers also contributed to the sport. Aubrey Beardsley in his *Story of Venus and Tannhauser* described an orgy involving children.[20] In *The Memoirs of Josephine Mutzenbacher*, attributed to Felix Salton, author of *Bambi*, Josephine, a prepubescent prostitute, graphically shares the details of her profession with her readers.[21] Guy de Maupassant in *The Colonel's Nieces* has a father assist his son in raping a child, " 'Give it to her,' muttered the father '. . . ain't she a beauty, boy. What a tight little cunt she's got.' "[22]

## PORNOGRAPHY AND VIOLENCE

One cannot prove with certainty that there is a causal connection between pornography and violence (or between violence and anything else, for that matter). But neither can one be sure that such a relationship does not exist. Pamela Hansford Johnson, who in 1966 covered the English trial of Ian Brady and his assistant Esther Hindley, convicted murderers of a youth and two children, was impressed by the fact that over fifty volumes of sadomasochistic material were found in Brady's room, with the Marquis de Sade his major hero. The "Moors Murders" (the mutilated bodies were found buried on the moors) elicited heated international discussion, pro and con, regarding the dangers of pornography. In Johnson's opinion, and in mine and many others, the violence found in pornography "is suggested to us, even urged upon us."[23] The influence of de Sade, who had a talent for making iniquitous ideas sound weighty, almost moral, is particularly perilous, especially since he has been resurrected as a "philosopher," and his brand of philosophy justifies cruelty:

*Crime is the soul of lust. What would pleasure be if it were not accompanied by crime? It is not the object of debauchery that excites us but rather the idea of evil.*[24]

De Sade articulated his ideology. He had gentlemen "depuce" (deflower) little girls between the ages of three and seven, immobilizing girls over a grill bringing them to a "light roast" until they lost consciousness, buggering them steadily while fathers were forced to publicly rape their own infant daughters. I will spare the reader descriptions of other such "pleasures" which go on in *The 120 Days of Sodom* for seven hundred and eighty-eight pages.[25]

    Although most psychiatrists, psychologists and sexologists concede that pornography essentially expresses hostility toward females, they mitigate this misogyny by relegating pornography to fantasy which is "nothing more than a representation of infantile sex life."[26] They prefer to believe that pornography serves as a healthy outlet, a safety valve which releases hostility and fantasy and restrains actual sexual aggression. Other scholars, however, understand that "there may be deeper affinities than we as yet understand between 'total freedom' of uncensored erotic imagination and the total freedom of the sadist."[27] I hold with this latter view. So many who have freely indulged in sadistic fantasies have in fact acted them out, thus verifying a "strong affinity" between their imagination and their behavior. If, for example, de Sade's sex life did not match his imagination it was not for lack of effort. After several episodes, he was finally arrested for sticking local teen-agers with knives, whipping them, feeding them dangerous aphrodisiacs and other such delights. Illustrating the same affinity, Frederick Hankey, nineteenth-century "erotomaniac" and distributor of pornography, provided his book-binder with little girls in lieu of payment;[28] while of Leonard Smithers, respectable publisher and collector of pornography, Oscar Wilde said, "He was a man who loved first editions; little girls are his passion."[29]

After the Moors Murder trial and the conviction of Brady and Hindley to life imprisonment, Pamela Hansford Johnson asked a friend:

*Do you suppose now it is demonstrated that a young man and woman may have played out the fantasies of dirty books in murdering a youth and two children, people will look around and wonder whether the total permissive craze toward violence and sexual cruelty oughtn't just possibly to be checked?*[30]

He replied gloomily, "Not a bit of it. They will try to sweep it all under the carpet and as quickly as they damned well can."[31] And he was quite right. Fifteen years later we can simply glance at news-stands to know that the craze toward violence and sexual cruelty has not been checked. The relationship between pornography and vio-lence has not been established to everyone's satisfaction, but even if it is merely suspected, Johnson has reasonably asked, "What price would we pay to prevent the torturing of one helpless child?"[32]

Anti-obscenity and anti-pornography laws do exist and one might ask why they are not enforced. But these rulings, which originated in England during the eighteenth century, were rarely taken seriously. John Cleland, author of *Fanny Hill*, wrote the story of a fifteen-year-old prostitute and was arraigned on an obscenity charge. When he explained that poverty had driven him to write the novel, the Privy Council granted him a pension of 100 pounds a year on condition that he would not repeat the offense. He took the pension and wrote another pornographic work, but was never troubled by the law again.[33] Trials which took place on charges of blasphemy or obscenity were almost always motivated by political rather than moral reasons. John Wilkes was fined 500 pounds ostensibly for his "obscene" *Essay on Women*, but in reality he was penalized because his political agitations disturbed King George III.[34] In fact it was not until the nineteenth century, when women agitated for female emancipation and disseminated literature demanding sexual equality, the right of women to control their own bodies and their reproductive functions, that obscenity rulings were sincerely enforced. Margaret Sanger in America, Annie Besant in England and Marie Stopes in Scotland were all arrested for writing and distributing "obscene" literature on birth control.[35] But while many women and some men were persecuted for advocating sexual equality, no one prevented the American and European markets from being flooded with hard-core pornography.

During the few short decades that literary censorship flourished in America, writers such as D. H. Lawrence and Frank Harris were condemned for their sexually explicit writings. When it became clear, however, that in their work and the work of others, the portrayal of "sexy women" was not aimed to promote sexual equality, censorship relaxed. By the mid-1950s a series of Supreme Court decisions resulted in progressively more lenient attitudes toward sexually explicit material,[36] and by 1970 the National Commission on Obscenity and Pornography published a report which concluded that pornography is not harmful; instead, it is seen as educational, encouraging frank discussions between parents and children, releasing "inhibitions"; it is "not a factor in the causation of crime," and therefore "is not a matter of public concern."[37]

Nothing could better illustrate the Commission's lack of moral interest than its refusal to deal with the exploitation and victimization of children. By denying the use of children in pornography, the Commission risked gross inaccuracies and its credibility. It is claimed that pedophilia is outside the interests of pornography in stag films; "the taboo against pedophilia however has almost remained inviolate, the use of prepubescent children is almost nonexistent."[38] It really takes very little to know that as soon as the camera was invented, dirty postcards of breastless, hairless children and of pregnant, naked child prostitutes appeared. And from the liberated 1960s until today publications are displayed on newsstands which advertise films entitled *Infant Love, Children and Sex, Little Girls*, and so on, where one can see shots of children from six to thirteen performing oral sex. I have never even found it necessary to browse in Forty-second Street sex shops for my research. From San Francisco to New York, in every airport, train and bus station, the most respectable bookstores and newsstands carry paperbacks entitled *Uncle Jake and Paula, The Child Psychiatrist, Lust for Young Girls,*

*Adults Balling Children*, ad nauseum. One can easily obtain *Lollitots*, in which you can get introduced to Patti, who we are told is the most exotic ten-year-old you'll ever meet, or *Little Girls*, which offers pictures of ten- and twelve-year-olds in intercourse with adult males; for forty-five dollars one can purchase a film in living color and see a nine-year-old being used by two Arab boys, then by an adult.

The Commission's ability to ignore child pornography could only stem from a conscious or unconscious determination to tolerate male sexual interest in children and to refrain from interfering in a lucrative industry. The Commission managed to rationalize this determination by assuming that legal restraints on pornography could be justified only by proving bad effects upon the consumer. Admittedly, pornography does not harm its all-male consumer population. It harms the items consumed. Unlike hair dyes and cigarettes, the items consumed in pornography are not inanimate objects but live women and children who are degraded and abused in the process. By adopting a "consumer beware" attitude, however, the Commission was satisfied with the fact that juveniles rarely purchase explicit materials. Therefore, once such materials were labelled "for adults only," or "parental guidance recommended," the Commission felt its obligation to the young was over.

Some members of the Commission produced studies, testimony and authoritative evidence establishing that pornography was physically dangerous to the young, encouraged child molestation and rape, destroyed the public image and the private self-image of children and could hardly be concealed from children when it appears everywhere.[39] The Commission paid little heed to the minority of its members and recommended the repeal of laws restricting the sale of pornography.[40]

By 1973 the Supreme Court abandoned a national standard definition of obscenity and allowed individual states to establish their own guidelines.[41] In face of mounting legal and academic criticism the United States cancelled funding for the Anti-Pornographic Center in California in 1975. Protests against the Center were made by the American Civil Liberties Union, the American Library Association and the American Association of University Professors for what they called infringement of academic freedom, fostering the threat of government-sponsored censorship and flouting the new Freedom of Information Act.[42]

Many jumped on this strange bandwagon in the name of

freedom, and currently our most progressive and radical elements prefer to defend pornographers rather than organize against them. Others have argued that if "forbidden fruit" is available, prurient material will soon become boring and interest will wane. Nothing could disprove this more than our current avalanche of child pornography. In 1977 Judianne Densen-Gerber unleashed a crusade against this overwhelming onslaught and produced 250 publications dedicated to sex with children aged three, four and five.*[43] She discovered, however, that putting this industry out of business was not easy. The Supreme Court ruling which permits communities to determine what is obscene allows individual judges to translate the sexual use of children as liberating and educational. The child pornography industry is today in excellent health.

It is estimated that 1.2 million children under sixteen are yearly involved in commercial sex, either prostitution, pornography or both.[44] Those who have been in the struggle for a woman's right to a legal abortion have said that if men could become pregnant abortion would be a sacrament. And if women and children were the prime consumers of pornography and men the objects to be degraded and endangered, would the Commission on Obscenity and Pornography not then have declared pornography to be a crime? I think it would.

---

*As a result, the New York State legislature enacted a law designed to protect children. To effect this law they omitted the word "obscene" and declared a person guilty of promoting any sexual performance by a child under age 16. In 1978, under this law, in the case of Ferber vs. New York, the defendant who was selling two kiddie films was convicted. Kiddie porn disappeared from the streets and was, at least, no longer available for popular consumption. The defendant appealed and in May, 1981, the New York Court of Appeals struck the law down. The Court argued that the section which omitted the word "obscene" "would prohibit the promotion of materials that are traditionally entitled to constitutional protection from government interference under the 1st amendment." Children will now again be sacrificed to legal technicalities. As of this printing, the New York State legislature plans to bring the child protective law to the U.S. Supreme Court for a more considered decision.

# 14. THE SEXUAL ABUSE OF BOYS

Sexuality is not the most intractible element in power relations, but rather one of those endowed with greater instrumentality; useful for the greatest number of maneuvers and capable of serving as a point of support, as a linchpin for the most varied strategies.

Michel Foucault, *The History of Sexuality*[1]

Traditionally women and children (male and female) have been cast together. They have shared the same minority status, have been exploited as domestic and wage slaves and for the greater part of history even wore the same clothing to distinguish them from adult males. Together they have been idealized, romanticized, infanticized, trivialized, sexualized and desexualized. Since both women and children have been lumped together as helpless, dependent and powerless, they even share the same "feminine" gender and consequently both have been sexually used and abused by men.

Gender is a flexible term. Masculine or feminine does not necessarily correspond to those who are male and female. Women and male and female children are often patiently, indulgently, condescendingly or angrily seen as weak, dependent and helpless. Gender difference, unlike sexual difference, implies masculine superiority and feminine inferiority, and since the prototype of romantic or sexual love contains the formula of one dominant and one subordinate partner, men sometimes select a person of the same sex but opposite gender as a sex partner. A man in prison will, without injury to his masculinity, rape another inmate who is young, thin, fair and vulnerable enough to be taken for "feminine"; a soldier will sometimes rape not only women and children, but also conquered men to assert himself as conqueror, and since antiquity men have sexually used male and female children. Even Freud who insisted that "anatomy is destiny" was able to tolerate sex between those of the same sex but opposite gender. He understood, for example, ancient Greek boy-love because "it was not the masculine character of the boys which kindled the love of man; it was the physical resemblance to women as well as his psychic shyness, demureness and need for instruction and help."[2] Love between equals, however, has either been despised, ridiculed or not regarded seriously.

During the 1940s Katharine Hepburn and Spencer Tracy sailed through several films in which hilarity was based upon conflicts believed to inevitably arise from a relationship between an equally mature man and woman; and when Walt Whitman envisioned a brotherhood of lovers who remained devoted through middle age, John Addington Symonds could not help but suppress a smile when he pictured "clashing beards and tinkling watch-chains" as adult men embraced.[3] "Vive la différence" does not necessarily applaud genital distinction; a couple of the same or opposite sex but unequal in status and age may be regarded more seriously than a matched pair of the same or opposite sex who share equivalent status and age. Thomas Mann's classic novella *Death in Venice*, the story of a middle-aged man who died of unrequited love for a sixteen-year-old to whom he had never spoken a word, has stood up as an enduring tragedy. Love poems to boys, just as those to women, are as passionate as they are condescending. Both admire lips, hair, skin, waist and other passive anatomical parts while they ignore the variable, complex unique aspects of the human personality such as talent, ambition, intellect, humor, in those they claim to adore. Edward Westermark, the Finnish philosopher and anthropologist who wrote the monumental *History of Marriage*, said:

*It should be noticed that the most common form of inversion, at least in Mohammedan countries, is love of boys and youths not yet the age of puberty, that is of male individuals who are physically like girls.*[4]

*Greek Love* by J. Z. Eglinton is an entire book devoted to sex between men and boys. Eglinton argued that asymmetry, which is implicit in marriage, where the groom is older, richer, stronger and better educated than his bride, is also featured in boy-love. And what is more, this temporary experience will prepare a boy for later normal heterosexuality; "where a man has fellated his boyfriend, often he has used this fact to further the boy's education in what to expect in heterosexual experience."[5]

Martin Hoffman in his study of *The Gay World* summed up the work of the Kinsey team as follows:

*Those individuals who were arrested for sexual offenses with boys under 12 are the least oriented towards their own sex of all males arrested for homosexual acts. They are generally bisexual; of those who had sexual relations with boys under 12 ultimately nearly 2/3 will marry. Of those who had sexual relations with boys between the ages of 12 and 15, slightly more than half will marry.* .... *In other words it is fair to say that the younger the male partner of the sex offender the more likely he is to be bisexual rather than* exclusively homosexual ... *Most adult males who have a sexual relationship with boys under 12 show a relative predisposition towards heterosexual offenses with girls under 16. In brief most of them are interested in young people.*[6]

The gay Canadian publication, *Body Politic*, issued an appeal for John Roestad, who, it said, was imprisoned because he "had sex" with hundreds of boys between the ages of eight and fourteen. In an editorial, *Body Politic* argued that if the heterosexual behavior is not considered dangerous then "you must consider that John Roestad's sexual preferences are as legitimate and as potentially fulfilling as your own."[7]

When we consider a substantive history, tradition and authoritative opinions which condone sex with boys because it is equivalent to heterosexual relationships, the plea on the part of the *Body Politic* is not so farfetched. Boy-lovers or pederasts today as in ancient Greece claim that they raise their young lovers to be courageous, upstanding citizens who will be released before maturity to marry. They point to a long list of esteemed emperors, kings, politicians, militarists, writers, artists, and such who enjoyed young boys, and to other cultures where, to this day, virile bold men make womanly use of a beardless boy.[8] Fortified by history, tradition and experts, pederasts have organized to find kindred spirits and, encouraged by our sexual revolution, have lobbied to rescind legislation which prohibits sex with minors, to lower or eliminate the legal age of consent and to halt apprehension and imprisonment of boy-lovers.

It is quite true that in this homophobic world, pederasts are incarcerated more than men who behave similarly with girls. But while I have sympathy for victims of prejudice, attempts to normalize objectionable behavior in one group because it mirrors objectionable behavior in a more privileged group puzzle me. If the gay male community could place a priority upon protecting children rather than defensively protecting their right to sexual preference, they might not go along with defending the "civil rights" of boy-lovers. When NAMBLA, or the North American Man/Boy Love Association, asked for support in 1979, many gay men objected, but no group that I know of came out with a strong public statement. The greatest split in the gay community over this issue came from organized lesbians, who publicly and unequivocably refused to support or be associated with the principles set forth by NAMBLA.* In March 1979, members of Lesbian Feminist Liberation of New York issued a press release which stated:

*The so called Man/Boy Lovers are attempting to legitimatize sex between children and adults by confusing the real needs of gay youth with a call to repeal all age of consent laws. Feminists easily recognize this as the latest attempt to make palatable the sexual exploitation of children.*

The group passed a resolution affirming:

*1. That the age of consent issue is a divisive to our coalition and our movement.*
*2. That it is diversion from the primary focus of the Lesbian and Gay movements.*
*3. That the Coalition opposes the sexual abuse of children by heterosexual or homosexual persons.*

This resolution was overwhelmingly approved.[9]

The ambivalence among gay men is unfortunate. As advocates of the sexual rights of equal adults they might offer a model for ethical human relationships, but as it is I find it difficult to support anyone's right to unequal sex, homosexual or heterosexual style. It would make far more sense for them to categorically condemn child molesting. I find the position taken by one social worker and therapist on the subject most reasonable. "A child molester is neither heterosexual nor homosexual," she said. "He is a *child* molester."[10]

It follows, however, that when a boy substitutes for a female he is as vulnerable to victimization as she is. Consequently, headlines screaming *Teacher Accused of Abusing Boys, Rapist Assaults Male Children, Boy of Five Slashed to Death by Sadist Sex Madman, Texas Toll of Boys in*

---

*This will be further discussed in the next chapter.*

*Nation's Biggest Sex Slaying* appear as frequently as those announcing atrocities committed against female children. Boys as well as girls are liberally traded in the white slave market. In Lebanon, Iraq and in Southeast Asia, Central Asia and Africa, there are as many boys in brothels from age eight to fourteen as there are girls. In Bombay one can find little boys in cages with darkened eyes and rouged lips, made up to look like girls. Once these children pass thirteen or fourteen they are cast out to survive as best they can, and they do so either by continued prostitution or by becoming pimps and procuring other little boys.[11] But let us not forget that Western civilization also functions according to the principles of supply and demand. Men in this country, as well as abroad, profit from the sale of boys. In 1972 in the "hinterlands" of Mineola, Long Island, a group of middle-class men who had for ten years been luring boys with expensive clothes and money into prostitution were exposed.[12] A year later a similar ring was uncovered in Suffolk County.[13] The curriculum vitae of men who conducted these operations is impressive. Among them one can find a psychiatrist associated with a reputable hospital, an athletic recruiter for a prominent university and a former organizer for the Big Brothers organization. In 1974 another ring was exposed in affluent Westchester County.[14] And from time to time the media informs us that a Chicago jury will probe pornography and prostitution involving boys; that three arrests were made in New York in a raid on an alleged prostitution ring and "call boy service"; that twelve men were arrested as child molesters in a Boston area ring.[15]

Men with a common interest in boys are so numerous that they are recognizable as a group called "chickenhawks." The boys, of course, are the "chickens." Chickenhawks can be found in every social and economic class; they are politicians, teachers, church officials, athletes, men in the working class and also derelicts and prowlers. The children, however, primarily from poor, ethnic, welfare families, may not be interested in sex but cannot resist the money. In every big city where there are poor children, young male hookers, from about eight to fourteen, patrol the streets in search of customers; and chickenhawks hang out where the kids are. Once past fourteen these boys, over the hill, also turn to pimping. With a constant demand for a fresh supply of young flesh, pimps cover deprived neighborhoods and bus and train stations on the lookout for runaways. These children, many of whom are rejected, abandoned or stranded without friends or money, may go along with procurers. If they resist they are often kidnapped, raped or otherwise coerced into prostitution.[16]

Some chickenhawks prefer not to scour the streets so they make contacts elsewhere. Newsletters or publications such as *Hermes* or *Straight to Hell*, which caters to pederasts, carry personal columns through which one can find others who can direct them to groups of boys, twelve to sixteen, preferably youngsters who enjoy "nudity and boyish freedom." For those who wish to conduct their transactions by phone, every major city which has a call-girl service provides call boys, ten to sixteen, who can be hired out by the hour, day, night, week or longer. For the more discriminating there are older, better educated, ambitious adolescent boys looking for men who can get them through school or procure them a decent job. This category of call boy, like the call girl, will try to make connections while he is still young and attractive. Where there is money, influence and power, boys as well as girls will sell themselves.

And of course the lucrative pornographic industry will eagerly pander to men with a taste for boys. *Boy Howdy*, "for those who think young," is plastered with photos of naked boys in every imaginable sexual position. For those who like their lads very young, *O Boy* provides pictures of seductively posed naked boys, six to twelve, looking pathetically awkward and vulnerable. Even the conservative publication, *The Gay Advocate*, has advertised films from the "lollypop" collection featuring Wayne and Carl, 2 thirteen-year-olds and Greg and Mickey, 2 fourteen-year-olds, in a large ad depicting two baby-faced boys sucking lollypops and nude from the waist down.[17] In their publications, organized pederasts advertise and recommend hard and soft pornographic slides, movies and books. *Boys Will Be Boys* is a photo essay of over 200 pages of pictures of boys in all stages of attire, semi-attire and nudity; *The Sex Book* is an encyclopedia with a relevant text and nude photos of children; *Legend of Paradise, The Boy, Chicken, The Asbestos Diary*, etc., all pander to men with a sexual attraction to children, particularly little boys.

Not all chickenhawks restrict themselves to commercial sex. Some get their pleasures closer to home and at no cost. As the 1970s began, it was estimated that of all reported cases, one boy was molested for every ten girls. This figure has now jumped to three boys for every ten girls. Some studies project that just as 25 percent of all females will be molested before age thirteen, 10 percent of all males will experience a sexual encounter with an adult in child-hood.[18] Currently there has also been a growing awareness of father-son incest. A study published in *The American Journal of Psychiatry* indicated that within a small sampling (six families), ten sons were involved in father-son incest and, the researchers stated, "We are aware of no cases of mother-daughter or mother-son incest in the same clinical population."[19] It has recently been estimated that approximately two thirds of all offenders against male children are family members or friends. Some authorities feel that male children may be even more reluctant to report than female children. One boy did not recount his experience because, he said, "I didn't want anyone to think I was queer"; and it has also been suggested that because boys have greater sexual freedom, greater sexual self-esteem, and are less inhibited they engage sexually with men more willingly. This may well be true. In the twenty-eight male testimonies I was able to obtain, there was a great variety of reactions even in this small sampling. Responses went from pleasure, pride, ambivalence, shame later mitigated by maturity to humiliation, frustration and anger. Of the 150 females interviewed all but one had strong negative reactions. This could be accounted for by the different social attitudes toward male and female children and therefore different subjective reactions. If a boy felt "feminized" by the experience, he was humiliated; if, by identifying with his male molester, he suffered no loss of masculine esteem through the encounter, the experience was either inconsequential or positive; and if humiliated as a child but able to compensate as a man for his childish helplessness, he could look back on the incident with amused indifference.

In a culture where male sexuality represents strength, super-iority, dominance and success, in a world where the desired image is a male image, it is not surprising that a male child will react differently to a sexual experience than a female child. The male knows that one day his sexuality will signify strength and superiority whereas to the female, sex with a male adult emphasizes her tradi-tional secondary status. In the Kinsey study of *Sexual Behavior in the Human Male* so few men reported childhood sexual abuse that the study concluded:

*The anatomy and functional capacities of male genitalia interests the younger boy to a degree that is not appreciated by older males who have become heterosexually conditioned and who are continuously on the defensive against reactions which may be interpreted as homosexual.* [20]

In contrast, however, consider the reactions of the 4,000 women interviewed in *Sexual Behavior of the Human Female*. One in four reported sexual encounters with men in preadolescence and all the reactions were negative. The investigators were puzzled:

*It is quite difficult to understand why a child except for its cultural conditioning should be disturbed by having its genitalia touched or seeing the genitalia of another person.* [21]

The researchers failed to account for the profound consequences arising from a deeply ingrained double standard. Males and females are defined not only as different, but as sexually unequal. Because she is regarded as castrated, organless, deficient and sexually inferior, the female child will react differently to what appears to be the same experience. The interpretations by men to their own molestation reflect this disparity.

Ray, a man in his early thirties, father of two children, came through his molestation with heightened self-esteem; he identified so positively with his molester that he, in turn, grew up to molest other children:

*My brother was ten years older than me and my hero. When I was nine, I was in the house of one of his friends who was about twenty. He asked me to come into his room. He had an erection. He said, "Why don't you put it in your mouth." I did and found it very interesting. I don't recall feeling anything sexual but I enjoyed it. Later he gave me presents and was really nice to me.*

*I never felt guilty about it. As a matter of fact, I forgot about it until I had some homosexual fantasies and suddenly flashed back. I could dig what it was like. I could feel the sense of it.*

*The only thing bad was that we never talked about it; it would have been healthier if we talked about it. But I understand it—I mean what he did to me. I understand it because I've molested little girls. I started when I was fifteen—there was this little girl who lived upstairs. She was about six and I would pretend I was playing rough housing but then I would rub up against her and get my rocks off that way. She didn't even know what I was doing. Why should I feel guilty? It can't hurt the kids and I enjoy it.*

**Sam, in his early** twenties, estimated that he contributed as much to the encounter as his molester. The experience validated his manhood and his attraction to men:

*When I was eight my parents sent me to boxing school. I was fascinated by my teacher's biceps. One day the kids asked him to flex his muscles and I think he noticed how I got into it.*

*I don't remember when it first happened but he would take me into the back room and pretty quickly we got to the genitals. I enjoyed it a great deal. I gave him all the encouragement I could. One of the things that was interesting was that he performed fellatio on me while I was lifting weights. It was like a new exercise. I liked it.*

*When I was fourteen I knew I was gay. I was always attracted to older men but recently I like younger ones too. I kept this experience a secret. I didn't tell my family because they would have taken me out of boxing school. After I had my first adult experience, I was about seventeen, I told my parents I was gay. I was really feeling good about it and very satisfied. My parents were pretty upset. I heard my mother sobbing in the next room; it sounded strange but it didn't bother me.*

If deviant behavior promotes self-worth and one's conscience does not object, deviance of itself does not necessarily create guilt. Therefore, Ray, a child molester, and Sam, a homosexual, were more satisfied than disturbed by their sexual encounters. Their deviance proved more rewarding than compliance with taboos or guilt from an uncomfortable identification with a child's fear and confusion or a mother "sobbing in the next room." What I find disturbing here, beyond deviance, taboos and social censure, is that in both instances the masculine image, presumed to be so vital, was attained without concern for the damage and suffering this attainment inflicted upon others.

Paul, a man in his later twenties, was molested at an early age. Unlike Ray and Sam, the incident frightened and shamed him:

*One day, at age nine, on my way to my music lesson, two teenaged boys declared me their prisoner and took me into a vacant shack. I was extremely frightened and began to cry. One of them shoved his penis in my face and ordered me to take it in my mouth. I was very frightened and did what I was told.*

*Then he told me to take off my pants, but this time I dashed for the door and ran to my lesson, crying all the way. My teacher asked me what was wrong. I told him some boys had hit me but did not tell him about the sexual part.*

In retrospect, however, after Paul had acquired the physical power, social strength and success that comes with maturity, the experience did not seem as damaging. As an adult he became a bachelor around town, obtained trophies for his skill in golf and tennis and achieved unusual financial success. At the time of the incident, Paul reacted with the same helplessness and shame as a female child, but unlike a little girl, it was not the sexual humiliation but his powerless immaturity that bothered him. "I was not ashamed because of the sex but because I was afraid and acted like a baby," he reported.

Once the temporary limitations of childhood passed, he looked back upon the incident without humiliation, anger or conflict.

*I would say that the experience taught me never to show fear and to attain physical, social and economic power and self-confidence; it reinforced my desire to be athletic and successful. And truth be told, I've gotten pretty much what I was after with women, in sports and in business. I guess I'm pretty lucky.*

Ralph, age thirty-nine, could not attain the success which might compensate for his humiliation. Unlike Paul, he never recovered from the indignity; the damage to his self-image never healed and the experience, symbolic of childhood helplessness, followed him into maturity.

*When I was about seven or eight a man in the candy store used to put his hand on my penis. Later when I was thirteen living in a small suburban community, I was part of a boys' softball, basketball and football club. The coach would sexually molest us. Nobody ever said anything about it till one day it all came out.*

*He was married with children and a sports writer for a big newspaper. He asked me to go to the movies with him and that was a big deal for me. During the movie he put his hand on me and kissed me. It was freaky, very embarrassing.*

*I was so embarrassed that I would not cooperate. Consequently I wasn't assigned to games and couldn't play ball but a lot of kids, not as good as*

*I, did play. One day when one of the boys and the coach didn't show up for practice, somebody said, "I wonder if he's doing to him what he did to me." Then it all came out. Every kid had a story to tell but the kids who did not cooperate did not get to play ball.*

*I'm not a homosexual. I'm married and have two kids of my own. Now I work in a theater and know that unless you "play ball" with certain people, you never can get ahead.*

Men are usually terrified at being taken for a woman. When addressing a group of high school students, I pointed to the similarities in treatment and discrimination of women and minors. I was surprised when the male students objected vehemently, almost violently, at being identified, no matter how sympathetically, with women. In the same vein, when Jackie, my eleven-year-old neighbor, was accosted by an exposed man, his immediate reaction was "Why me? I'm not a girl." A group worker reported that many sexually molested boys were concerned that something in their demeanor and carriage betrayed feminine traits and invited the incident. To Tom, age sixteen, being mistaken for a woman was the core of his humiliation:

*I know women get raped, but I'm not a woman. I'm a boy. I'm sixteen and still have had more than my share of being molested. When I was nine and coming home from school, this boy, a teen-ager, asked me to come to his apartment. When we got there no one was home. He sat me on the bed, took my pants down and did it. It hurt bad and I was scared but while he did it he was talking; talking all the time about his hobbies and other things.*

*A few years ago at camp some of the boys were talking about experiences like that and when I told them my story they said I was raped. I was shocked. I never told my parents. God forbid you should mention the word sex in front of them.*

*Now I'm sixteen and I'm not a virgin or homosexual. I'm an usher at a movie theater and like a day won't go by when I don't feel someone's hand on me. I'll be sitting in the theater and the next thing I know a man has his hand in my crotch. It's upsetting; I don't know what to do; make a scene and interrupt everything? It makes me feel ashamed. Why do men fool around with me? I know I'm young but I don't look like a woman.*

Both Ralph and Tom were reduced to infantile effeminate impotence. Perhaps with added height, weight and a beard, Tom will eventually be protected from further insult. Though no longer sexually molested or harassed, just as females who were molested in childhood, Ralph's maturity did not erase the damage to his ego.

While collecting my research, I was unable to obtain testimony from men who were sexually used by women, but in *The First Time*, a collection of initial sexual experiences, I found some examples of men who had early sexual encounters with women. These men, however, were so titillated by the experience that even if they had been coerced, they did not feel victimized. Joseph Cotten, the actor, was taught the "facts of life" at age eight by a nineteen-year-old woman and boasted, "If it was a shock then it was a delightful shock." And he was pleased to think that "I was her star pupil."[22] Liberace, TV and nightclub entertainer, lost his virginity at thirteen to "this big chesty broad . . . I didn't know what was happening but I liked it."[23] Whether or not these men truly reacted to their experience as claimed, in retrospect they felt the incident warranted bragging. Lou Rawls, the singer, was embarrassed when at age thirteen he lost his virginity to an older woman. He consoled himself, however, with the thought that "losing your cherry wasn't a big thing with us except the thing was not to lose your cherry to a faggot."[24] No matter how uncomfortable, he was still a superior male; the real danger lay in being used as a woman—and only another man could reduce him to that level.

Even the female molester of a female child does not have the status of the male molester. In the one testimony of a girl molested by a woman, the child did not find her abuser as menacing as a man. Carol, now age twenty-six, named four childhood incidents and one was with a woman:

*She was a teacher. What she made me do struck me as bizarre, but not terribly frightening. Sometimes I think I imagined it but I know I didn't because she did it to my sister too. It really wasn't pleasant and I hated it but it was only one time. Being molested by men is scary because a man can kill you and besides it's something that goes on all your life.*

When a male child does feel sexually exploited by a woman, he later manages to exorcise the insult and validate his manhood by taking sexual revenge upon all women. Iceberg Slim, modernday pimp, and Lord Byron, late-eighteenth-century English poet, both suffered sexual abuse by women. Slim was forced to perform cunnilingus at age three, and in his autobiography he attested to his subsequent cruelty toward women generally and prostitutes in particular.[25] Byron, said by his biographers to have been used by his nursemaid for over a year at about age eight,[26] was notorious for his misogyny and torment of the opposite sex. Virginia Woolf, however, after prolonged molestation by George Duckworth, raged not against men, but against herself and died by her own hand. Depressed women who were raped in childhood are said to have turned their anger resulting from violation against themselves.[27]

I make no claim that women cannot commit sexual offenses against children. The few examples presented here illustrate that it is possible; but women who are socialized to surrender seldom demand or impose their sexual desires or compulsions upon others. The female sex offender is rare.* I would agree with David Finkelhor, who in his study of *Sexually Victimized Children* said, "The most obvious characteristic of sexual abusers has been one of the least analyzed; they are almost always men. It is older males who initiate sexual contact with younger children. . . . This finding is just as true for boys as girls. . . . Women do not make sexual advances towards children."[28]

For all practical purposes pedophilia does not affect either lesbians or heterosexual women. As we look back through history it is men, not women, who sexually pursue children. It is men who create the demand that produces the supply and in that peculiar bit of farmland known as Times Square, there would be no chickens if there were no hawks.

---

*I deal here only with overt sex acts between adults and children. To get into the fantasies or seductive behavior on the part of either men or women, would be quite debatable and unmanageable.*

# 15. FROM THE SENSUOUS WOMAN TO THE SENSUOUS CHILD: LIBERATION OR BACKLASH?

People whose spirit may resist an erroneous conviction
that they are doing something new and revolutionary
may be unhappy to learn when told that they are the
most recent expression of what is by now an old tradition.
Bennett Berger, "Hippie Morality—More Old Than New"[1]

Diana Russell, author of *The Politics of Rape*, warns that "sexual liberation without sex-role liberation can actually result in the greater oppression of women."[2] Given certain attitudes in vogue today, I should like to add that the sexual liberation of children without regard for sex or age inequities can be dangerous to our young. Nonetheless, the alleged "right" of children to have sex with adults (and vice versa) is currently touted as harmless or a civil-rights and revolutionary issue.

In the 1930s, Drs. Lauretta Bender and Abram Blau, after studying sexually assaulted children, concluded that since the myth of childhood innocence seems in the main to have been rejected, the suggestion is made that sexually assaulted children by adults does not have a particularly detrimental effect on a child's subsequent behavior. And because the children studied were unusually attractive, Bender and Blau considered the possibility that the child might have been the "seducer rather than the seduced."[3] Dr. Karl Menninger,

drawing upon this study, suggested that in light of scientific investigation, children exposed to premature sexual experiences frequently
turn out to be unusually charming, attractive and emotionally healthy.⁴
René Guyon, who wrote *Ethics of Sexual Acts* in the 1930s, is regarded as having made an important contribution to the "new
morality." Guyon went back in history to the time when girls were
married at twelve, and the age of consent was between six and ten; to
Bombay, where 74,000 children married before age five and 350,000
between six and ten, and to China, where it was customary for
children of both sexes to discreetly masturbate dinner guests under
the table. Guyon saw these practices as examples of sexual freedom.⁵

When advocates of the new morality employ the past, they
seem to yearn for the good old days when children could be legally
exploited and raped.

The *Satyricon* by Petronius, written in Nero's time, details a
night of debauchery enjoyed by Trimalcho and his young friend
Giton. When Giton was presented with the prospect of deflowering
the seven-year-old Pannychis, he questioned the propriety of taking
one so young. His doubts were soon allayed by an experienced
prostitute, who said, "Is she any younger than I when I submitted to
my first man? Juno, my patroness, curse me if I can remember the
time I was ever a virgin for I diberted [sic] myself with others of my
own age when I was a child." Convinced, Giton achieved his "bloody
victory" and the child's screams so aroused a passing soldier that he
joined the revelers and demanded his turn. Pannychis pleaded with
the soldier to consider her extreme youth but "her entreaties inflamed
him all the more," so she covered her head and "endured what the
fates had in store for her."⁶

Those struggling against sexual prudery and hypocrisy today are basically demanding that we permit sexual exploitation to
operate above rather than underground as in Petronius' time. But
whether sexual liberationists turn to the alleged freedom of the
past or protest the alleged repression of the past 150 years, in
common they support sex between the generations. By the mid-
1960s the Kinsey team was equating animal and human behavior
and looking to the lower species to rationalize child-adult sex. "The
horror with which society views the adult who has sexual relations
with young children is lessened when one examines the behavior of
other mammals," we were told. "Sexual activity between adult and
immature animals is common and appears to be biologically nor-

mal."[7] And what is more, "Disregard for age, sex, and species need not be regarded as biologically pathological; it is precisely what we see in various animals, particularly monkeys."[8] Along the same line, Dr. Robert S. de Ropp in 1969 suggested that animal and human behavior were not far removed. "The craving of the elderly male for the young female is not necessarily confined to the human species," he said. "Old stags are always after little ones and the young does are always willing."[9] De Ropp matched this with Frank Harris' avowed desire for half-fledged girls in his later years. And in 1978, Dr. Alayne Yates in her book *Sex Without Shame* saw "an enormous erotic potential in infants," warned against exploiting this potential, but found that "non-coercive father-daughter incest can in fact produce competent and notably erotic young women. Childhood is the best time to learn."[10] Dr. H. Wells, author of *The Sensuous Child*, feels that "children have the right to sexual pleasure" but that "most of this sexual trauma stuff is nonsense." Wells had a patient who was gang-raped at fourteen, then later abused by an older brother but she grew up, had children and presented "no observable problems."[11] Warren Farrell, who is completing a book on incest, found that experiences reported by females were predominantly negative. However, he states that in his four years of examining hundreds of incest participants:

*I found a daughter often cooperated with her father's sexual caresses when she was younger, but as she got older and learned that "incest is wrong," she translated that into her father's violating her. As society treated her as a sex object, she wondered if she was only worthwhile as a sex object. "After all, that was when Daddy paid most attention to me."*[12]

Farrell notes that "Unfortunately, Daddy often did pay most attention to her when he was being sexual," followed by the questionable rationale, "But for him, being sexual was often the only way he knew how to express his affection."[13]

To me the most puzzling approach to adult-child sex comes from Richard Farson, author of *Birthrights*. Farson is dedicated to the emancipation of children. "What children need," he writes, "is the option to refuse. The freedom not to engage in sexual activity is as important as any other aspect of freedom." But, he continues, "children are raised in such a way that they cannot refuse adults." Farson therefore unconditionally objects to adults who insensitively pick up, fondle, hug and kiss powerless children. He explains that children have little experience in saying no. They also have little experience in trusting their own reactions to people and in resisting the promise of rewards. They are not informed about sexual matters, do not understand their own sexuality or that of others and cope ineffectively in this area.

I totally agree. However, when genital contact occurs between an adult and child, Farson inconsistently allows that the child may often be a "willing participant."[14] And although he finds the nuclear family detrimental and oppressive to offspring, incest, he claims, is less traumatic than we have been led to believe. In a situation where the mother is an invalid, for example, father-daughter incest may keep the father from straying and function to keep the family together; or, in his own words, "Sometimes incest occurs because it becomes functional to the preservation of the family."*[15]

Except for mother-son incest, which is always regarded as pathological, I have never found a work on children's liberation, children's rights or children's sexual freedom which unconditionally opposes sex between children and adults.

I believe the term *liberation* as it is carelessly applied to children is both dangerous and absurd. Born helpless and vulnerable, the young have always relied upon the greater capacity of adults for survival. One way or another, every society must deal with growth from infancy to maturity, and every culture establishes a period during which infants are nurtured and protected until they can be left to their own devices. To equate the oppression of children with oppressed blacks and women is to confuse the nature of childhood. Even if given every opportunity, the very young cannot fend for themselves, whereas given an even chance most adults will survive and function. I grant that adults most frequently do not understand the special needs of children; however, damage cannot be prevented by equalizing what is perhaps the only true biological asymmetrical human condition. Children have the right, not to equality with adults, but to considerate adult understanding, custody and protection. They have the right to alternatives to punitive parents or guardians; to legislation which will prevent and prohibit

---

*The concept of "functional incest" originated with Dr. Christopher Bagley, sociologist at the Institute of Psychiatry in London. His work on the subject has led many "progressive" thinkers to believe that the dangers of father-daughter incest have been highly overstated.

the abuse of power which the mature implicitly hold over the immature; and to be guided as soon as possible toward early independence. Unless we recognize that the fully grown hold all the power and therefore all the responsibility (which includes the responsibility to say "no," no matter how persuasive a child may be) children's liberation is meaningless. Unless we understand that children, though not easily duped, lack the capacity to resist adult pressure, granting a child the so-called "right" to freely choose an adult sex partner is much like liberating the chicken from its coop only to be devoured by the fox.

The call for the sexual freedom of children, in the name of child welfare, is transparently focused upon adult gratification. Lars Ullerstam, a Scandinavian physician and philosopher, has found it "regrettable that there is no way to supply the pedophiliacs with the objects of their sexual desire but I don't know how this can be arranged in practice. I oppose," he said, "the view that it is an a priori fact that these individuals should not be allowed to gratify their sexual urge."[16] Choosing to ignore power and age disparities, pedophiles have confused the justified right of sex between consenting adults with the unjustified right of sex between men and children, and are organizing to gratify their urges in the name of civil rights. PIE, or Pedophile Information Exchange, and PAL, or Pedophile Action for Liberation, operate out of England. Other groups are based in Switzerland and Germany, while in the United States we have CSC, or Childhood Sensuality Circle, which promotes child-child and child-adult sex, and BL, which stands for both Better Life and Boy Love.

The René Guyon Society promotes heterosexual child-child and child-adult sex and promises that sex at an early age will prevent divorce and delinquency. The group's motto is, "sex by age eight or else it's too late." Members have lobbied in Sacramento, California, and claim to have found support among some legislators in their attempt to alter laws prohibiting sex with minors.[17] And in September 1977, at an international conference on "Love and Attraction" sponsored by the University of Swansea in Wales and the British Psychological Society, a disturbance was created when organized pedophiles came forth as an oppressed minority.

When pedophiles at the Swansea conference advocated the legalization of sex between children and adults and reduction of the age of consent to four, the cooks, porters and caretakers of the

University of Swansea threatened to strike. "Either Tom O'Carroll, Chairman of Pedophile Information Exchange leaves," said the spokesman of the National Union of Public Employees, or "we stop work on the entire campus."[*18] Community disapproval was so strong that when O'Carroll entered the Crockett Arms Bar, a woman poured a pint of beer over him,"thumped him three times" and made his nose bleed.[19] O'Carroll was forced to leave the conference and the time allotted to pedophiles was drastically cut. Two officers of PIE were "aggrieved and shocked" at their reception. In an interview with Polly Toynbee of the *Guardian Women,* a Welsh newspaper, they protested that "children are highly sexual creatures whose natural sexuality is repressed by the society we live in"; that "loving kind relations with adults outside the family can be good for children"; and stressed that though "almost all children are far more capable of anal and vaginal intercourse than they are given credit for," most pedophile relationships don't involve penetration, only mutual masturbation. After the interview, Polly Toynbee "had that sinking feeling that in five years or so their aims might be acceptable." Ms. Toynbee had that "sinking feeling" for good reason. Child-adult sex is being considered with increasing openness.[†20]

In Philadelphia, shortly before this writing, a coalition for gay rights met to plan a march on Washington to protest discrimination against homosexuals. In addition to protesting job discrimination and laws against sex between consenting adults, a group of men proposed to demand the right of adults to have sex with children. David Thorstad, spokesman for the coalition, said:

*Our tactics and strategy must be based not only on protecting the rights of members of our community . . . but on fighting for the rights of all people regardless of sex, color or age.*

*We are engaged in a war between the forces of sexual liberation on the*

---

*[*]Tom O'Carroll has recently written a book,* Paedophilia: The Radical Case, *in which we are told he describes his own attraction to children, exposes the misconception that paedophiles are monsters, presents proposals for changes in the law, discusses children's rights, and the nature of consent and presents a detailed history of the "paedophile movement."*

*[†]I wish to thank Dorothy Tennov, author of* Psychotherapy: The Hazardous Cure *for bringing me all the newspaper reports and data from the Swansea conference.*

*one hand and the forces of sexual repression on the other. Man/Boy love and cross generational sex have become the cutting edge of that war.*

> *Repeal all age of consent laws!!!*
> *Freedom of sexual expression for all!!![21]*

In December 1978 several Boston men were charged with illegal sexual acts with boys. A defense committee and conference, attended by about 150 persons, evolved. The turnout included a priest, a labor organizer, an artist, a social worker and other representatives of middle-class intellectual America. Dr. Richard Pillard of the Department of Psychiatry at Boston University reminded the conferencees that "Freud pointed out 70 years ago that sexuality begins in childhood, even infancy."[22] Another speaker defended teen-age hustling because for him it was the only way to get sex with men. It was "very fulfilling," he said.[23]

Though most who attended were supportive, the conference did not go smoothly. An uproar erupted when radical feminist Jon Schaller objected. She said:

*At this point we still live in a society which is dominated by adults, where adults make the laws and regulations and where young people have no practice making decisions about their lives. Any relationship between an adult and young person where the adult is not consciously trying to overcome the power difference is going to be oppressive. And that's the important issue for anybody in that kind of situation.[24]*

At the close of the conference, thirty-two men and two teen-agers caucused and organized the Man/Boy lovers of America, a newsletter and a New York conference for March 1979. I went to the New York conference. About one hundred men and five women attended. Of the five women, four, like myself, were researching. As in Boston, the group appeared to be a cross section of respectable, academic Bohemia. One participant gave a scholarly discourse on the glories of Greek love. Another bemoaned the fact that his advanced age reduced his capacity for sexual pleasure with boys; he was saddened by the opposition from certain gay brothers, almost all Lesbians and radical feminists. Two teen-agers, one about eighteen, the other fourteen, testified that it was they who seduced older men. The fourteen-year-old had always been attracted to mature males. After his parents divorced, he chose to stay with his father. His father, more permissive than his mother, liked girls about seventeen years younger than himself. Father and son recognized that while Dad liked them young, junior preferred them old. Another man objected to the use of the word *love* in a relationship between man and boy. Love, he said, is a euphemism for sex. Sex is the center of where we are at, he continued, because sex with boys is beautiful, healthy, good and fun. We want no restrictions on age. Children at any age, five, six, seven or eight, are entitled to sexual freedom. Sex between men and boys eliminates ageism, closes the generation gap, and challenges authority and patriarchy because it is the "fullest expression of humanity" and the "truest revolution."

Since groups favoring Man/Boy love represent a small number I hesitate to emphasize their importance. Nor do I wish to join those who plague gay men as child molesters; they are no greater child molesters than straight men. Nonetheless, the combination of organizations, conferences, books, articles, and professional opinions cited above indicate to me a dangerous and growing trend.

Freud's theories on infant sexuality, as we have seen, did indeed influence our estimation of childhood sexuality. Freud, however, never meant for the sexual impulses of children to be directly gratified by adults. Sex energy of children was to be channelized so that adult males would contribute to the economy and politics of society and females would become proper wives and mothers. It was Wilhelm Reich who, in the 1930s, advocated that children be permitted to sexually explore and gratify themselves. According to Reich, the repression and redirection of sexual energy created neurotic, serflike adults who fed totalitarianism and fascism. "One has to liberate the instincts. This is a prerequisite to cure,"[25] he said. In his decline, the obsessed Reich insisted that free sexual expression was a panacea for all individual and social ills.

But no matter how much Reich encouraged orgiastic freedom, in terms of the young he proposed no more than nonintervention in childhood masturbation or peer sex play. He vehemently opposed sexual seduction, coercion, pornography, exhibitionism, sexual inequality and sex between children and adults. He was always fearful that his theories might be misconstrued and result in sexual anarchy or what he called "the fucker chaos."[26] Eventually, after being cruelly persecuted, he died, quite mad, in prison.

When the New Left suggested that it is better to "make love, not war," they failed to demand that sexism be smashed along with imperialism. Free sex, just as free food and free dope, was to be distributed in a fantasized, emancipated but macho utopia. The movement advised its followers "never to trust anyone over thirty" and addressed itself not only to flower children and college students, but to high school, junior high and grade-school students. Their sexual doctrine was succinctly articulated by a spokesman of the White Panthers:

*Fuck God in the ass, fuck your woman until she can't stand. Fuck everybody you can get your hands on. Our program of rock and roll, dope and fucking in the streets is a program of total freedom for everyone.* [27]

But when these young radicals approached thirty, they discovered that their love-ins and fuck-ins neither freed the poor, the parks nor liberated Washington, D.C.; they cut their hair, put on business suits, joined established politics, religious groups, EST, and allied themselves with bourgeois civil libertarians and pornographers in the cause of sexual liberation. However, those who are convinced that sexual liberation is a radical outlook fail to notice that it is an ancient, reactionary, exploitative custom.

The current concept of sexual liberation has no relationship whatsoever to political freedom. To the contrary, since sex is an inexpensive diversion, tyrants and rulers have always encouraged men to sexually use women and children in order to divert them from their poverty and subjugation, so as to prevent possible rebellion. The poor and enslaved were never prevented from violating their own women and children.

There is an old saying that "bed is the poor man's opera," and in our increasing hostile, loveless day-to-day life, sex, as a substitute for love, is mistaken for intimacy and offered as a cure for loneliness. The myth that freedom begins in bed belies the fact that most of our valid frustrations stem from complicated social problems. However, in this world where so many are powerless, "bed" may be the only arena where one can prop a faltering ego, heal damaged self-esteem or prove a cause. Unable to prevent the irresponsible use of nuclear power, to eliminate poverty and the agony of starving, abandoned, deprived and brutalized children, the most radical elements of our society have chosen to defend rapists, pornographers and child molesters.

The concept of sexual liberation as the last frontier in the struggle for freedom closed the 1960s with *The Sensuous Woman*. The concept of children's sexual liberation has closed the 1970s with *The Sensuous Child*. When sexual liberation becomes synonymous with political revolution a movie such as *Pretty Baby* can pass as a radical, intelligent work of art and the new avant-garde can advise that "Every child has the right to loving relationships including sexual, with a parent, sibling, other responsible adult or child."[28] Today's idea of sexual liberation and the sexual freedom of children is a euphemism for sexual exploitation, and at the rate we are going, today's sexual freedom may well become tomorrow's "opiate of the masses."

# 16. THE FIRST STEP

Unlike puppets, we have the possibility of stopping our movements, looking up and perceiving the machinery by which we have been moved. In this act lies the first step towards freedom.

Peter L. Berger, *Invitation to Sociology.*[1]

The purpose of a revolution is to unseat an entrenched political power. But no sooner do some of us, women and men, begin to expose and challenge the male abuse of sexual power than this effort is co-opted and dissipated as it is swept under the "sexual liberation" umbrella. From D. H. Lawrence to Hugh Hefner, it is Lady Chatterley, the superbunny or the bachelor girl who insists that the offer of her body plus a bottle of wine is "downright upright," who is projected as the model of the liberated woman. Similarly, the little girl who is said to be free of sexual hangups will giggle at the flasher because he's "just plain silly," understand that Uncle Teddy touched her all over because he is "friend sick"[*2] and will not be disturbed when Daddy crawls into her bed and fondles her. In this male ıtopia, men will never be burdened by emotional traumas, venereal disease, pregnancy, commitments, responsibilities, charges of rape, statutory rape or child molestation as the consequence of their sexual behavior.

Fortunately there are enough prudes, busybodies and concerned adults about to alarm the public with frequent accounts of child molestation or child prostitution and pornography. To counter an unsavory male image, however, films appear in which mothers turn on to their sons, such as *Luna* and *Flesh and Blood*. These maneuvers evolve not from a conscious conspiracy but from an ingrained attitude and time-proven successful strategy of blaming

---

*The term "friend sick" originated with Frederick Storaska, a self-appointed authority on the prevention and protection of women and children from sexual assault. He has adopted the stance of "savior" of women and children who he sees as inevitable victims.

females for what men do; they evolve from a long tradition of female archetypes such as Eve and Pandora who beset the world with evil. Some modern therapists, sexologists and criminologists who assert that "the roots of paedophiliac tendencies in the individual can be traced to an early situation between mother and child,"[3] that "victims of sex crimes have a hidden psychological need to be victimized,"[4] and that father-daughter incest is instigated by the mother who is unwilling to sexually gratify her husband, draw from this tradition. One researcher described her incestuous father subjects as having broken a radio over a mother's head, burned the children with hot irons, locked a mother in the closet while sexually abusing their child, yet, nevertheless, concluded that a father's incestuous behavior is the result of "the failure of the mother to protect her child."[5] This relentless tendency to blame women for male sexual transgression enabled Drs. Bell and Hall in their study *The Personality of a Child Molester* to attribute their subject's molesting behavior to his "fixation at an early age in psychosexual development due to his mother's intimacy."[6] The doctors arrived at this conclusion even though Norman claimed that he might have gone on to college, a career and marriage had not his father sexually assaulted him when he was four.[7]

Because mothers are seen as responsible for male violations, even child victims focus their rage against their mothers. As Adrienne Rich pointed out when quoting the observations of a psychologist in her book *Of Women Born*:

*When a female child is passed from lap to lap so that all the males in the room (father, brother, acquaintances) can get a hard-on, it is the helpless mother standing there and looking on that creates the sense of shame and guilt in the child. One woman at a rape conference in New York City testified that her father put a series of watermelon rinds in her vagina when she was a child to open it up to his liking and beat her if she tried to remove them. Yet what that woman focuses her rage on today is that her mother told her "never say a word about it to anyone."[8]*

As interest in child-adult sex increases, so do attempts to divert the responsibility from men onto the victim, her mother or the offender's wife and/or mother.

The time has come for us to refuse to enter this no-win contest. It is time for us to stop believing that, in a world which eroticizes children, which is bombarded with pornographic, artistic and commercial images of sadistic men and masochistic women, where little boys are expected to "despise" little girls and misogyny is accepted as a reflection of natural differences, mothers, who hold almost all the responsibility for children and almost no authority, have the power to create rapists, child molesters and even child victims. It is time we rejected reactionary programs which masquerade as progress and refuse to "liberate" our children from adult concern, care, discipline and protection. We must begin to understand that if women are to rear children and be responsible for their later adult behavior, mothers must at least be fortified with economic and social support necessary to protect them from an avalanche of detrimental outside influences and from direct sexual assault. And, of course, we must face and accept the fact that it is men, not women, who actually seduce, rape, castrate, feminize and infantilize our young, and it is time for them, rather than for women, to be held responsible for destructive, exploitative sexual behavior. Most of all, it is time for us to break the silence which protects molesters and endangers children; for us to disclose those secrets which have filled so many closets with skeletons and have transformed so many streets, towns and cities into Peyton Place.

I am aware that the identification of men as child molesters will provoke cries of protest. However, not all men are child molesters; many love children and have enriched their lives, and therefore many men of conscience can identify with and help prevent the pain and humiliation inherent in the violation of the human body. All of us, men, women and children alike, are guided by a mutable culture rather than immutable biology. Unlike the lower species, we have the ability to change, to look about, perceive what is going on and to question and challenge. Once we perceive, question and challenge the existence of the sexual abuse of children, we have taken the first crucial step toward the elimination of the degradation, humiliation and corrosion of our most valuable human resource—our young.

# Afterword

When viewed within the context of history, the scope of the sexual abuse of children is overwhelming. Had I not set out to present the subject in a comprehensive form, each chapter could have developed into a book and that book been expanded into volumes. There is still much work to be done regarding child-adult sex. Without an understanding of how we have moved from the past to the present, we tend to react to known incidents of this age-old practice as a series of odd, inexplicable, spontaneous eruptions. Consequently, agencies authorized to help those involved, see and treat adults who are sexually attracted to children as criminals, deviants, or persons suffering from particular hormonal imbalance and other individual aberrations. To my thinking, a program of total reeducation, a debriefing from centuries of programming total populations in the belief of a man's right to exercise sexual power and privilege, would be more to the point.

But even if such a program became miraculously operative, it would take several generations to exorcise past indoctrination. Meanwhile, for those "tip of the iceberg" individuals who do come forth, immediate help is needed. Where can they turn?

With the current recognition of the prevalence of sexual assault and family violence, attempts are being made to provide the necessary aid by many existing agencies offering family, child protective, criminal rehabilitation, and health services. The National Center for Child Abuse and Neglect, DHEW, Washington, D.C. 20013, and the Center for the Prevention and Control of Rape, DHEW, Washington, D.C. 20013, both affiliated with the National Department of Health, Education and Welfare, disperse information, literature and resources for concerned citizens and professionals. The National Law Enforcement Administration, a branch of the United States Department of Justice, Washington, D.C. 20051, funds and supports prevention and assistance programs. Each state has at least one state-wide agency authorized to investigate suspected cases, and every city and most smaller localities provide some sort of child protective service; such services are either incorporated in the local Department of Welfare or in private and public family or child protective agencies. Currently, public and privately funded rape crisis centers and sexual assault centers have emerged independently or within women's centers or as adjuncts to city or state sex crime units and hospitals. (Consult your telephone directory for appropriate listings.) Susan Griffin in her book *Rape: The Power of Consciousness*[1] lists approximately 1,000 such agencies. This number indicates an eagerness to deal with the problem but unfortunately, those unaffiliated with established organizations, despite their excellent work, usually cannot manage on their limited grants and meager fund raising. They are often compelled to discontinue their services or operate sporadically.

The National Center on Child Abuse and Neglect, in its pamphlet "Child Sexual Abuse, Incest, Assault and Sexual Exploitation," published by the Department of Health, Education and Welfare, warns that trauma to the victim and family can sometimes be increased by well-established professional intervention. It points out that medical examinations often routinely and insensitively performed by some hospitals can be perceived by the child as yet another brutal bodily intrusion, and that in the legal process, accusations made by children are often viewed with suspicion. Furthermore, in some communities, for reasons of protection an assaulted child may be removed from a family, leading young victims to conclude that they are being punished for the crimes committed against them. And in cases where the father, the prime breadwinner, is the offender and he is incarcerated without financial provisions being made for the family, crippling poverty can result.

In her book *Kiss Daddy Goodnight*,[2] Louise Armstrong selectively lists resources for those needing counseling, but cautions those who wish to report an incident first to make an anonymous contact with a related community service (rape crisis service, child protective service, hospital, etc.) for preliminary information. Most agencies will offer a rundown of available services and resources to the anonymous inquirer, but it may take perseverance to find the appropriate help.

For the patient researcher, past and present information regarding the sexual abuse of children, however maddeningly and distressingly scattered, is there. Hopefully, this work will help inspire others to investigate and expand upon the problem and create a workable structure with which to implement its elimination.

# Chapter Notes

## 1. A LOOK AT THE PROBLEM

1. Carolyn Swift, "Sexual Assault of Children and Adolescents." From testimony prepared for the Subcommittee on Science and Technology of the United States House of Representatives on January 11, 1978, in New York City.

2. Philip Nobile, Introduction to William Kraemer and others, *The Normal and Abnormal Love of Children* (Kansas City: Sheed Andrews and McMeel, Inc., 1976), p. x.

3. Ibid., p. xi.

4. Ibid., p. ix.

5. Ibid.

6. *The Report of the Commission on Obscenity and Pornography,* A New York Times Book (New York: Bantam, 1970), p. 611.

7. Lois Mark Stalvey, "The Child Molester," *Woman's Day*, November 1973.

8. Tony Parker, *The Hidden World of Sex Offenders* (New York: Bobbs-Merrill, 1969), p. 23.

9. Vincent De Francis, *Protecting the Child Victim of Sex Crimes Committed by Adults* (Denver: The American Humane Society, 1969), p. vii.

10. Carolyn Swift, "Sexual Assault of Children and Adolescents."

11. Alfred Kinsey and others, *Sexual Behavior of the Human Female* (New York: Pocket Books, 1953), p. 121.

12. David Finkelhor, *Sexually Victimized Children* (New York: Free Press, 1979), p. 53.

13. Mary L. Keefe, "Police Investigation in Child Sexual Assault," in Ann Wolbert Burgess and others, *Sexual Assault of Children and Adolescents* (Lexington, Mass.: Lexington Books, 1978), p. 159.

14. Paul Gebhart and others, *Sex Offenders* (New York: Harper and Row, 1965), p. 9.

15. National Abortion Rights Action League, "The Facts About Rape and Incest," Washington, D.C.

16. Queens Bench Foundation, *Sexual Abuse of Children* (San Francisco: 1976), p. 5.

17. "The Ultimate Violence," KPFA radio station folio, San Francisco.

18. Brooklyn Society for the Prevention of Cruelty to Children, Annual Report, 1977.

19. Lucy Berliner and Doris Stevens, "Advocating for Sexually Abused Children in the Criminal Justice System" (Seattle, Washington: Sexual Assault Center, Harborview Medical Center).

20. "Sexual Abuse of Children Common, Study Finds," *Bergen (N.J.) Record*, November 15, 1977.

21. Margaret C. McNeese, M.D. and Joan R. Hebeler, M.D., "The Abused Child" Clinical Symposia, CIBA, New Jersey, vol. 27, No. 5, 1977, pp. 14-15.

22. "Medical Symptoms of Sexual Abuse in Children," in *Medical Aspects of Human Sexuality*, p. 139.

23. Ann Wolbert Burgess and others, *Sexual Assault of Children and Adolescents*, pp. 146-47.

24. Alan Guttmacher Institute, Research and Development Division of Planned Parenthood, *One Million Teen-Agers* (New York, 1976), p. 10.

25. Katherine B. Oettinger, *Not My Daughter: Facing Up to Adolescent Pregnancy* (Englewood Cliffs, N.J.: Prentice-Hall, Inc., 1979), pp. 10-11.

26. Joseph J. Peters, "Children Who Are Victims of Sexual Assault and the Psychology of Offenders," *American Journal of Psychotherapy*, vol. 30, No. 3, July 1976, pp. 407-8.

27. Ibid., p. 402.

28. In a letter distributed by David Finkelhor, Ph.D., of the Family Violence Research Program of the University of New Hampshire and Judith Herman, M.D., of the Women's Mental Health Collective, Inc., Somerville, Mass.

29. Ann Wolbert Burgess, Lynda Lytle Holmstrom and Maureen P. Causland, "Divided Loyalty in Incest Cases," ed. Ann Wolbert Burgess and others, *Sexual Assault of Children and Adolescents*, p. 125.

30. Ibid., p. 123.

31. Ibid., p. 122.

32. Katherine Brady, *Father's Days: A True Story of Incest* (New York: Seaview Books, 1979), pp. 58, 59.

33. Inge K. Boverman and others, "Sex Stereotypes and Clinical Judgments of Mental Health," *Journal of Consulting and Clinical Psychology*, 1970, vol. 34, No I., pp. 5–7.

34. Louise Armstrong, *Kiss Daddy Goodnight* (New York: Hawthorn Books, 1978), p. 24.

35. Lady Murasaki, *The Tales of Gengi* (New York: Doubleday Anchor, 1955), p. 146.

36. Anonymous, "Young Girl's Song" in Louis Untermeyer *Collection of Great Poems* (New York: Permabooks, 1961), p. 32.

37. Charlotte Mews, "The Farmer's Bride" in E. M. Cole, *Erotic Poetry* (New York: Random House, 1962).

38. Linda Brent, "The Trials of Girlhood," in Nancy F. Scott, ed. *Roots of Bitterness* (New York: Dutton, 1972), p. 261.

39. Ruth Rosen and Sue Davidson, eds. *The Maimie Papers* (New York: Feminist Press, 1977), p. 193.

40. Agnes Smedley, *Daughters of Earth* (New York: Feminist Press, 1973), p. 116.

41. Susan Brownmiller, *Against Our Will* (New York: Simon and Schuster, 1975), pp. 273–75.

42. Quentin Bell, *Virginia Woolf* (New York: Harcourt Brace Jovanovich, 1972), p. 44.

43. Claudia Dreifus, *Woman's Fate* (New York: Bantam, 1973), pp. 75–81.

44. Ingrid Bengis, *Combat in the Erogenous Zone* (New York: Knopf, 1972), p. 11.

45. Kate Millett, *Flying* (New York: Knopf, 1974), pp. 8, 9.

46. Joyce A. Ladner, *Tomorrow's Tomorrow* (New York: Doubleday Anchor, 1972), p. 63.

47. Susan Griffin, *Rape: The Power of Consciousness* (Hagerstown, New York: Harper & Row, 1979), p. 4.

48. Robin Morgan, "The Father." *Lady of the Beasts* (New York: Random House, 1976), p. 6.

49. Linda Marie, *I Shall Not Rock* (New York: Daughters Publishing, 1977), pp. 24–25.

50. Nancy Gager and Cathleen Schurr, *Sexual Assault: Confronting Rape in America* (New York: Grosset and Dunlap, 1976), p. 7.

51. Brownmiller, *Against Our Will*, p. 281.

52. Sandra Butler, *Conspiracy of Silence, the Trauma of Incest* (San Francisco: New Glide Publications, 1978), passim.

53. Armstrong, *Kiss Daddy Goodnight*, pp. 234–35.

54. Ibid., p. 235.

55. Linda Tschirhart Sanford, *The Silent Children* (New York: Doubleday, in press).

56. *The Discreet Gentlemen's Guide to the Pleasures of Europe* (New York: Bantam Books, 1975), p. 51.

57. Allan H. Mankoff, *Mankoff's Lusty Europe* (New York: Viking, 1973), pp. 51–53.

58. "Peaches and Daddy Browning," *Liberty*, Winter 1974, pp. 48–51.

59. A. Nicholas Groth, "Guidelines for the Assessment and Management of the Offender." In Burgess, ed., *Sexual Assault of Children and Adolescents*, p. 32.

60. A. Nicholas Groth, "Patterns of Sexual Assault Against Children and Adolescents." In Burgess, ed., *Sexual Assault of Children and Adolescents*, p. 23.

61. Joseph J. Peters, "Children Who Are Victims of Sexual Assault," p. 410.

62. Edward M. Brecher, *Treatment Programs for Sex Offenders* (Washington, D.C.: National Institute of Law Enforcement and Criminal Justice, U.S. Department of Justice, 1977), p. 29.

63. Ibid., p. 55.

## 2. THE BIBLE AND THE TALMUD: AN INFAMOUS TRADITION BEGINS

1. Noah Kramer, *History Begins at Sumer* (New York: Doubleday Anchor, 1959), p. 85.

2. Ibid., p. 86.

3. Ibid., p. 133.

4. Numbers 31:19.

5. Seder Nezikin, ed., *The Babylonian Talmud* (translated by I. Epstein). (London: The Soncino Press, 1935), p. 376.

6. Cited from Allen Edwardes and R. E. L. Masters, *The Cradle of Erotica* (London: The Odyssey Press, 1970), p. 77.

7. Maimonides, *The Book of Women* (Book Four). (New Haven: Yale University Press, 1972), p. 18.

8. Exodus 20:17.

9. Eugene J. Lipman, ed. and trans., *The Mishna* (New York: W. W. Norton, 1970), p. 191 (Kiddishin 1:1).

10. David M. Feldman, *Marital Relations, Birth Control, and Abortion in Jewish Law* (New York: Schocken Books, 1974), p. 178.

11. Ibid., p. 179.

12. Maimonides, *The Book of Women*, p. 20.

13. Feldman, *Marital Relations*, p. 67.

14. Deuteronomy 22:29.

15. Exodus 22:16, 17.

16. Louis M. Epstein, *Sex Laws and Customs in Judaism* (New York: KTAV Publishing, 1967), p. 182.

17. Ibid.

18. Ibid.

19. Ibid., p. 183.

20. Ibid., pp. 164–65.

21. Ibid., p. 167.

22. Ibid., p. 166.

23. Lev. 21:9.

24. Deuteronomy 22:20–22.

25. Genesis 20:2–21, 34.

26. Ezekiel 16:34.

27. Maimonides, *The Book of Women*, p. 335.

28. Ibid.

29. Ibid.

30. Epstein, *Sex Laws and Customs*, pp. 158–59.

31. Maimonides, *The Book of Women*, p. 18.

32. Epstein, *Sex Laws and Customs*, pp. 212–15.

33. Maimonides, *The Book of Women*, pp. 238–45.

34. Epstein, *Sex Laws and Customs*, p. 185.

35. Maimonides, *The Book of Women*, p. 68.

36. Fred Rosner, *Sex Ethics of Maimonides* (New York: Bloch Publishing, 1974), p. 122.

37. Hayyim Schneid, *Marriage* (Philadelphia: Jewish Publication Society of America, 1973), p. 95.

## 3. THE CHRISTIANS

1. Henry Charles Lea, *History of Sacerdotal Celibacy in the Christian Church* (Secaucus, New Jersey: University Books, 1966), p. 526.

2. Eileen Power, *Medieval People* (New York: University Paperbacks, 1966), p. 97.

3. G. G. Coulton, *Medieval Panorama* (New York: W.W. Norton, 1974), p. 639.

4. Ibid., p. 631.

5. Ibid., p. 644.

6. John C. O'Dea, *The Matrimonial Impediment of Nonage* (Washington, D.C.: Catholic University of America Press, 1944), p. 6.

7. Ibid., p. 46.

8. Ibid., p. 69.

9. Ibid., p. 69.

10. Rev. H. A. Ayrinhac, *Marriage Legislation in the New Code of Canon Law* (New York: Benzinger Brothers, 1919), p. 313.

11. Charles Edward Smith, *Papal Enforcement of Some Medieval Marriage Laws* (Baton Rouge, La.: Louisiana State University, 1940), p. 41.

12. V.H.H. Green, *Medieval Civilization in Western Europe* (New York: St. Martin's Press, 1971), pp. 183–84.

13. O'Dea, *Matrimonial Impediment,* p. 101.

14. Ibid., p. 22.

15. Matthew 19:5.

16. 1 Corinthians 6:16.

17. Ayrinhac, *Marriage Legislation,* p. 203.

18. John Fulton, *Laws of Marriage* (London: Weel, Gardner, Darton and Co., 1883), p. 111.

19. Smith, *Papal Enforcement,* p. 142.

20. Sir Matthew Hale, *The History of the Pleas of the Crown* (Philadelphia: Robert H. Small, 1847), p. 650.

21. Mortimer Levine, "A More Than Ordinary Case of Rape," *The American Journal of Legal History,* Vol. 7, April 1963, p. 162.

22. Hale, *The History of the Pleas of the Crown,* p. 631.

23. Ibid., p. 633.

24. Lea, *History of Sacerdotal Celibacy,* pp. 501–2.

25. Ibid.

26. Julia O'Faolain and Laura Martines, *Not in God's Image* (New York: Harper Torchbooks, 1973), p. 240; also Power, *Medieval People,* pp. 73–78.

27. Lea, *History of Sacerdotal Celibacy,* p. 533.

28. Ibid.

29. Heinrich Kramer and James Sprenger, *Malleus Malificarum* (New York: Dover, 1971), pp. 41–48.

30. Ibid., p. 47.

31. Reginald Scot, *The Discoverie of Witchcraft* (New York: Dover, 1972), p. 4.

32. Kramer/Sprenger, *Malleus Malificarum,* p. 144.

33. Russell Hope Robbins, *The Encyclopedia of Witchcraft and Demonology* (New York: Crown, 1974), pp. 55–56.

34. Ibid., p. 56.

35. Nicholas Remy, *Demonalatry* (Secaucus, New Jersey: University Books, 1947), p. 95.

36. Montague Summers, *Geography of Witchcraft* (New York: Citadel, 1973), p. 153.

37. Ibid., p. 302.

38. Robbins, *Encyclopedia of Witchcraft*, p. 462.

39. Ibid., p. 555.

40. Robbins, *Encyclopedia of Witchcraft*, p. 348.

41. Summers, *Geography of Witchcraft*, pp. 502–3.

42. Remy, *Demonalatry*, p. 166.

43. Charles Kirkpatrick Sharpe, *Witchcraft in Scotland* (New York: Barnes and Noble, 1972), p. 152.

44. Margaret A. Murray, *The Witch-cult in Western Europe* (London: Oxford University Press, 1971), p. 36.

45. Ibid., p. 37.

46. J.S.F. Forsyth, *Demonologia* (London: A. K. Newton, 1831), p. 259.

47. Julio Caro Barja, *World of Witches* (Chicago: University of Chicago Press, 1965), p. 193.

48. Robbins, *Encyclopedia of Witchcraft*, p. 395.

49. William W. Sanger, *History of Prostitution* (New York: Medical Publishing, 1899), p. 103.

50. Robbins, *Encyclopedia of Witchcraft*, p. 255–56.

51. Summers, *Geography of Witchcraft*, p. 509.

52. Robbins, *Encyclopedia of Witchcraft*, p. 412.

53. I have used three sources to document these accounts: *Satanism and Witchcraft* by Jules Michelet; *Geography of Witchcraft* by Montague Summers; and *The Encyclopedia of Witchcraft and Demonology* by Russell Robbins. *The Devils of Loudon* by Aldous Huxley was also used for the Loudon incident. These sources at times contradict one another. For example, one claims that Madeline of the Gaufridi affair was nine, whereas another says she was thirteen, when first seduced.

54. Robbins, *Encyclopedia of Witchcraft*, p. 195.

55. Kurt Seligman, *Magic, Supernaturalism and Religion* (New York: Pantheon Books, 1971), p. 169.

56. Peter Blos, *On Adolescence* (New York: Free Press, 1962), p. 39.

57. Ibid., p. 49.

58. Jacob Burckhardt, *The Civilization of the Renaissance in Italy* (New York: Harper Colophon Books, 1975), Vol. II, 444.

## 4. GREEK LOVE

1. Selected essays of Plutarch, *On Love, the Family and the Good Life* (New York: A Mentor Book, New American Library, 1957), p. 17.

2. Arno Karlin, *Sexuality and Homosexuality* (New York: W.W. Norton, 1971), p. 130.

3. Casper J. Kramer, Jr., ed., *The Complete Works of Horace* (New York: Modern Library, 1936), p. 11.

4. Willis Barnstone, trans., *Greek Lyric Poetry* (New York: Schocken Books, 1972), p. 40.

5. J. D. Kaplan, ed., *Dialogues of Plato* (New York: Washington Square Press, 1963), pp. 174-75.

6. Thucydides, *The Peloponnesian Wars*, trans. Hubert Wetmore Wells (Baltimore: Penguin Books, 1959), p. 118.

7. Ibid., p. 117.

8. Hans Licht, *Sexual Life of Ancient Greece* (London: The Abbey Library, 1971), pp. 440-63.

9. Morton Hunt, *The Natural History of Love* (New York: Knopf, 1959), pp. 45-46.

10. Barnstone, *Greek Lyric Poetry*, p. 125.

11. *The Greek Anthology*, trans. W. R. Paton (Cambridge, Mass.: The Harvard University Press, Loeb Classical Library, 1918), Vol. IV, bk. XII, no. 34.

12. Ibid., no. 5

13. Ibid., no. 205.

14. Barnstone, *Greek Lyric Poetry*, p. 101.

15. *The Greek Anthology*, bk. X, no. 20.

16. Licht, *Sexual Life of Ancient Greece*, p. 415.

17. Hunt, *Natural History of Love*, p. 47.

18. Plutarch, *Selected Essays*, pp. 47-48.

19. Polybius, *The Histories*, Hugh R. Trevor-Roper, ed., Mortimer Chambers, trans. (New York: Twayne, 1966), p. 306.

20. Herodotus, *The Histories*, Robert Baldick and Betty Radice, eds., Aubrey de Sélincourt, trans. (Baltimore: Penguin, 1971), pp. 533-34.

21. *The Greek Anthology*, bk. XI, no. 51.

22. Plato, *Phaedrus and the Seventh and Eighth Letters*, Robert Baldick and Betty Radice, eds., Walter Hamilton, trans. (Baltimore: Penguin, 1973), p. 41.

23. Karlin, *Sexuality and Homosexuality*, p. 56.

24. Suetonius, *The Twelve Caesars*, Robert Baldick and Betty Radice, eds., Robert Graves, trans. (Baltimore: Penguin, 1975), pp. 131-41, p. 223.

25. *Rochester's Poems on Several Occasions*, James Thorpe, ed. (copyright 1950 © 1978. Reprinted by permission of Princeton University Press, song on pp. 59 and 60.

## 5. A VICTORIAN CHILDHOOD

1. William Blake, "The Mental Traveller." In David Perkins, ed., *English Romantic Writers* (New York: Harcourt, Brace and World, 1967), p. 112.

2. Graham Ovenden and Robert Melville, *Victorian Children* (New York: St. Martin's Press), p. 10.

3. Richard von Krafft-Ebing, *Psychopathia Sexualis* (New York: Putnam's, 1965), p. 518.

4. August Bebel, *Women Under Socialism* (New York: Schocken, 1971), p. 165.

5. Simone de Beauvoir, *The Second Sex* (New York: Bantam, 1968), pp. 298-99.

6. Ronald Pearsall, *Worm in the Bud* (New York: Macmillan, 1969).

7. Ibid,. p. 361.

8. Peter Coveney, *The Image of Childhood* (Baltimore: Penguin, 1967), p. 81.

9. Thomas Swann, *Ernest Dowson* (New York: Twayne, 1964), pp. 32-39.

10. Desmond Flower and Henry Mans, *The Letters of Ernest Dowson* (London: Cassell, 1967), pp. 116-18.

11. Allen Hervy, *Israfel* (New York: Rinehart, 1934), p. 300.

12. Charles Haines, *Edgar Allen Poe* (New York: Franklin Watts, 1975), p. 17.

13. Ada Nisbet, *Dickens and Ellen Ternan* (Berkeley, Cal.: University of California Press, 1952).

14. Pearsall, *Worm in the Bud*, p. 359.

15. Joan Evans, *John Ruskin* (New York: Oxford University Press, 1955), pp. 317-34.

16. Helmut Gernsheim, *Lewis Carroll* (New York: Dover, 1969), p. viii.

17. Florence Brecher Lennon, *The Life of Lewis Carroll* (New York: Dover, 1972), pp. 237-54.

18. Leslie Fiedler, Introduction to *Beyond the Looking Glass*, ed. Jonathan Cott (New York: Stonehill, 1973), p. xx.

19. Lennon, *Life of Lewis Carroll*, p. 394.

20. Pearsall, *Worm in the Bud*, p. 65.

21. Ibid., p. 612.

22. Honoré de Balzac, *The Physiology of Marriage* (New York: Société des Beaux-Arts, n. d.: introduction written in 1829), p. 140.

23. Fernando Henriques, *Prostitution and Society*, vol. III, (London: Macgibbon and Kee, 1968), p. 280.

24. Anonymous (Walter), *My Secret Life* (New York: Grove Press, 1966), pp. 383-84.

25. William Acton, *Prostitution* (New York: Praeger, 1968, first published 1857), pp. 12, 116.

26. Ibid., pp. 71-73.

27. Ibid., p. 136.

28. James Laver, *The Age of Optimism, 1848-1914* (New York: Harper and Row, 1966), pp. 104-5.

29. Bebel, *Women Under Socialism*, p. 162.

30. Abraham Flexner, *Prostitution in Europe* (New York: Century, 1914), pp. 78-79.

31. Milton Rugoff, *Prudery and Passion* (New York: Putnam's, 1971), pp. 321-39.

32. Edwin Seligman, *The Social Evil* (New York: Putnam's, 1912), p. 239.

33. *Pall Mall Gazette*, London, July 7, 1885.

34. Vern L. Bullough, *The History of Prostitution* (New Hyde Park, New York: University Books, Inc., 1964), p. 176.

35. *Pall Mall Gazette*, London, July 6, 1885.

36. Henriques, *Prostitution*, pp. 285-87.

37. Laver, *Age of Optimism*, p. 105.

38. Theodore A. Bengham, *The Girl That Disappears* (New York: Gorham, 1911), p. 8.

39. *Pall Mall Gazette*, London, July 6, 1885.

40. Reginald Wright Kauffman, *The House of Bondage* (New York: Grosset and Dunlap, 1912), pp. 459-60.

41. Ibid., pp. 68-69.

42. Kathleen Barry, "Did I Ever Really Have a Chance?" *Chrysalis*, Los Angeles, No. 1.

43. Olive Banks and J. A. Banks, *Feminism and Family Planning* (New York: Schocken, 1972), p. 114.

44. Aileen S. Kraditor, *Up From the Pedestal* (Chicago: Quadrangle, 1968), p. 159.

45. Glen Petri, *A Singular Iniquity—the Campaigns of Josephine Butler* (New York: Viking, 1971), p. 113.

46. Ibid., p. 114.

47. Ibid., p. 114.

48. Ibid., p. 116.

49. David J. Pivar, *The Purity Crusade* (Westport, Conn.: Greenwood, 1973), p. 105.

50. Petri, *A Singular Iniquity*, p. 149.

51. The account of Butler, Stead, the abolitionists and the revolt of the women was derived from several sources. They are Petri, *A Singular Iniquity*, op. cit.; Pearsall, *Worm in the Bud*, op. cit.; Banks and Banks, *Feminism and Family Planning*, op. cit.; Henriques, *Prostitution and Society*, op. cit.; William L. O'Neil, *The Woman Movement* (Chicago: Quadrangle, 1969); Michael Pearson, *Five Pound Virgins* (New York: Saturday Review Press, 1972).

## 6. CHILD MARRIAGE IN INDIA

1. Sarvepalli Radhakrishnan and Charles A. Moore, eds., *A Sourcebook in Indian Philosophy* (New Jersey: Princeton University Press, 1957), p. 190.

2. Irene H. Frieze and others, *Women and Sex Roles* (New York: W.W. Norton and Co., 1978), pp. 128-34.

3. Julia O'Faolain and Lauro Martine, *Not in God's Image* (New York; Harper Torchbooks, 1973), p. 5.

4. Ibid., p. 48.

5. Katherine Mayo, *Slave of the Gods* (New York: Harcourt, Brace and Co., 1929), pp. 256-57.

6. Ibid., p. 259.

7. Cited from William J. Fielding, *Strange Customs of Courtship and Marriage* (New York: Hart Publishing Co., 1942), p. 194.

8. Vatsyana, *Kama Sutra* (New York: Lancer Books, 1964), p. 61.

9. Ibid., p. 77.

10. Walter T. Wallbank, *A Short History of India and Pakistan* (New York: A Mentor Book, 1965), p. 92.

11. Vera and David Mace, *Marriage East and West* (Garden City, New York: Doubleday and Co., Inc., 1960), pp. 194-200.

12. Katherine Mayo, *Mother India* (New York: Harcourt, Brace and Co., 1927), passim.

13. Ibid., p. 46.

14. Ibid., p. 56.

15. Louis Fischer, *Gandhi* (New York: A Mentor Book, 1960), p. 125.

16. Mayo, *Slave of the Gods*, op. cit. p. 266.

17. Ibid., p. 268.

18. Mace, *Marriage East and West*, op. cit. p. 196.

19. Katherine Mayo, *The Face of Mother India* (New York: Harper and Brothers, 1936), pp. 1-41.

20. Mary Daly, *Gyn/Ecology* (Boston: Beacon Press, 1978), p. 438.

21. Evelyn Sullerot, *Women, Change and Society* (New York: McGraw-Hill, 1971), p. 60.

22. Daly, *Gyn/Ecology*, op. cit. p. 438.

23. Bernard Weinraub, "Married at Ten, Deserted at Fifteen, She Lives in the Delhi Streets," *The New York Times*, April 14, 1973.

24. Daly, *Gyn-Ecology*, op. cit. p. 438.

25. Wallbank, *A Short History of India and Pakistan*, op. cit. p. 265.

## 7. THE FREUDIAN COVER-UP

1. Joseph J. Peters, M.D., "Children Who Are Victims of Sexual Assault and the Psychology of Offenders." *American Journal of Psychotherapy*, vol. xxx, No. 3, July 1976, pp. 398–421.

2. Sigmund Freud, *The Complete Introductory Lectures of Psychoanalysis* (New York: Norton, 1966), p. 584.

3. Ibid., p. 584.

4. Ibid., p. 584.

5. Marthe Robert, *The Psychoanalytic Revolution*, trans. from French, Kenneth Morgan (London: Allen & Unwin, 1966), p. 63.

6. Sigmund Freud and Josef Breuer, *Studies on Hysteria*, trans. Joan Riviere (New York: Avon, 1966), p. 174.

7. Ibid., p. 211.

8. Sigmund Freud, "Fragment of an Analysis of a Case Hysteria," trans. Joan Riviere, in *Collected Papers*, vol. III (London: Hogarth, 1953).

9. Walter A. Stewart, *Psychoanalysis: The First Ten Years: 1888-1898* (London: Allen & Unwin, 1969), p. 2.

10. Marie Bonaparte, Anna Freud, and Ernst Kris, eds., *The Origins of Psycho-analysis, Letters to Wilhelm Fliess, Drafts and Notes: 1887-1902*, by Sigmund Freud, translated by Eric Mosbacher and James Strachey (New York: ©1954 by Basic Books), editors note, p. x.

11. Ibid., pp. 77–80.

12. Ibid., p. 126.

13. Sigmund Freud, "The Aetiology of Hysteria," in *Collected Papers*, I-203.

14. Ibid., p. 203.

15. Marie Bonaparte and others, *Origins*, pp. 195–96.

16. Sigmund Freud, "On the History of the Psychoanalytic Movement," in *Collected Papers,* I, 303–4.

17. Freud, "Aetiology of Hysteria," pp. 203–4.

18. Ibid., pp. 203–4.

19. Freud, *Introductory Lectures,* pp. 584–85.

20. Bonaparte and others, *Origins,* p. 170.

21. Ibid., p. 219.

22. Ernest Jones, *The Life and Work of Sigmund Freud* (New York: Basic Books, 1961), p. 211.

23. Bonaparte and others, *Origins,* pp. 206–7.

24. Ibid., pp. 215–17.

25. Ibid., pp. 223–24.

26. Hans Licht, *Sexual Life in Ancient Greece* (London: Abbey Library, 1971), p. 134.

27. Freud, "History of the Psychoanalytic Movement," p. 300.

28. Sigmund Freud, "Psycho-Analysis," in *Collected Papers* (London: Hogarth Press, 1974), V, 118.

29. Janine Chassequet-Smirgel, "Feminine Guilt and the Oedipus Complex," J. Chassequet-Smirgel and others, eds., *Female Sexuality* (Ann Arbor: University of Michigan Press, 1970), pp. 94–112.

30. Helene Deutsch, *The Psychology of Women* (New York: Bantam Books, 1973), I, 258.

31. Karl Abraham, "The Experiencing of Sexual Trauma as a Form of Sexual Activity," in *Selected Papers on Psychoanalysis* (New York: Basic Books, 1954), p. 53.

32. Ibid., p. 62.

33. Freud, "History of the Psychoanalytic Movement," p. 300.

34. Anonymous, *A Young Girl's Diary* (New York: Barnes and Noble, 1961), preface.

35. Paul Roazen, *Freud and His Followers* (New York: Knopf, 1975), pp. 442–43.

36. John James, *The Facts of Sex* (Princeton, N.J.: Vertex, 1970), p. 118.

37. Lindy Burton, *Vulnerable Children* (London: Routledge & Kegan Paul, 1968), pp. 87–98, passim.

38. Peter Blos, "Three Typical Constellations in Female Delinquency," in *Family Dynamics and Female Sexual Delinquency,* Otto Pollak and Alfred S. Friedman, eds., (Palo Alto, California: Science and Behavior Books, 1969), pp. 103–5.

39. Max Schur, *Freud, Living and Dying* (New York: International Universities, 1972), pp. 125–36.

40. Bronislaw Malinowski, *Crime and Custom in Savage Society* (Totowa, N.J.: Littlefield, Adams, 1966), pp. 77–80.

41. Roazen, *Freud and His Followers,* p. 335.

42. Ibid., p. 359.

## 8. MYTHS, FAIRY TALES AND FILMS

1. Lucy Larcom, *A New England Girlhood* (Magnolia, Mass.: Peter Smith, 1973), p. 106.

2. Simone de Beauvoir, *The Second Sex* (New York: Bantam, 1968), p. 269.

3. All stories from Francis Jenkins Olcott, ed., *Grimms' Fairy Tales* (New York: Follett, 1968).

4. Ibid., p. 86.

5. Ibid., p. 86.

6. Bruno Bettelheim, *The Uses of Enchantment* (New York: Knopf, 1976), p. 219.

7. Hans Christian Andersen, *Andersen's Fairy Tales* (New York: Grosset and Dunlap, 1955), p. 69.

8. Ibid., passim.

9. Barbara Standford, *Myths and Modern Man* (New York: Pocket Books, 1972).

10. Walter Harrelson, *From Fertility Cult to Worship* (New York: Doubleday, 1969), p. 68.

11. Susan Brownmiller, *Against Our Will* (New York: Simon and Schuster, 1975), p. 292.

12. Kurt Ranke, ed., *Folktales of Germany* (Chicago: University of Chicago Press, 1968), Foreword pp. xvii–xviii.

13. Ibid., pp. xvii–xviii.

14. Kay Stone, "Things Walt Disney Never Told Us," in *Journal of American Folklore* (special issue on women and folklore) vol. 88, No. 374, January–March 1975.

15. Andrew Lang, ed., *The Grey Fairy Book* (New York: Longmans, Green, 1900), pp. 332–44.

16. Ibid., pp. 275–80.

17. Jean Corcoran, adapter, *Folk Tales of England* (Indianapolis: Bobbs-Merrill, 1968), pp. 44–49.

18. Ibid., p. 124.

19. Helene Deutsch, *The Psychology of Women* (New York: Bantam, 1973), I-11.

20. Ibid., p. 32.

21. Ibid., p. 33.

22. Martha Finley, *Elsie Dinsmore* (New York: A. L. Burton, 1896), pp. 170–71.

23. Frances Hodgson Burnett, *A Little Princess* (New York: A Yearling Book, 1975), p. 17.

24. Ibid., p. 222.

25. Johanna Spyri, *Heidi* (New York: E. P. Dutton, 1921), p. 153.

26. George Eliot, *Silas Marner* (New York: Pocket Books, 1948), p. 169.

27. Robert Windeler, *Sweetheart* (New York: Praeger, 1974), passim; and Raymond Lee, *The Films of Mary Pickford* (New York: Castle Books, 1970), passim.

28. Jeanne Basinger, *Shirley Temple* (New York: Pyramid, 1970), passim.

29. Mark Best, *Those Endearing Young Charms* (New York: A. S. Barnes, 1971), passim.

30. Ibid., passim.

31. Nora Sayre, "Graham Greene on Film," *The New York Times Book Review*, December 17, 1972, p. 3.

32. Anne Sexton, *Transformations* (Boston: Houghton Mifflin, 1971), p. 112.

## 9. THE DEMON NYMPHETTE

1. Vladimir Nabokov, *Lolita* (New York: Putnam, 1958), p. 64.

2. Hart Crane, *The Complete Poems of Hart Crane* (New York: Doubleday, 1958), p. 10.

3. John Dryden, "Song for a Young Girl," in *Erotic Poetry,* William Cole, ed. (New York: Random House, 1962), p. 418.

4. Ibid., p. 37.

5. Graham Ovenen and Robert Melville, *Victorian Children* (New York: St. Martin's Press, 1972).

6. Fyodor Dostoyevsky, *The Possessed,* trans. Constance Garnette (New York: Laurel Books, 1964), p. 711, plates 111 and 112.

7. Fyodor Dostoyevsky, *Crime and Punishment,* trans. Constance Garnette (New York: Laurel Books, 1962), p. 537.

8. Edward Lucie-Smith, *Eroticism in Western Art* (London: Thames and Hudson, 1972), pp. 150, 182.

9. Arthur Miller, *The Crucible* (New York: Bantam, 1963), passim.

10. David Hamilton, *Sisters* (New York: William Morrow, 1974), p. 15.

11. Wilson Bryan Key, *Media Sexploitation* (Englewood Cliffs, N.J.: Prentice-Hall, Inc., 1976), pp. 55–56.

12. Advertisements in *Seventeen* magazine, August 1977, and other publications.

13. Marylin Bender, *Beautiful People* (New York: Dell, 1967), p. 229.

14. Rosemary Kent, "Clothes Conscious Kids," *Harper's Bazaar,* January 1977, p. 111.

15. *The New York Times,* August 11, 1977.

16. Mary Vespa, "The Littlest Vamp," New York *Daily News,* January 9, 1975, p. 27.

17. Kent, "Clothes Conscious Kids," p. 110.

18. Pauline Kael, *I Lost It at the Movies* (Boston: Atlantic Monthly, 1965), p. 157.

19. Pauline Kael, *Kiss Kiss Bang Bang* (New York: Bantam, 1971), p. 98.

20. Steven Marcus, *The Other Victorians* (New York: New American Library, 1974), p. 274.

21. Hannah Arendt, *On Violence* (New York: Harcourt Brace and World, 1970), p. 75.

22. Mike Childs, "De Palma has the Power," in *Cinefantastique,* vol. 6, no. 1, p. 29.

23. Don Shay, "Robert Wise on Audrey Rose," ibid., p. 26.

24. Nabokov, *Lolita,* p. 316.

25. Benjamin Karpman, *The Sexual Offender and His Offenses* (New York: Julian Press, 1957), pp. 416–57.

26. Nabokov, *Lolita,* p. 136.

27. Ibid., p. 144.

28. Ibid., p. 194.

29. Ibid., p. 316.

30. Molly Haskell, *From Reverence to Rape* (New York: Holt, Rinehart & Winston, 1974), p. 346.

31. Edgar Z. Friedenberg, "The Image of the Adolescent Minority," in *Youth and Sociology,* Peter K. Manning and Marcello Truzzi, eds. (Englewood Cliffs, N.J.: Prentice-Hall, 1972), pp. 36–37.

32. *Ms.,* October 1974.

33. Vincent Canby, "Pretty Baby by Louis Malle," *The New York Times,* April 5, 1978.

34. Judith Crist, "Beauty in Baby," *New York Post,* April 5, 1978.

35. Christina Rossetti, "In an Artist's Studio," in *The World Split Open,* Louise Bernikow, ed. (New York: Vintage, 1974), p. 125.

36. John H. Gagnon and William Simon, *Sexual Conduct* (Chicago: Aldine, 1973), p. 304.

## 10. FATHERS AND DAUGHTERS

1. *Sexual Assault: The Target Is You,* brochure prepared by the Hennepin County Attorney's Office, Minneapolis, Minnesota.

2. Phyllis Chesler, *Women and Madness* (New York: Doubleday, 1972), pp. 74–75.

3. Ruth Benedict, *Patterns of Culture* (Boston: Houghton Mifflin, 1959), pp. 32–36.

4. Raphael Patai, *Sex and Family in the Bible and the Middle East* (New York: Doubleday, 1959), p. 26.

5. Kirson S. Weinberg, *Incest Behavior* (New York: Citadel, 1965), p. 14.

6. Patai, *Sex and Family,* p. 35.

7. Lev., 18:15.

8. Lev., 18:6.

9. 2 Samuel 13:13.

10. Patai, *Sex and Family,* p. 25.

11. Genesis, 49:4.

12. 2 Samuel 15:23.

13. Patai, *Sex and Family,* p. 25; and Weinberg, *Incest Behavior,* p. 13.

14. Patai, *Sex and Family,* p. 25.

15. Genesis 19:30–38.

16. Herodotus, *The Histories,* eds. Robert Baldick and Betty Radice, trans. Aubrey de Sélincourt (Baltimore: Penguin, 1971), p. 153.

17. Herbert Maisch, *Incest* (New York: Stein and Day, 1972), p. 22.

18. Ibid., p. 29.

19. R.E.L. Masters, *Patterns of Incest* (New York: Ace, 1963), pp. 34–35.

20. Geoffrey Chaucer, "The Canterbury Tales" in *The Portable Chaucer* (New York: Viking, 1979), pp. 259–64.

21. Giovanni Boccaccio, *The Decameron* (New York: Laurel, 1971), pp. 624–35.

22. Masters, *Patterns of Incest,* p. 56.

23. Wardell B. Pomeroy, "A New Look at Incest," *Forum,* November 1976, p. 12.

24. Abigail van Buren, "Dear Abby," *New York Post,* November 13, 1977.

25. Margaret Mead, *Male and Female* (New York: Morrow, 1975), pp. 198–99.

26. Ruby Rohrlich Leavitt, *The Puerto Ricans* (Tucson: University of Arizona Press, 1974), p. 60.

27. Susan Brownmiller, *Against Our Will* (New York: Simon and Schuster, 1975), p. 281.

28. Harry Kalven and Hans Zeisel, *The American Jury* (Boston: Little, Brown, 1966), p. 304.

29. Weinberg, *Incest Behavior,* p. 40.

30. Maisch, *Incest,* p. 92.

31. P. H. Gebhard and others, *Sex Offenders* (New York: Bantam, 1965), p. 207.

32. Barbara Campbell, "Incest Case Haunts Critics of City System," *The New York Times,* January 19, 1976.

33. Ann Landers, "Ann Landers," New York *Daily News,* October 8, 1975, p. 57.

34. Abigail van Buren, "Dear Abby," *New York Post,* November 13, 1977, April 14, 1976.

35. "State Senate Passes Bill on Abortion," *New York Post,* March 31, 1976, p. 32.

36. Judith Herman and Lisa Hirshman, "Father Daughter Incest," in *Signs, Journal of Women and Culture in Society,* June 1977.

37. Richard von Krafft-Ebing, *Psychopathia Sexualis* (New York: Putnam's, 1965), p. 101.

38. Alfred M. Freedman and others, *Modern Synopsis of Comprehensive Textbook of Psychiatry II* (Baltimore: The Williams and Wilkins Company, 1976), p. 772.

39. Clelland S. Ford and Frank A. Beach, *Patterns of Sexual Behavior* (New York: Harper Colophon Books, 1972), p. 123.

40. Richard von Krafft-Ebing, *Psychopathia Sexualis,* p. 103.

41. Pomeroy, "A New Look at Incest," op. cit.

42. Abigail van Buren, "Dear Abby," *San Francisco Chronicle,* June 28, 1976.

43. Freedman, *Modern Synopsis,* p. 770.

## 11. SEX EDUCATION AND THE CHILD MOLESTER

1. Mary Breasted, *Oh! Sex Education* (New York: Praeger Publishers, Inc., 1970). Reprinted by permission of Holt Rinehart and Winston.

2. Child Study Association of America, *What to Tell Your Children About Sex* (New York: Pocket Books, 1970), pp. 20–21.

3. Benjamin Spock, M.D., *A Teenager's Guide to Life and Love* (New York: Pocket Books, 1971), p. 107.

4. Committee on Adolescence, Group for the Advancement of Psychiatry, *Normal Adolescence* (New York: Scribner's, 1968), p. 22.

5. Ibid., p. 25.

6. Herant A. Katchadourian and Donald T. Lunde, *Fundamentals of Human Sexuality* (New York: Holt, Rinehart and Winston, 1972), p. 86.

7. Mary S. Calderone, M.D., "Sex and Social Responsibility," in Pat G. Powers and Wade Baskin, *Sex Education: Issues and Directives* (New York: Philosophical Library, 1969), p. 101.

8. Sex Information and Educational Council of the United States, *Sexuality and Man* (New York: Scribner's, 1970), pp. 83–98 passim.

9. Ibid., p. 98.

10. Ibid., p. 97.

11. Michel Foucault, *The History of Sexuality* (New York: Pantheon, 1978), p. 157.


## 12. A HARD LOOK AT THE LAW

1. Herant A. Katchadourian and Donald T. Lunde, *Fundamentals of Human Sexuality* (New York: Holt, Rinehart and Winston, 1972), p. 423.

2. Frances E.W.Harper, "A Double Standard," ed. Louise Bernikow, *The World Split Open* (New York: Random House, Inc., 1974), p. 213.

3. Vincent de Francis, *Protecting the Child Victim of Sex Crimes Committed by Adults* (Denver, Colorado: American Humane Association, Children's Division, 1969), pp. 18–24.

4. Susan C. Ross, *The Rights of Women* (New York: Avon, 1973), pp. 164–70.

5. D. J. West, *The Young Offender* (London: Penguin, 1967), p. 197.

6. Matthew Hale, *History of the Pleas of the Crown* (Philadelphia: R. H. Small, 1847), I, 634.

7. Russell Hope Robbins, *The Encyclopedia of Witchcraft and Demonology* (New York: Crown, 1974), pp. 240–41.

8. Hale, *History of the Pleas,* p. 633.

9. "A Judge's Teen Shocker," *San Francisco Chronicle,* June 24, 1976, p. 26.

10. Earle Prevost, "Statutory Rape: A Growing Liberalization," *South Carolina Law Review,* 1966, vol. 18, 259.

11. Harry Kalven, Jr. and Hans Zeisel, *The American Jury* (Boston: Little, Brown, 1966), pp. 276–81.

12. Leo Kanowitz, *Women and the Law* (Albuquerque: University of New Mexico Press, 1971), p. 7.

13. Ibid., p. 23.

14. Ibid., p. 22.

15. Federal Bureau of Investigation, U.S. Department of Justice, *Uniform Crime Reports for the United States* (Washington, D.C.: 1975), pp. 6, 185.

16. Albert Moll, *The Sexual Life of the Child* (New York: Macmillan, 1921), p. 233.

17. Ibid., pp. 219–34.

18. Ibid., p. 225.

19. Ibid., p. 192.

20. Ibid., p. 228.

21. Frank S. Caprio and Donald R. Brenner, *Sexual Behavior: Psycho-Legal Aspects* (New York: Citadel, 1961), p. 213.

22. Alfred M. Freedman and others, *Modern Synopsis of Comprehensive Textbook of Psychiatry II* (Baltimore: Williams and Wilkins, 1976), p. 1213.

23. Caprio and others, *Sexual Behavior,* p. 211.

24. Louise J. Despert, *The Emotionally Disturbed Child* (New York: Doubleday Anchor, 1970), p. 128.

25. Kenneth S. Carpenter, "Children's Reliability in Sex Offense Accusations," in *Medical Aspects of Human Sexuality,* January 1979.

26. Ann Wolbert Burgess and Anna T. Lazlo, "When the Prosecutrix is a Child in Cases of Sexual Assault," in Emilio C. Viano, *Victims and Society* (Washington, D.C.: Visage, 1976), p. 387.

27. Fred Inbau and John E. Reid, *Criminal Interrogations and Confessions* (Baltimore: Williams and Wilkins, 1976), p. 111.

28. Vincent de Francis, *Protecting the Child Victim,* pp. 181–94.

29. Charles Dickens, *Oliver Twist* (Garden City: Sun Dial Press, 1948), p. 327.

## 13. CHILD PROSTITUTION AND KIDDY PORN

1. Polly Adler, *A House Is Not a Home* (New York: Holt, Rinehart and Winston, Publishers, 1953).

2. Alix Kates Shulman, ed., *Red Emma Speaks* (New York: Vintage, 1972), p. 43.

3. Lillian Ambrosino, *Runaways* (Boston: Beacon Press, 1971), pp. 3–4.

4. Ann Landers, "Treatment Center for Child Prostitutes," *New York Daily News,* February 26, 1979, p. 38.

5. Alton Slagle, "Chewed Up then Spat Out," *New York Daily News,* March 14, 1977, p. 25.

6. Dick Bass, "The Short Little Life of a Prostitute, 15," *New York Post,* March 1, 1975, p. 3.

7. Selwyn Raab, "Veronica's Short, Sad Life—Prostitution at 11, Death at 12," *The New York Times,* October 3, 1977.

8. Selwyn Raab, "Pimps Establish Recruiting Link to the Midwest," *The New York Times,* October 3, 1977.

9. Adler, *A House Is Not a Home.*

10. "Youth for Sale on the Streets," *Time* magazine, November 28, 1977.

11. Judy Klemesrud, "Midtown Beat: Stalking the Pimp," *The New York Times,* February 2, 1977.

12. Paul Tabori, *Secret and Forbidden* (New York: New American Library, 1966), pp. 147–48.

13. Charles Winick and Paul M. Kinsie, *The Lively Commerce* (Chicago: Quadrangle, 1971), pp. 53–54.

14. Simone de Beauvoir, *The Second Sex* (New York: Bantam, 1968), p. 578.

15. Barbara Campbell, "Officials Consider Child Pornography Hard to Prosecute," *The New York Times,* January 15, 1977.

16. Ron Sproat, "The Working Day in a Porno Factory," *New York Magazine,* March 11, 1974, p. 40.

17. Ian Bloch, *The Sexual Extremities of the World* (New York: Award, 1964), pp. 339–56.

18. Steven Marcus, *The Other Victorians* (New York: New American Library, 1974), p. 237.

19. Anonymous, *The Romance of Lust* (New York: Grove Press, 1972), passim.

20. Aubrey Beardsley, *The Story of Venus and Tannhauser* (New York: Award, 1967), pp. 124–5.

21. Paul J. Gillette, *The Encyclopedia of Erotica* (New York: Award, 1969), pp. 309–16.

22. Guy de Maupassant, *The Colonel's Nieces* (California: Brandon Books, 1972), p. 2.

23. Pamela Hansford Johnson, *On Iniquity* (New York: Scribner's, 1967), p. 125.

24. Marquis de Sade, *The 120 Days of Sodom* (New York: Grove Press, 1966), p. 28.

25. Ibid., passim.

26. Marcus, *The Other Victorians,* p. 286.

27. George Steiner, "Night Words," in *The New Eroticism,* Philip Nobile, ed. (New York: Random House, 1970), p. 130.

28. Ronald Pearsall, *The Worm in the Bud* (New York: Macmillan, 1969), p. 386.

29. Ibid., p. 289.

30. Johnson, *On Iniquity,* p. 132.

31. Ibid., p. 132.

32. Ibid., p. 136.

33. Vern Bullough and Bonnie Bullough, *Sin, Sickness and Sanity* (New York: New American Library, 1977), p. 166.

34. Ibid., p. 166.

35. Ibid., p. 171.

36. Ibid., pp. 173–74.

37. *The Report of the Commission on Obscenity and Pornography,* A New York Times Book. Introduction by Clive Barnes (New York: Bantam, 1970), p. xi.

38. Ibid., p. 139.

39. Ibid., pp. 456–700.

40. Ibid., pp. 75–85.

41. Bullough, *Sin, Sickness and Sanity,* p. 174.

42. Everett R. Holles, "Anti-Pornography Center Losing U.S. Aid," *The New York Times,* April 30, 1975.

43. Barbara Campbell, "Aid Asked in Blocking Use of Children in Pornography," *The New York Times,* November 14, 1977.

44. Mitchell Ditkoff, "Child Pornography," *The American Humane Society,* vol 16, no. 4, 1978.

GENERAL REFERENCES ON ORGANIZED CHILD PROSTITUTION

Marin Arnold, "13 Accused Here of Torturing Girls to Force Them Into Prostitution," *The New York Times,* April 6, 1971.

Marvin Smilon, "Hooker Pipeline Pair Indicted," *New York Post,* April 12, 1978.

"Bust Teen Sex Ring: Arrest Couple in New Jersey," New York *Daily News,* October 13, 1977.

David Black, "The White Slave Trade in the East Village," *The Village Voice,* January 13, 1972.

"9 Men Indicted in Los Angeles for Running an International Child Prostitution Ring that Allegedly Used Children as Young as Four." *Gaysweek,* August 21, 1978.

James P. Sterba, "U. N. Aid Asks Inquiry on Forced Prostitution."

OTHER RESOURCES ON CHILD PROSTITUTION AND RUNAWAYS

Christine Chapman, *America's Runaways* (New York: William Morrow, 1976).

Celeste MacLeod, "Street Girls of the 70's," *The Nation,* April 20, 1974.

David Black, "Running Away," *The New Ingenue,* July 1973.

Kathy McCoy, "The Runaways," *Teen,* July 1976.

Jacob A. Goldberg and Rosamond W. Goldberg, *Girls of the City Streets* (New York: Foundation Books, 1940).

14. THE SEXUAL ABUSE OF BOYS

1. Michel Foucault, *The History of Sexuality*, trans. Robert Hurley (New York: Pantheon, 1978), p. 103.

2. Sigmund Freud, *Three Contributions to the Theory of Sex* (New York: E. P. Dutton, 1962), p. 10.

3. Brian Reade, *Sexual Heretics* (New York: Coward-McCann, 1970), p. 8.

4. Arno Karlin, *Sexuality and Homosexuality* (New York: Norton, 1971), p. 240.

5. J. Z. Eglinton, *Greek Love* (New York: Oliver Layton, 1965), p. 151.

6. Martin Hoffman, *The Gay World* (New York: Bantam, 1971), pp. 91–92.

7. "Opinion Outrage," *The Body Politic,* Toronto, Canda, September/October 1974.

8. Allen Edwards, *The Jewel in the Lotus* (New York: Lancer, 1969), pp. 239–254.

9. Lesbian Feminist Liberation, Inc., "Man/Boy Lovers," press release, New York, March 1979.

10. Linda Tschirhart Sanford, *The Silent Children* (New York: Doubleday, in press).

11. Sean O'Callaghan, *The White Slave Trade* (London: Robert Hale, 1965), passim.

12. "Six Indicted in Sexual Club Using Boys," *The New York Times,* May 23, 1972.

13. David A. Andelman, "8 Indicted in 'Boys-for-Sale' Ring," *The New York Times,* May 4, 1973, p. 45.

14. "Police Charge Boys Procured by Four Men," *Standard Star* (New Rochelle), February 1, 1974.

15. *The New York Times,* May 23, 1977; December 1, 1977; December 9, 1977.

16. "The Chickenhawks," *Newsweek* magazine, April 30, 1973; "Chickenhawk Trade Found Attracting More Young Boys to Times Square Area," *The New York Times,* February 14, 1977.

17. *The Gay Advocate,* July 1976, p. 12.

18. Carolyn Swift, "Sexual Assault of Children and Adolescents," Testimony prepared for subcommittee on Science and Technology of the U.S. House of Representatives, January 11, 1978. (Dr. Swift is Director of Prevention Projects, Wyandot Mental Health Center, Wyandot, Kansas.)

19. Katherine N. Dixon and others, "Father-Son Incest: Underreported Psychiatric Problem?" *American Journal of Psychiatry,* July 1978, p. 835.

20. Alfred C. Kinsey and others, *Sexual Behavior of the Human Male* (Philadelphia: W. B. Saunders, 1949), p. 168.

21. Alfred Kinsey and others, *Sexual Behavior of the Human Female* (New York: Pocket Books, 1953), p. 121.

22. Karl Fleming and Anne Taylor Fleming, *The First Time* (New York: Simon and Schuster, 1975), p. 74.

23. Ibid., p. 172.

24. Ibid., p. 222.

25. Iceberg Slim, *Pimp, The Story of My Life* (Los Angeles: Holloway House, 1969), passim.

26. André Maurois, *Byron* (New York: D. Appleton, 1969), pp. 32–34.

27. Anna Katan, "Children Who Were Raped," in *The Psychoanalytic Study of the Child,* Ruth Eissler and others, eds. (New Haven: Yale University Press, 1973), pp. 208–24.

28. David Finkelhor, *Sexually Victimized Children* (New York: Free Press, 1979), p. 75.

## 15. FROM THE SENSUOUS WOMAN TO THE SENSUOUS CHILD: LIBERATION OR BACKLASH?

1. Bennett Berger, "Hippie Morality—More Old Than New," in *The Sexual Scene,* John H. Gagnon and William Simon, eds.

2. Diana E. H. Russell, *The Politics of Rape* (New York: Stein and Day, 1975), p. 208.

3. L. Bender and Abram Blau, "The Reactions of Children to Sexual Relations with Adults," *American Journal of Orthopsychiatry,* 1937, vol. 7.

4. Nancy Gager and Kathleen Schurr, *Sexual Assault: Confronting Rape in America* (New York: Grosset and Dunlap, 1976), p. 45.

5. René Guyon, *Ethics of Sexual Acts* (New York: Blue Ribbon, 1941), pp. 44–72.

6. Petronius, *The Satyricon,* trans. W. C. Firebaugh (New York: Washington Square Press, 1966), pp. 36–38.

7. Paul Gebyart, *Sex Offenders* (New York: Harper and Row, 1965), p. 54.

8. Ibid., p. 276.

9. Robert S. de Ropp, *Sex Energy* (New York: Delta, 1969), pp. 111–12.

10. Alayne Yates, *Sex Without Shame* (New York: William Morrow, 1978), p. 121.

11. Hal M. Wells, *The Sensuous Child* (New York: Stein and Day, 1978), p. 152.

12. Warren Farrell, "The Americanization of Oedipus," *Cue* magazine, 1979.

13. Ibid.

14. Richard Farson, *Birthrights* (New York: Macmillan, 1974), p. 147.

15. Ibid., p. 149.

16. Lars Ullerstam, *The Erotic Minorities* (New York: Grove Press, 1966), p. 74.

17. René Guyon, *Bulletin,* September 1, 1975.

18. Geoffrey Lakeman, "Union Strike Over Child Sex Leader," *Daily Herald* (Wales), September 7, 1977.

19. "Child Sex, Man Attacked in Pub by Woman," *Western Mail* (Wales), September 9, 1977.

20. Polly Toynbee, "Sex Offender Can Aid Child—Good Can Come from Pedophilia Priest Claims," *Guardian Women* (Wales), September 12, 1977.

21. David Thorstad, "A Statement to the Gay Liberation Movement on the Issue of Man/Boy Love," *Gay Community News,* January 6, 1979.

22. "Men and Boys: The Boston Conference," *Gaysweek,* February 12, 1979.

23. Ibid.
24. Ibid.
25. Wilhelm Reich, *The Sexual Revolution* (New York: Octagon, 1971), p. 12.
26. David Zane Mairowitz, *The Radical Soap Opera* (New York: Avon, 1974), pp. 217–18.
27. Ibid., pp. 224–25.
28. Valida Davila, "A Child's Sexual Bill of Rights," Sexual Freedom League Childhood Sexuality Circle.


16. THE FIRST STEP

1. Peter L. Berger, *Invitation to Sociology* (New York: Doubleday Anchor, 1963), p. 176.
2. Frederick Storaska, *How to Say No to a Rapist* (New York: Warner, 1976), p. 199.
3. William Kraemer and others, *The Normal and Abnormal Love of Children* (Kansas City: Sheed Andrews and McMeel, Inc., 1976), p. 2.
4. Georgia Dullea, "Child Prostitution: Causes Are Sought," *The New York Times,* September 4, 1979, p. C11.
5. Yvonne Tormes, *Child Victims of Incest* (Denver: The American Humane Association, Children's Division, 1969), p. 27.
6. Alan P. Bell and Calvin S. Hall, *The Personality of a Child Molester* (New York: Aldine, 1971), p. 93.
7. Ibid., p. 76.
8. Jean Mundy, Ph.D., "Rape—For Women Only" as cited in Adrienne Rich, *Of Woman Born* (New York: W. W. Norton, 1976), p. 244.


AFTERWORD

1. Susan Griffin, *Rape: The Power of Consciousness* (Hagerstown, New York: Harper & Row, 1979).
2. Louise Armstrong, *Kiss Daddy Goodnight* (New York: Hawthorn Books, 1978).

# Index